CRISIS MANAGEMENT
AND
BRIEF TREATMENT

CRISIS MANAGEMENT

AND

BRIEF TREATMENT

Theory, Technique, and Applications

Albert R. Roberts

Editor

NELSON-HALL PUBLISHERS
Chicago

Typesetter: Precision Typographers
Printer: Capital City Press
Cover Painting: Ivan Whitkov, "Duo"

Library of Congress Cataloging-in-Publication Data

Crisis management and brief treatment : theory, technique, and
  applications / Albert R. Roberts, editor.
      p.   cm.
  Includes bibliographical references.
  ISBN 0-8304-1429-0
  1. Crisis intervention (Psychiatry) 2. Brief psychotherapy.
  I. Roberts, Albert R.
  RC480.6.C758   1996
  616.89'14—dc20   95-40746
                                                                                          CIP

Manufactured in the United States of America

10 9 8 7 6 5 4 3 2

™ The paper used in this book meets the
minimum requirements of American
National Standard for Information
Sciences—Permanence of Paper for
Printed Library Materials, ANSI
Z39.48-1984.

DEDICATION

This book is dedicated to the memory of two very caring people—William C. Roberts and Robert Nevin.

In loving memory of my brother Bill, who cared deeply about his family and friends. Growing up in the Bronx together taught us about adventure, goal setting, overcoming adversity, and risk taking. I miss our meaningful discussions. His work ethic and strength of spirit during chemotherapy are an ongoing source of inspiration to his children Evie and Harrison and all who knew him. Bill would be very proud of his daughter and son, who have followed in his footsteps to become successful optics engineers.

In fond memory of my friend and former colleague, Dr. Robert S. Nevin, one of the most thoughtful and considerate colleagues I have ever known. His sudden death is mourned by his wife, children, colleagues, and M.S.W. students at Indiana University.

CONTENTS

SECTION I
Overview   1

Contents

SECTION II
Acute Psychological Crisis, Crisis Intervention, and Brief Therapy Applications   35

SECTION III
Acute Situational Crisis, Crisis Management, and Brief Treatment Applications   103

Contents

FOREWORD

Crisis Management and Brief Treatment

In recent years, our colleagues in Social Work and the other Health Professions have begun to appreciate the efficacy of various forms of short-term intervention. Indeed we have moved from a position of mourning the diminution of the status of long-term treatment, so long the sought-for model of intervention, to a realization that much of our work with clients is short-term. Hence rather than second best, as was frequently suggested in an earlier day, in its various forms it is the treatment of choice for many of the presenting situations of current practice.

At times this transition to a much more prevalent use of short-term intervention was accompanied by rhetoric either decrying or praising the perceived advantages and disadvantages of time-limited or open-ended therapy. However, in fact, the shift to this model was not the result of who spoke best but, as befits responsible practice in any profession; it emerged from a large number of well-designed and implemented research projects across a broad spectrum of settings and situations.

Again, as befits service-oriented professions, practice evolved into the development of theory and emerging theories aided in the strengthening and enrichment of practice.

Dr. Roberts' volume reflects well these developments! He has built an outstanding model of intervention drawing upon the important theoretical bodies that have aided in the emergence of various strategies of short-term intervention. In particular, he has placed emphasis on crisis work. He has then asked a group of highly experienced practitioners to apply his model to a range of situations, all of which are associated with high stress and acute crisis. He is to be highly commended for this, for it gives the volume a strong conceptual unity not always found in edited books. This unity permits a carryover from one type of case to another, again something that a good theory and its planned application should facilitate.

Dr. Roberts has chosen his authors well for they, too, have been consistent in building their chapters in a conceptually consistent manner while at the same time focusing on the individuality of the various situations that comprise their area of focus.

His opening chapter sets the theme for the volume by identifying the prevalence of crises in our society. He then makes a strong case that all practitioners in the helping professions need to have some competence in this type of theory. His targeting of the book to a broad range of practitioners is another of its strengths and important contributions

Since short-term and crisis intervention are not the sole purview of any profession, the psychology, social work, and counseling professions need to work together to overcome the turf boundaries between them. Social work authors need to do more interdisciplinary writing. So often we have written only for each other, thus failing in our responsibility to assist our colleagues in other professions, who, over the decades, have taught us much.

As effective practice increasingly becomes founded on tested and developing theory, responsible practice will of necessity demand highly honed diagnostic skills. For just as good theory can enhance our effectiveness, it also helps us to understand more precisely its limitations and thus its ability to harm when improperly utilized.

This volume will be of great value to various groups of readers, students, clinicians, and professors. The case examples are well chosen and help us to understand the area of problem functioning that is being discussed. What is of particular importance is the way that many of the interventive strategies discussed by each author have usefulness for other types of clients. Again it is this type of thinking that helps to strengthen practice. Dr. Roberts and his coauthors have served us well in this regard.

In summary, the book reminds us of how much we already know about how to practice effectively in this complex world of treating crises and unbearable stresses. It emphasizes the need for good theory to underpin practice. But as well, it tells us that theories are living, not closed, systems. Thus they change and develop as we learn more from our practice about what is and is not effective in what circumstances, and with which clients. It is an excellent example of how theory and practice are inexorably interlinked, something that is not always evident in our writing, our teaching, and our practice. It is a superb example of the kind of writing of which we need more: writing that is very client- and practitioner-oriented, is readable, and is extremely useful.

I commend Dr. Roberts for his work and that of his colleagues in developing a timely and important contribution to the therapeutic literature.

Francis J. Turner, Dean
Faculty of Social Work and Director, International Programs
Wilfrid Laurier University
Waterloo, Ontario, Canada

PREFACE

We live in an era in which acute crisis events related to AIDS, alcoholism, suicide attempts, child abductions, incest, gun shot wounds, woman battering, and unemployment have become far too commonplace. Everyday, millions of people are struck by intense stressors and crisis events that they are not able to resolve without short-term help from social workers and psychologists.

This book has three primary objectives:

1. To present the latest estimates and official prevalence rates of acute crisis episodes in American society today. For example, the annual rate of emergency room visits for gunshot wounds and woman battering, drug overdoses, child abductions, rape, and murder will be discussed.
2. To review and integrate basic theory and practice models underlying the planning and implementation of brief time-limited interventions.
3. To present the latest information about crisis management and brief treatment strategies applied to high-risk groups.

Crisis management, brief treatment, and other short-term modalities have evolved considerably over the past decade to help health care, mental health, and criminal justice practitioners address a wide range of serious psychological problems. Crisis management and brief treatment approaches are particularly timely now as economic factors make long-term psychotherapy increasingly unaffordable. In view of the increasing limitations placed by health insurance providers on the number of reimbursable sessions per client with particular diagnoses, clinicians do their best to resolve their clients' problems in a short amount of time. The overwhelming majority of individuals and families with a serious emotional problem seek help only after their problems have escalated into a full-blown crisis. Therefore, the editor planned this book to meet the needs of students, professors, and clinicians. The book includes all specially written chapters on the latest applications of Roberts' Seven-Stage Crisis Intervention Model and other popular forms of brief treatment.

Social work and psychology educators and their students have been searching for a textbook that thoroughly reviews the latest crisis management techniques and brief treatment applications to high risk populations. This is the first text to apply the seven-stage crisis intervention model, as well as task-centered and brief psychotherapeutic approaches to specific acute crisis episodes. Several books have been published on crisis intervention during the past decade. Other books have been published on brief treatment. However, this is the first up-to-date, interdisciplinary volume presenting a wealth of information on acute psychological crises, acute situational crises, crisis management techniques, and other brief treatment approaches.

ABOUT THE CONTRIBUTORS

Alan L. Berman, Ph.D., is executive director of the American Association of Suicidology. Prior to 1995, Dr. Berman served as director of the National Center for the Study and Prevention of Suicide at the Washington (D.C.) School of psychiatry and was a professor of psychology at The American University. Dr. Berman has published extensively in the field of suicidology, is a past president of the American Association of Suicidology, and was a recipient of the Association's Edwin Schneidman Award.

Elaine P. Congress, D.S.W., is director of the doctoral program at Fordham University Graduate School of Social Service in New York City, where she teaches social work ethics, clinical practice, and family-oriented treatment to master and doctoral students. Before becoming a professor, Dr. Congress was director of the Mental Health Clinic at Lutheran Medical Center in Brooklyn, New York for eighteen years. She is one of the associate editors of the journal *Crisis Intervention and Time-Limited Treatment.* Currently completing a book on *Multicultural Perspectives in Working with Family,* Dr. Congress has published numerous book chapters and journal articles.

Barry R. Cournoyer, D.S.W., is associate dean for quality improvement at Indiana University School of Social Work, where he evaluates various aspects of all three of the school's educational programs (B.S.W., M.S.W., and Ph.D.) and attempts to encourage excellence in teaching, service and scholarship. He is the author of *The Social Work Skills Workbook*, second edition (Brooks/Cole, 1996), and continues to teach courses at both the master's and doctoral levels. He is also a practitioner to a small clientele in the city of Indianapolis.

Sophia F. Dziegielewski, Ph.D. , is associate professor at the School of Social Work, University of Alabama. In 1995, Dr. Dziegielewski was selected as the NASW Social Worker of the Year for the state of Tennessee. She also developed and conducted the sixteen-hour preparation course for the social work licensure exam in six states.

Gilbert Greene, Ph.D., is an associate professor in the College of Social Work at The Ohio State University. Previously, he held faculty positions in the Schools of Social Work at Michigan State University and University of Iowa. Dr. Greene teaches courses on clinical social work with individuals, couples, families, and crisis intervention and time-limited treatment. He is the book review editor for *Crisis Intervention and Time-Limited Treatment,* and has published numerous articles and book chapters.

Geoffrey L. Greif, Ph.D., is professor, School of Social Work, University of Maryland at Baltimore. He is the author of four books and more than seventy articles and book chapters. His current writing focuses on parents who drop out after divorce and on academically successful African-American males and their families.

Fred J. Hanna, Ph.D., is currently Assistant Professor in the Department of Counseling and Human Services at Johns Hopkins University. He has had clinical experience in a variety of settings, ranging from crisis counseling to chemical dependence and private practice. Dr. Hanna has published several articles on the factors of psychotherapeutic change and the phenomenological aspects of counseling practice.

David A. Jobes, Ph.D., is an Associate Professor of psychology at the Catholic University of America in Washington, D.C., where he is a member of the clinical faculty of CUA's Ph.D. clinical psychology training program. As an expert in suicide, Dr. Jobes speaks widely on the topic, conducts training workshops in suicidology, and has published numerous journal articles, book chapters, and two books in the field. Dr. Jobes was the 1995 recipient of the Edwin Schneidman Award.

Rick Myer, Ph.D., received his doctorate in Counseling Psychology from the University of Memphis in 1987 and is a licensed psychologist in the state of Illinois. He is currently an Associate Professor at the Department of Educational Psychology, Counseling, and Special Education at Northern Illinois University, where he serves as director of the Counseling lab. He has worked in a variety of clinical settings and currently has a private practice in the Chicago suburbs. Dr. Myer's research interests include assessment for crisis intervention and therapists' social relationships.

Albert R. Roberts, D.S.W., is professor of Social Work and Criminal Justice at the School of Social Work, Rutgers University, New Brunswick, New Jersey, where he conducts seminars and courses on research methods, crisis intervention, stress and coping skills, family violence intervention, adolescence, victimology, and juvenile justice. Dr. Roberts is the founding editor-in-chief of the journal *Crisis Intervention and Time-Limited Treatment*. He has approximately 100 published articles and book chapters to his credit. He has authored or edited eighteen books, and is founder and current editor of the Springer Publishing Company's twenty-five volume series on social work. Dr. Roberts is a fellow of the American Orthopsychiatric Association, a lifetime member of the Academy of Criminal Justice Sciences, and an active member of the National Association of Social Workers, the Council on Social Work Education, the American Association of Suicidology, and the American Society of Criminology.

Cheryl Resnick, D.S.W., is an assistant professor in the Department of Social Work at Georgian Court College in New Jersey. Her professional interests primarily center around the practice of hospital social work and other health-related issues. Dr. Resnick was formerly on the faculty at the University of Tennessee School of Social Work. She has several other publications on crisis intervention, including a chapter in Dr. Roberts' recently published book, *Helping Battered Women*.

Kate Wambach, Ph.D., is currently an assistant professor in the School of Social Work at The University of Texas at Austin. She teaches in the school's mental health and chemical dependence services concentration. Along with numerous program evaluation projects, her research interests are focused on interventions for family members with relatives experiencing severe and chronic mental health and/or substance abuse problems.

SECTION I

Overview

CHAPTER 1

Converging Themes in Crisis Intervention, Task-Centered and Brief Treatment Approaches

BARRY R. COURNOYER

Over the course of the past decade, helping professionals, including many who are psychoanalytically oriented, have increasingly begun to use short-term treatment approaches with a wide range of populations and psychosocial problems (Bradey, 1985; Cornett, 1991; Dane, 1989; Gilbar, 1991; Jackson, 1981; Newhill, 1989; Podell, 1989; Sefansky, 1990; Sussal and Ojakian, 1988; VanHook, 1987; Weiss and Parish, 1989; Woldrich, 1986; and Zakus and Wilday, 1987). Indeed, "short-term psychotherapy is increasingly being called the wave of the future" (Strupp and Binder, 1984, p. 3). Previously, many psychologists, psychiatrists, social workers, and counselors—unless they worked on emergency, crisis intervention, information and referral, or discharge planning services—tended to adopt practice models that were, more or less, *open-ended* in nature. In other words, as the practitioner and client reached an understanding as to the direction and focus for their work together, the time frame remained indeterminate. Budman and Gurman (1988) aptly refer to this as *time-unlimited* practice.

Even behavior therapists, presumably among the more time efficient of clinicians, commonly expect treatment to be in the twenty-five to fifty visit range (Wilson, 1981, as cited in Pekarik, 1993). Most clients, however, do not remain clients for the many months or years envisioned in open-ended models. Clients tend to discontinue treatment long before that. The global research findings on this are quite clear. Regardless of the presenting problem, treatment goal, or theoretical orientation and professional affiliation of therapists, the length of outpatient psychotherapeutic service is usually less than twenty sessions. Even in private practice, outpatient psychotherapeutic treatment is typically less than twenty-six sessions (Pardes and Pincus, 1981). Garfield (1978) found that most settings lose 50 percent of their clients before the eighth session. The median number of sessions for clients in most treatment contexts is five to six. This is consistent with clients' expectations prior to beginning treatment. As Pekarik suggests, "the professional treatment expectations of most people are shaped by their experience with general health care" (1993, p. 412). In managed mental health care contexts, for example, 88 percent of clients expected no more than five visits (Pekarik, 1991, as cited in Pekarik, 1993). Most clients expect service to last two to three months at the most and, in this regard, they tend to conform to their own, rather than to therapists', expectations (Budman and Gurman, 1988).

Recently, however, the divergent expectations of therapists and clients have begun to merge—toward those of clients. In a dramatic shift, short-term treatment is becoming the preferred approach for an extraordinarily wide range of presenting problems, client populations, and service contexts. This growing trend toward brief forms of psychotherapeutic practice has come about for several reasons. First, there is an enormous and probably increasing demand for crisis intervention and short-term treatment services. (Note Roberts' reference in chapter 2 to more than "130 million situational crisis events" experienced each year in the United States and to the incidence rate cited in his "Scope of the Problem" section.) Second, insurance companies, agency boards and administrators, legislators, and other policy makers have increasingly emphasized *accountability, productivity,* and *efficiency* in the provision of psychotherapeutic services. The use of Diagnostic Related Groups (DRGs) in hospitals, the spread of managed health care systems and Health Maintenance Organizations (HMOs), and the possibility of greater governmental oversight of the provision of mental health services are affecting both the philosophy and nature of helping services. Third, consumers of psychotherapeutic services are increasingly demanding greater therapeutic efficacy and efficiency, and more cost-effectiveness. Fourth, both clinicians and administrators are becoming aware of the expectations and actual patterns of clients to attend psychothera-

4

peutic sessions for approximately six to twelve sessions. Fifth, professionals are becoming more knowledgeable concerning the research on treatment effectiveness.

For some time now, clinical researchers (see Budman and Gurman, 1988; Pekarik, 1993) have been aware that (1) short-term psychotherapeutic service is typically at least as effective as long-term treatment; (2) short-term treatment is far more efficient in both outpatient and inpatient contexts; (3) for most clients, the greatest amount of progress for psychotherapeutic treatment occurs within the first six to eight sessions; and (4) although progress may continue to occur with additional sessions, the rate of progress slows significantly after the initial six to ten sessions and then drops off dramatically after approximately sixteen or eighteen sessions.

In spite of the powerful evidence in support of short-term treatment, there are, appropriately, professionals who criticize at least some elements of the short-term approaches. Indeed, there are several challenging arguments and some research findings that deserve careful considerations (see, for example, Good, 1987; O'Conner and Reid, 1986; Sachs, 1983; and Strean, 1981). The most compelling criticisms are those that question the universal application of short-term treatment to *all* presenting problems and to *all* clients or patient populations, and those that argue that many clients will be *screened in* or *screened out* in order to maximize efficiency and effectiveness of short-term treatment. It is indeed, unfortunately, quite likely that as individual helping professionals and helping organizations move toward greater accountability, effectiveness, and efficiency through the utilization of short-term treatment approaches, there will be pressure to discriminate against certain client populations and presenting problems perceived to be "difficult" or "intractable." To counter that tendency, proponents of short-term approaches need to discover ways to adapt the basic principles and processes of brief treatment to specific problems and populations. Many short-term clinicians and researchers have done just that. (See, for example, Benbenishty, 1988; Bromley, 1987; Cornett, 1991; Greenberg et al., 1988; Jackson, 1981; Trafford, 1992; Tsui and Schultz, 1985; and Weiss and Parish, 1989.)

In spite of the appropriate challenges to short-term treatment approaches, the overwhelmingly positive findings in support of their efficacy and utility are leading clinicians, agency administrators, and practice theoreticians toward short-term models of practice *and* toward a more eclectic orientation. Without question, brief treatment approaches will become the modal forms of intervention in the second half of the 1990s and the early 2000s.

Interestingly, many of the components of these emerging models of brief psychotherapy have long been key elements of *task-centered* practice as taught in many schools of social work throughout the country (Reid and Epstein, 1972, 1977; Reid, 1978, 1986, 1988). They are also consistent with many of the major elements of crisis intervention (Golan, 1978, 1986; Roberts, 1990, 1995).

When crisis intervention, task-centered, and brief psychotherapeutic approaches are compared, remarkable similarities emerge. Clinical psychologists Budman and Gurman (1988) identify several dimensions of brief time-limited psychotherapy that can serve as a guide for the consideration of these three perspectives in short-term treatment.

DEVELOPMENT AND MAINTENANCE OF A CLEAR AND SPECIFIC FOCUS

"Setting and maintaining realistic goals are very important in the brief therapy process" (Budman and Gurman, 1988, p.17). Among the more common therapeutic mistakes or "errors in technique" (Sachs, 1983) in psychotherapy generally is the "failure of the therapist to *structure* or *focus* the treatment sessions" (Budman and Gurman, 1988, p. 17). Although the development and maintenance of clear therapeutic focus represents a departure from both traditional psychodynamic (i.e., "Please express, without censor, anything that comes to mind") as well as several of the existential and phenomenological therapies (i.e., "What would you like to explore today?"), focusing (Perlman, 1957) has a lengthy history as a practice principle in social work. It is consistent with social work's tradition of *contracting* with clients. Contracting "yields clearly identified problems, specific goals for work, a change program through which the goals may be pursued, and, often, one or more discrete action steps" (Cournoyer, 1991, p. 224). *Focusing*, as used in social work practice, "is a skill through which the worker helps to direct or maintain the attention of the client and worker upon the work at hand" (Cournoyer, 1991, p. 289). The task-centered model, especially, helps workers and clients maintain focus by negotiating specific tasks that clients undertake in working toward goal achievement.

The notion of a clear and specific focus is also inherent in crisis intervention work. Golan (1978) and Roberts (1990) emphasize as a major principle in the beginning phase of crisis intervention a focus upon the precipitating factor or problem (the event, incident, or situation that led to professional involvement). Golan (1978) further sug-

6

gests that the client and professional together select one target problem for work. She also recommends the development of a specific and concrete contract. The targeted problem and the contract then serve to keep both the professional helper and the client clearly focused throughout the course of their work together.

THERAPIST IS HIGHLY ACTIVE

Unlike longer term approaches, in brief treatment, the therapist actively provides structure to sessions, guides clients "back" toward the problems and goals for work, asks leading questions, gives advice, offers suggestions, and, in collaboration with clients, negotiates "homework" and other activities. The brief therapist is not "inscrutable," "passive," or "inactive." Rather, she or he is highly active, attempting to exploit for the client's benefit each minute of each session. This is extremely similar to task-centered practice in its emphasis upon workers' active structuring of each session and energetically encouraging clients to undertake jointly determined tasks designed to resolve problems and achieve defined goals.

In crisis intervention too, the professional helper is extremely active, proceeding through predictable phases of work in a structured and often sequential fashion. Roberts (1990), for example, suggests seven "procedural steps" for helping people in crisis. These include, (1) making psychological contact and rapidly establishing the relationship, (2) examining the dimensions of the problem in order to define it, (3) encouraging an exploration of feelings and emotions, (4) exploring and assessing past coping attempts, (5) generating and exploring alternatives and specific solutions, (6) restoring cognitive functioning through implementation of action plan, and (7) following up.

MAINTENANCE OF AN AWARENESS OF TIME

In brief psychotherapeutic treatment, both the professional helper and the client recognize that the relationship is a time-limited one. The therapist periodically reminds the client of the "time status" (e.g., "We have now completed four sessions together. We have four left to go"). Therefore, each session is viewed as extremely significant (e.g., one-eighth or one-twelfth of the whole). Professionals adopting a task-centered approach also view time and time limits as vital elements in effective practice. As an essential part of the process, workers actually *contract* with clients for a specific number of sessions (often eight and seldom more than twelve).

Recognition of the significance of time is reminiscent of an important historical theme in the profession of social work. During the period from approximately 1930 through 1955, an intense struggle between the "diagnostic" and the "functional" schools of thought was fought out in social work schools and journals. Proponents of the "diagnostic" school were strongly influenced by Freudian psychology. They envisioned social workers as, essentially, therapists whose role was to apply psychodynamically oriented psychotherapy to a wide range of psychological and social problems.

Social workers advocating a "functional" approach opposed the diagnostic school's heavy reliance upon Freudian psychoanalytic theory. They preferred the views of Otto Rank, who was a faculty member at the Pennsylvania School of Social Work. Virginia Robinson, Jesse Taft, and other social workers who affiliated with the functional school rejected Freudian notions of scientific determinism and the "psychology of illness." Instead, they promulgated a psychology of human potential and emphasized each individual person's capacity to determine his or her own life. They replaced the notion of "treatment" with the concept of "service," changed "patient" to "client," and realigned the center of change from the "therapist" and the "therapeutic relationship" to the "client." The client then became a major actor and a determining factor in the process of change. Also, the conscious and planned use of *structure*, including *time-limits*, became an important part of the provision of service. As active, responsible participants in the helping process, clients were fully informed of the limits to both the professional-client relationship and the extent of services provided. Such "limits" were viewed as important elements in the change and growth processes, as clients were thought to benefit from the realistic experience of certain boundaries in the nature of the relationship with the worker and in the use of agency resources. It is interesting to note how popular the concept of planned limit-setting or boundary clarification has become in psychotherapy with persons diagnosed as personality or character disordered. It is indeed likely that such processes might also be useful to a much wider range of client populations, diagnostic categories, and presenting problems.

The significance of time and time limits as vital factors in helping is also both explicitly and implicitly recognized by crisis intervention theorists. Roberts (1990), for example, emphasizes a ''rapid'' establishment of the relationship between helper and client. And Golan (1978), envisions a typical process of crisis intervention that involves approximately five or six interviews.

THERAPIST ENCOURAGES CLIENT'S ''BEING'' OUTSIDE THERAPY

In another change from some traditional psychotherapeutic models, the brief psychotherapist recognizes the therapy may not necessarily be the most important aspect of the client's life. Whereas some traditional psychotherapists have encouraged patients to view ''therapy as the most significant and important part of your life,'' brief therapists tend to view the world outside the consulting office as replete with potential resources. Extra-office (i.e., ''homework'') assignments are routinely negotiated. Frequently, the brief psychotherapist requests that significant others participate in at least some of the treatment sessions. Clients may be encouraged to join self-help and support groups (e.g., ACOA, Al-Anon, etc.) during and following the course of psychotherapeutic intervention. Of course, such activities are entirely consistent with social work's traditional ''person-in-environment'' concept of practice. They are especially congruent with the task-centered approach in its emphasis upon ''tasks'' and ''activities'' undertaken by the client during the interval between interview sessions. Indeed, the concept of the brief therapist-patient relationship is similar to the predominant social work view concerning therapeutic relationships in that profound transference is not encouraged, is not considered necessary, and is certainly not considered sufficient for positive change.

Crisis intervention theorists also tend to emphasize ''being'' and ''doing'' in the real world outside the context of the professional helping relationship. For example, as part of the process of contracting Golan (1978) suggests that the crisis intervener and client negotiate an ''agreement on joint activity: specific goals at which to aim, tasks on which to focus. Set up a working plan of what the client will do . . . and what others involved will contribute'' (p. 87). She encourages the worker and client to ''be as specific and concrete as possible'' (p. 87). During the implementation of work phase, she notes that the tasks or goal directed activities can be ''*action* oriented and geared to bring about change in performance'' and they ''can also be *thinking* oriented, to help the client decide on a course of action or ways to implement it'' (pp. 90–91).

EVALUATION AND TREATMENT ARE INEXTRICABLY BOUND

In several brief psychotherapy models, as in task-centered practice, evaluation of progress begins immediately and continues throughout the treatment process. As goals are defined, preferably in specific and concrete terms, some means for identifying progress toward them are also identified. This, of course, contrasts with several traditional psychotherapeutic approaches that tend to avoid specific goal setting and view evaluation from the rather abstract and often subjective perspective of the therapist's assessment and theoretical formulation (e.g., resolution of an Oedipal conflict or working through an inferiority complex).

Crisis intervention theorists also recognize the importance of evaluation and the relationship of that process to the therapeutic work. Golan (1978), for example, specifically suggests that the crisis worker and client jointly evaluate progress by reviewing, typically in the fourth or fifth interview, how things are now compared to how they were when they first began their work together. Progress is also evaluated in relation to key themes, feelings and emotions. Tasks and activities that were undertaken are reviewed and evaluated in terms of their impact on goal achievement and their effects upon the person and his or her environment. Significantly, work that was not completed or remains to be undertaken is also identified in order that the client may continue to address it following the termination of the relationship with the crisis worker.

FLEXIBLE USE OF INTERVENTIONS AND TIME

In brief psychotherapy, the therapist is eclectic and pragmatic in the use of interventive strategies and techniques. Similarly, the ''50-minute hour'' is not considered sacrosanct. Brief therapists may meet with clients for shorter (or longer) sessions and at intervals that may be less (or more) than once per week. Often, the intervals between sessions become longer as the work progresses. Such flexibility is well known to social workers who make home visits or interview clients while providing transportation to medical appointments or food pantries. They may see a particular client every day for a week, then once a week for a month, then once a month for six months, and so on. Brief therapists and task-centered practitioners tend toward flexible eclecticism, incorporating interventive techniques from other professions and from various, often theoretically incongruent but pragmatically compatible schools of thought (see, for example, Fischer, 1986; Fuhriman, Paul, and Burlingame, 1986). Commonly, there is a much greater emphasis upon the present and the future than upon the past, and increasingly more attention is paid to *solutions* than to *problems* (see, for example, Bergman, 1985; de Shazer, 1985; de Shazer, Berg, and Lipchik, 1986; de Shazer and Berg, 1992; Fraser, 1984; Nunnally and Lipchik, 1989).

Crisis workers also tend to be flexible, eclectic, and creative in their approach to intervention. Roberts (1990), for example, encourages the crisis counselor and the client to generate alternative strategies and identify a range of potentially more adaptive coping behaviors. Frequently, this "brainstorming" process results in the identification of creative, innovative, and often unique action steps. Not surprisingly, many of the strategies and activities that emerge from this collaborative process between worker and client are not identifiable psychotherapeutic techniques *per se*. Rather, they are specific, pragmatic, and eclectic, solution-oriented action steps intended to help resolve the identified problem.

PLANNED FOLLOW-UP OF BRIEF THERAPY

In the brief psychotherapy envisioned by Budman and Gurman (1988), the therapist suggests a follow-up session approximately one year after the termination of the therapeutic work. Clients are informed of this during the last meeting. Crisis intervention theorists also recommend such a step, although the time frame may be less than one year (Roberts, 1990).

Regardless of the specific time interval preferred, routine follow-up with former clients serves several beneficial functions. In fact, the knowledge that the professional helper intends to follow up at a later point may, in itself, provide many clients with a sense of security and transitional support, aiding in the maintenance and generalization of change. Follow-up helps in the process of evaluating the effectiveness of the service provided, especially in regard to the durability of whatever changes have occurred. And, follow-up conveys to clients that they have been and continue to be significant to the professional helpers who served them.

SUMMARY

Brief treatment approaches are emerging as the preferred, perhaps even prototypical, models of intervention for a variety of psychosocial problems, especially those of a crisis or acutely stressful nature. We may confidently predict that during the late 1990s and early 2000s, brief therapies will represent the modal forms of psychotherapeutic treatment. Many factors have contributed to this phenomenon. First, there is a large, and probably increasing, incidence of acute situational crises and a concomitant need for crisis intervention and short-term services for the more than 100 million people affected by them each year. Second, there are growing demands, from several constituencies, for accountability and efficiency in psychotherapeutic practice. Third, the research findings that suggest at least as effective outcomes for short-term when compared to long-term approaches are becoming more widely known.

These and other factors have led toward a convergence of practice principles from among several models of short-term practice. Brief psychotherapy, task-centered practice, and crisis intervention each emphasize therapeutic structure and focus, clear specificity of problems and goals, time limits, high activity on the part of the professional helper, evaluation as part of the treatment process, flexible and eclectic interventive strategies, incorporation of goal-directed activities or action steps by clients outside of the interview context, inclusion of significant others as part of the treatment, consideration of the unique cultural and socioeconomic factors of the client population, and planned follow-up subsequent to termination. These principles may be expected to guide the modal treatment approaches of the remainder of the twentieth and the early part of the twenty-first centuries.

REFERENCES

Benbenishty, R. (1988). Assessment of task-centered interventions with families in Israel. *Journal of Social Service Research, 11* (4), 19–43.

Bergman, J. S. (1985). *Fishing for barracuda: Pragmatics of brief systemic therapy.* New York: Norton.

Bradey, R. (1985). Crisis social work intervention with families experiencing sudden infant death. *Australian Social Work, 38* (2), 35–37.

Bromley, M. A. (1987). New beginnings for Cambodian refugees—or further disruptions? *Social Work, 32* (3), 236–239.

Budman, S.H. and Gurman, A.S. (1988). *Theory and practice of brief therapy.* New York: Guilford.

Budman, S.H. (Ed.). (1981). *Forms of brief therapy.* New York: Guilford.

Cornett, C. (1991). Self object intervention in brief treatment with patients inappropriate for traditional brief psychotherapy models. *Clinical Social Work Journal, 19* (2), 131–147.

Cournoyer, B. (1991). *The social work skills workbook.* Belmont, CA: Wadsworth.

Dane, B. O. (1989). New beginnings for AIDS patients. *Social Casework, 70* (5), 305–314.

Davanloo, H. (Ed.). (1978). *Basic principles and techniques in short-term dynamic psychotherapy.* New York: Spectrum.

————— (Ed.). (1980). *Short-term dynamic psychotherapy.* New York: Jason Aronson.

De Shazer, S. (1985). *Keys to solution in brief therapy.* New York: W.W. Norton.

De Shazer, S., Berg, I. K., Lipchik, E., Nunnally, E., Molnar, A., Gingerich W., and Weiner-Davis, M. (1986). Brief therapy: Focused solution development. *Family Process, 25* (2), 207–221.

De Shazer, S. and Berg, I. K. (1992). Doing therapy: A post-structural re-vision. *Journal of Marital and Family Therapy, 18* (1), 71–82.

Eysenck, H. J. (1993). Forty years on: The outcome problem in psychotherapy revisited. In T. R. Giles (Ed.), *Handbook of effective psychotherapy* (pp. 3–20). New York: Plenum Press.

Fischer, J. (1986). Eclectic casework. In J. C. Norcross (Ed.), *Handbook of eclectic psychotherapy* (pp. 320–352). New York: Brunner/Mazel.

Fraser, J. S. (1984). Paradox and orthodox: Folie a deux? *Journal of Marital and Family Therapy, 10* (4), 361–372.

Fuhriman, A., Paul, S.S. and Burlingame, G. M. (1986). Eclectic time-limited therapy. In J. C. Norcross (Ed.), *Handbook of eclectic psychotherapy* (pp. 226–259). New York: Brunner/Mazel.

Garfield, S. L. (1978). Research on client variables in psychotherapy. In S. I. Garfield and A. E. Bergin (Eds.), *Handbook of psychotherapy and behavior change* (2nd ed., pp. 191–232). New York: Wiley.

Gilbar, O. (1991). Model for crisis intervention through group therapy for women with breast cancer. *Clinical Social Work Journal, 19* (3), 293–304.

Giles, T. R. (1993). Consumer advocacy and effective psychotherapy: The managed care alternative. In T. R. Giles (Ed.), *Handbook of effective psychotherapy* (pp. 481–489). New York: Plenum Press.

Goldfried, M. R. (Ed.). (1982). *Converging themes in psychotherapy: Trends in psychodynamic, humanistic, and behavioral practice.* New York: Springer.

Golan, N. (1978). *Treatment in crisis situations.* New York: Free Press.

————— (1986). Crisis theory. In F.J. Turner (Ed.), *Social work treatment: Interlocking theoretical approaches* (3d. ed.). New York: Free Press.

Good, P. R. (1987). Brief therapy in the age of Reagapeutics. *American Journal of Orthopsychiatry, 57* (1), 6–11.

13

Greenberg, L., Fine, S. B., Cohen, C., Larson, K., Michaelson-Baily, A., Rubinton, P. and Glick, I. D. (1988). An interdisciplinary psychoeducation program for schizophrenic patients and their families in an acute care setting. *Hospital and Community Psychiatry, 39* (3), 277–282.

Gustafson, J. P. (1986). *The complex secret of brief psychotherapy.* New York: Norton.

Horowitz, M., Marmar, C., Krupnick, J., Wilner, N., Kaltreider, N., and Wallerstein, R. (1984). *Personality styles and brief psychotherapy.* New York: Basic Books.

Jackson, J. A. (1981). Helping troubled teenagers in blended and single-parent families. *Social Work Papers, 16* (Spring), 43–52.

Kreilkamp, T. (1989). *Time-limited intermittent therapy with children and families.* New York: Brunner/Mazel.

Malan, D. H. (1963). *A study of brief psychotherapy.* New York: Plenum Press.

————— (1976). *The frontiers of brief psychotherapy: An example of the convergence of research and clinical practice.* New York: Plenum Press.

Mann, J. (1973). *Time-limited psychotherapy.* Cambridge, MA: Harvard University Press.

Mann, J. and Goldman, R. (1982). *A casebook in time-limited psychotherapy.* New York: McGraw-Hill.

Newhill, C. E. (1989). Psychiatric emergencies: Overview of clinical principles and clinical practice. *Clinical Social Work Journal, 17* (3), 245–258.

Nunnally, E. and Lipchik, E. (1989). Some uses of writing in solution focused brief therapy. *Journal of Independent Social Work, 4* (2), 5–19.

O'Conner, R. and Reid, W. J. (1986). Dissatisfaction with brief treatment. *Social Service Review, 60* (4), 526–537.

Pardes, H. and Pincus, H. A. (1981). Brief therapy in the context of national mental health. In S. H. Budman (Ed.), *Forms of brief therapy* (pp. 7–24). New York: Guilford Press.

Pekarik, G. (1991). Treatment impact at a managed mental health care clinic. Unpublished manuscript. Metropolitan Clinics of Counseling, Topeka, KS.

Pekarik, G. (1993). Beyond effectiveness: Uses of consumer-oriented criteria in defining treatment success. In T. R. Giles (Ed.), *Handbook of effective psychotherapy* (pp. 409–436). New York: Plenum Press.

Perlman, H. H. (1957). *Social casework: A problem-solving process.* Chicago, IL: University of Chicago Press.

Podell, C. (1989). Adolescent mourning: The sudden death of a peer. *Clinical Social Work Journal, 17* (1), 64–78.

Reid, W. J. (1978). *The task-centered system.* New York: Columbia University Press.

Reid, W. J. (1986). Task-centered social work. In F.J. Turner (Ed.), *Social work treatment: Interlocking theoretical approaches* (3d. ed., pp. 267–295). New York: Free Press.

————— (1988). Brief task-centered treatment. In R. A. Dorfman (Ed.), *Paradigms of clinical social work* (pp. 196–219). New York: Brunner/Mazel.

14

————— and Epstein, L. (1972). *Task-centered casework*. New York: Columbia University Press.

————— and Esptein, L. (1977). *Task-centered practice*. New York: Columbia University Press.

————— and Shyne, A. W. (1969). *Brief and extended casework*. New York: Columbia University Press.

Roberts, A. R. (Ed.). (1995). *Crisis intervention and time-limited cognitive therapy*. Thousands Oaks, CA: Sage.

Roberts, A. R. (Ed.). (1990). *Crisis intervention handbook: Assessment, treatment, and research*. Belmont, CA: Wadsworth.

Sachs, J. S. (1983). Negative factors in brief psychotherapy: An empirical assessment. *Journal of Consulting and Clinical Psychology, 51* (4), 557–564.

Sefansky, S. (1990). Pediatric critical care social work: Interventions with a special plane crash survivor. *Health and Social Work, 15* (3), 215–220.

Sifneos, P. (1972). *Short-term psychotherapy and emotional crisis*. Cambridge, MA: Harvard University Press.

————— (1979). *Short-term dynamic psychotherapy: Evaluation and technique*. New York: Plenum Press.

Small, L. (1979). *The brief psychotherapies*. 2nd ed. New York: Brunner/Mazel.

Smith, M. L., Glass, G. V. and Miller, T. I. (Eds.). 1980. *The benefits of psychotherapy*. Baltimore, MD: Johns Hopkins University Press.

Strean, H. S. (1981). A critique of some of the newer treatment modalities. *Clinical Social Work Journal, 9*, (3), 15–171.

Strupp, H. H. and Binder, J. (1984). *Psychotherapy in a new key: A guide to time-limited dynamic psychotherapy*. New York: Basic Books.

Sussal, C. M. and Ojakian, E. (1988). Crisis intervention in the workplace. *Employee Assistance Quarterly, 4* (1), 71–85.

Trafford, A. (1992). Violence as a public health crisis. *Public Welfare, 50* (4), 16–17.

Tsui, P. and Schultz, G. L. (1985). Failure of rapport: Why psychotherapeutic engagement fails in the treatment of Asian clients. *American Journal of Orthopsychiatry, 55* (4), 561–569.

Van-Hook, M. P. (1987). Harvest of despair: Using the ABCX model for farm families in crisis. *Social Casework, 68* (5), 273–278.

Weiss, B. S. and Parish, B. (1989). Culturally appropriate crisis counseling: Adapting an American method for use with Indochinese refugees. *Social Work, 34* (3), 252–254.

Wilson, G. T. (1981). Behavior therapy as a short-term therapeutic approach. In S. H. Budman (Ed.), *Forms of brief therapy* (pp. 131–166). New York: Guilford.

Woldrich, W. W. (1986). Adolescent suicide: Crisis intervention and prevention. *School Social Work Journal, 10* (2), 107–116.

Zakus, G. and Wilday, S. (1987). Adolescent abortion option. *Social Work in Health Care, 12* (4), 77–91.

CHAPTER 2

Epidemiology and Definitions of Acute Crisis in American Society

ALBERT R. ROBERTS

This chapter provides an overview of the epidemiology of the most prevalent mental health problems and acute crisis situations in American society. Health care and mental health professionals have become increasingly cognizant of the magnitude and impact of crisis situations on individuals, groups, and communities. Due to the varied methods of counting and estimating the incidence and prevalence of different types of crises, it is difficult to compile definitive counts. Despite the limitations of epidemiology studies and the problems of defining acute crises, advances have been made during the past decade in operationally defining the different types of crisis-producing events and in collecting up-to-date national statistics.

In recent years, several health, family, financial, psychiatric, and crime-related crises have been recognized by authorities as reaching epidemic proportions. The primary focus of this chapter is on acute psychological and situational crises that are precipitated by an unexpected and sudden traumatic event, for example, a diagnosis of a life-threatening illness, a sexual assault, a child being abducted, or a suicide attempt. A crisis situation can occur to anyone at any point in the life cycle. The most important feature of an acute situational crisis is that the triggering incident often poses a serious threat to the person's safety and survival.

An acute situational crisis can be operationally defined as follows: A sudden and unpredictable event takes place (being sexually assaulted at knife point, being held hostage by terrorists, having one's house and possessions destroyed in an earthquake); the individual or family members perceive the event as an imminent threat to their life, psychological well-being, or social functioning; the individual tries to cope, escape the dangerous situation, gain necessary support from a significant other or close relative or friend, and/or adapt by changing one's lifestyle or environment; coping attempts fail and the person's severe emotional state of imbalance escalates into a full-blown crisis. In the eloquent words of Professors Ann Burgess and Aaron Lazare (1976): "A crisis may occur when an unexpected traumatic external event is effective in disrupting the balance between a person's internal ego adaptation or homeostatic state and the environment. . . . The unexpected nature of the event and the coping resources of the person will determine the dimensions of the crisis experience (p.64)." Burgess and Lazare recommended that nurses, physicians, psychologists, social workers, educators, and clergy use crisis intervention, telephone crisis counseling, and/or hospital-based intervention in order to help the patient in acute crisis to regain psychological equilibrium and mastery of the situation.

Epidemiologists currently focus on such questions as who commits forcible rape, woman battering, or homicide and what types of risk reduction prevention strategies can be implemented to lessen the occurrence of these violent crimes. Epidemiologists also continue to uncover and measure risk factors of mental illness, AIDS, and cancer. Whether an epidemiologist is studying the number of people diagnosed with a certain disorder or life-threatening illness, he or she will encounter two major problems:

> The first is to differentiate as carefully as possible new cases from cases that have continued over some long period of time. The epidemiologist distinguishes incidence (the number of new cases that occur during a particular interval) from prevalence (all cases existing during a particular period of time). The prevalence rate includes all new cases that develop in the interval as well as those that began at some earlier time but continued. While prevalence gives some indication of the total magnitude of the problem and the need for services, incidence is a more useful statistic for the study of causation. The second problem is having clear criteria for identifying cases of a particular disorder and differentiating it as precisely as possible from other disorders. (Mechanic, 1989; 45–46)

Because acute crisis episodes are exceptionally varied and complex, it is difficult to accurately measure the total number of crisis

17

episodes occurring each year. For example, the chain of events directly preceding adolescent suicide attempts varies considerably from the events directly preceding a brutal battering. The problem of estimating the annual prevalence rate of crisis episodes is further compounded by the fact that many episodes are not reported to official agencies such as hospitals, mental health centers, and police departments. Professor David Mechanic points out that epidemiologists are not able to obtain records from primary care physicians and other private practitioners. In addition even data from central or state registries of child abuse cases or the mentally ill have serious limitations because of the reliability of persons making the diagnoses (Mechanic, 1989). Nevertheless significant progress has been made in refining some of the preliminary and crude national estimates of psychiatric disorders, violent crime victimizations, addictive disorders, and acute crisis events.

Over 130 million acute crisis events are encountered by over half of the population in the United States. The cumulative sources of this estimate are delineated in the ''Scope of the Problem'' section of this chapter. Initially, a number of these individuals are emotionally numb, confused, anxious, threatened, fearful, and suffering from intrusive thoughts or flashbacks. They often have difficulty concentrating and continually avoid stimuli related to the crisis event such as thoughts, feelings, conversations, activities, and places that arouse recollections of the crisis or traumatic event. Many of these individuals in acute crisis also seem to fit the new diagnosis of Acute Stress Disorder in DSM-IV (American Psychiatric Association, 1994). The crucial distinguishing feature of Acute Stress Disorders is the occurrence ''of characteristic anxiety, dissociative, and other symptoms that occurs within one month after exposure to an extreme traumatic stressor'' (American Psychiatric Association, 1994, p. 429). In addition, the individual persistently reexperiences the traumatic event, and also shows recurring symptoms of anxiety, avoidance of usual life tasks, and decreased emotional responsiveness. Within a few weeks some of the individuals experiencing an acute crisis event adapt by talking with close friends and/or relatives. Other individuals need the help of a social worker, psychologist, nurse, or clergyman. Without the intervention of a health care or mental health professional, some of these individuals in crisis will have difficulty regaining equilibrium and daily social functioning. The many individuals who become significantly distressed, clinically depressed, or impaired in their functioning at home or at work would certainly benefit from crisis intervention and short-term therapy.

18

DEFINITION OF CRISIS

There are several thorough definitions of crisis. One general and two specific definitions are summarized below. The first definition is from the *Dictionary of Psychology* (Reber, 1985) and is much too general.

> Strictly speaking, a crisis can be either a sudden improvement in things or a sudden deterioration. . . . Any sudden interruption in the normal course of events in the life of an individual or a society that necessitates re-evaluation of modes of action and thought. This general sense of a loss of the normal foundations of day-to-day activity is the dominant connotation of the term and is broadly used. For example, an individual is said to undergo a psychological crisis when abrupt departures from normality occur such as the death of a loved one, the loss of one's job, and the like. (p.166)

In fact, Professor Reber's definition of a crisis makes it sound like all sudden interruptions or stressful life events are synonymous with a psychological crisis. This is inaccurate. The meanings of the two concepts, stressful events and crisis, are frequently misunderstood. A hazardous or stressful life event can be only one major component of a pre-crisis stage.

Professors Gilliland and James (1993), in their comprehensive text entitled *Crisis Intervention Strategies*, provide a very complete and practical definition of crisis:

> Crisis is a perception of an event or situation as an intolerable difficulty that exceeds the resources and coping mechanisms of the person. Unless the person obtains relief, the crisis has the potential to cause severe affective, cognitive, and behavioral malfunctioning. Crisis is a danger because it can overwhelm the individual to the extent that it may result in serious pathology, including homicide and suicide. It is also an opportunity because the nature of the pain it induces impels the person to seek help. Individuals can react in any one of three ways to crisis. Under ideal circumstances, many individuals can cope effectively with crisis by themselves and develop strength from the experience. They change and grow in a positive manner and come out of the crisis both stronger and more compassionate. Other people appear to survive the crisis, but effectively block the hurtful affect from awareness, only to have it haunt them in innumerable ways throughout the rest of their lives. There are also those who break down psychologically at the onset of the crisis and clearly demonstrate that they are incapable of going any further with their lives unless provided with immediate and intensive assistance. (pp.3-4)

19

In the Glossary to *Crisis Intervention Handbook*, Roberts provides a definition that takes into account the five important components of a crisis:

> The subjective reaction to a stressful life experience that compromises the individual's stability and ability to cope or function. The main cause of a crisis is a stressful or hazardous event, but two other conditions are also necessary: (1) the individual's perception of the stressful event as the cause of considerable upset and/or disruption; and (2) the individual's inability to resolve the disruption by previously used coping methods. Crisis also refers to an "upset in the steady state." It often has five components: a hazardous event, a vulnerable state, a precipitating factor, an active crisis state, and the resolution of the crisis. Crisis seems to be derived from the Greek word for "decision," or more broadly, "a turning point." In addition, a Chinese ideograph for crisis can be interpreted both as a "danger," in the sense that it threatens to overwhelm the individual and may result in serious consequences, and as an "opportunity," because during periods of crisis one tends to become amenable to outside influence. (Roberts, 1990, p. 329)

A crisis is based on an unpredictable and arbitrary event, and a person's rapid rise of tension, sense of confusion, feeling of intense anxiety, and/or a state of disequilibrium from the impact of the event. Certain stressful or hazardous events cause a crisis in some individuals and not in others.

CASE STUDY

Dominic is a forty-five-year-old New Jersey State Trooper who works very hard. He is obese at 260 pounds. Dominic's wife calls him at work and asks him to come home immediately because his thirteen-year-old son Anthony has been suspended from school. She reports that the assistant principal found cocaine in Dominic, Jr.'s locker. Within seconds, Dominic, Sr. has severe chest pains and breaks into a cold sweat. Dominic, Sr. learned in his childhood that deviant acts will not be tolerated and that "children are a reflection of their parents." He also was socialized with the belief that it is extremely shameful when any family member is in trouble with the law. He is rushed to the nearest hospital emergency room. The symptoms in this crisis situation were consistent with a panic attack.

Another parent of a thirteen-year-old son who is suspended may

20

react very differently when hearing the bad news. He may suggest to his wife that she remain calm and offer to work it out after work in the evening. The father in this case denies there is a major life crisis and assumes that some other youth placed the drugs in his son's locker as a sick joke.

On the other hand, a parent with different socialization experiences during childhood and resulting beliefs might rush to school or home, and as soon as he or she sees the son, start hitting him. Child abuse puts the youth in crisis and possibly both the nonabusive and abusive parent as well.

CASE STUDY

Joann is a thirty-five-year-old homemaker with two children. She has been told by her husband that he just got the promotion he has been waiting for and they would be moving from New Jersey to Indiana. Joann has lived in the New Jersey area all her life and she doesn't know anyone in Indiana. Within a few days, she has an acute depressive episode with suicidal ideation.

Julie, a different thirty-five-year-old homemaker with two children, views the same event mentioned above—her husband's new job and the family's upcoming relocation—as an adventure and chance to learn about a different region of the United States. Upon hearing of her husband's promotion, Julie starts calling real estate agents, her rabbi, and the president of the local chapter of the National Council of Jewish Women (N.C.J.W.). By networking, Julie soon finds several new friends in Indiana, people who had relocated from the Northeast to Indiana in the past.

It is difficult to count the number of crises occurring in any one day because some event may produce a crisis in one person and not another. Even the most stressful and threatening of events may lead to a crisis in one person and not in another. For example, a divorce or an automobile accident would seem to produce a crisis in most people. However, the author has found that some people will not go into a crisis as a result of either of the above events. Whether or not an unpredictable event produces a crisis or unsteady state for a person depends on their physical and emotional condition, attitude, temperament, values, beliefs, expectations, ego strengths, and coping skills. Even when people are in crisis states, the length of the crises vary from several hours to several weeks or months. It should be noted that some events cause crisis symptoms and reactions in nearly everyone. For example, Foy et. al. (1992) found that one week after being raped, 94 percent of the women assessed met full symptom criteria for post-traumatic stress disorder (PTSD).

PUBLIC HEALTH PROBLEMS AND CRISIS PRONE INDIVIDUALS

During the past two decades, several major public health problems have received widespread public attention from both informed citizens and mental health professionals. The most threatening and hazardous public health problems, such as child abuse, AIDS, cancer, substance abuse, woman battering, sexual assault, suicide attempts, and intense family disorganization also seem to be the most pervasive. All races, religions, and socioeconomic groups are profoundly affected by these major problems. Many of the millions of individuals experiencing the above events are particularly prone to acute crisis episodes. The extent of the adult population encountering acute crisis episodes is not known and is impossible to measure precisely. Nevertheless, there is increasing evidence of a direct link between persons suffering from the above events and the onset of acute crisis episodes (Roberts, 1991; Gilliland and James, 1993).

Persons of all ages are susceptible to emotional crisis. Some people are more crisis-prone and vulnerable to the negative impact of highly stressful events than others. A person's vulnerability to a stressful life event is dependent to a certain extent on the newness, intensity, and duration of the stressful event. In addition, a person's risk and vulnerability increase markedly as a result of physical and emotional exhaustion, a dearth of prior experience in resolving a crisis, and a lack of material resources (e.g., shelter, food, or money to pay for medical services). But the most important factor in preventing a major stressful event from becoming a crisis is each person's ability to tap his or her inner ego strengths and support system, and to develop alternative coping mechanisms.

People have limits placed on their coping skills and resources as a result of such problems as serious physical illness, suicide attempts, psychiatric disorders, incest and repeated sexual assaults, and alcoholism. Some of these traumatic and hazardous crisis-inducing events can be too overwhelming to be handled with any normal coping strategies. At other times these problems can drain people of their coping

22

skills, especially when life's demands exceed their skills and resources. Epidemiologic data indicate that over one-half of the adult population of the United States has suffered from the above mentioned medical and mental health problems. The epidemiologic reports are based on national studies with representative samples from every region of the United States. Therefore, they are widely accepted as the most reliable prevalence estimates, and they provide some indication of those who may be at risk of acute crises throughout the nation. Each specific prevalence estimate is documented later in this chapter.

For many people, a hazardous or stressful life event is the last straw or the precipitating event to the crisis reaction. Persons suffering from anxiety or depressive disorders, drug addictions, or repeated violent assaults often experience a chain of life stresses and personal problems. When these individuals are overwhelmed and view their problems as insurmountable and unresolvable, they can rapidly deteriorate to a crisis state. The active state of acute crisis is characterized by confusion, tension, helplessness, inadequacy, imbalance, disequilibrium, and severe emotional disorganization. The onset of a crisis state is sudden and typically is resolved in "several weeks to several months" (Roberts, 1990, p. 11). A crisis can well be a pivotal point in a person's life. Effective resolution of an acute crisis can provide ego bolstering and very positive growth so that the individual is better prepared to cope with the successive stresses of daily living. In contrast, failure to successfully resolve a crisis may lead to recurring and chronic problems such as post-traumatic stress disorder (PTSD), chronic depression, and eating disorders, or physical symptoms such as headaches and musculoskeletal pains, or lethal incidents such as homicide or suicide.

The remainder of this chapter will focus on the personal and situational variables that relate to crises. Epidemiologic data is presented on situational variables (e.g., crime, illness, family problems, etc.) as well as data on personal variables (e.g., psychopathology and substance abuse). Information is also provided about the individuals who typically offer crisis intervention services. Finally, cognitive therapy is presented as a method for understanding the personal variables involved in crises.

SCOPE OF THE PROBLEM

Numerous situational variables may precipitate a crisis, including health emergencies, life-threatening illnesses, family problems, crime-related problems (including violent crime victimizations), and community disasters. The Bureau of Justice Statistics of the United States Department of Justice provides national prevalence estimates on violent crime victimizations.

- 959 children are abducted each day of the year (this finding is based on the recent estimates that 350,000 children are abducted each year).
- 357 individuals are victims of forcible rape each day of the year (this finding is based on the Bureau of Justice Statistics [B.J.S.] Annual Criminal Victimization Rates of over 130,000 rapes each year).

The National Center for Health Statistics and the American Hospital Association each provide nationally representative data on certified suicide fatalities, suicide attempts, and emergency room visits.

- Between 685 and 1,645 individuals attempt suicide each day of the year (this finding is based on the Maris & Associates, 1992 estimates that there are between 250,000 and 600,000 suicide attempts each year).
- 254,820 persons visit emergency rooms each day of the year (American Hospital Association, 1992). The majority of men and women visit a hospital emergency room because of a traumatic event or an acute psychiatric or medical crisis (e.g., gunshot wound, rape, car accident, drug overdose, sexually transmitted disease, or serious life-threatening illness).

The National Cancer Institute, the American Cancer Society, Inc., and the Center for Disease Control (C.D.C.) each provide up-to-date reports on annual incidence rates for the various types of cancer and AIDS.

- 3,205 new cancer cases are diagnosed each day of the year.
- 140 patients with AIDS die each day of the year and in 1994 alone the CDC projects that there will be 43,000–93,000 newly diagnosed AIDS cases.

Personal variables affect the severity and duration of a crisis. These variables include cognitive processes, behavioral coping skills, typical affective processes (i.e., mood), and prior history of psychopathology. One-year prevalence rates for mental and addictive disorders in the United States were recently reported by a group of prominent epidemiologists. The national prevalence rates are based on a five-year N.I.M.H. Epidemiological Catchment Area (ECA) Program at five study sites in different regions of the United States. In addition to one-year prevalence rates, the researchers measured the percentage of the United States population who utilized medical, mental health, and addiction treatment services over the course of one year (Reiger et al., 1993).

- 41,488 adults are diagnosed with affective disorders (bipolar, unipolar major depression, dysthymia) each day of the year. A total annual prevalence rate of 15,143,000 was estimated for affective disorders.
- 54,887 adults are diagnosed with anxiety disorders (phobia, panic disorder, obsessive-compulsive disorders) each day of the year. A total annual prevalence rate of 20,034,000 was estimated for anxiety disorders.
- 41,244 adults are diagnosed with substance abuse disorders each day of the year. A total annual prevalence rate of 15,054,060 was estimated for alcohol and drug-related disorders.

The national prevalence rates of 15.14 million affective disorders, 20.03 million anxiety disorders, and 15.05 million alcohol and drug-related addictions documented above from the ECA studies may well be significantly underestimated. Ronald Kessler and associates in their lifetime and twelve-month prevalence study of fourteen DSM-III-R psychiatric disorders reported that the prevalence of psychiatric disorders is much higher than previously suspected (Kessler, et al., 1994). This comorbidity survey was based on a stratified, multistage area probability sample of 8,098 noninstitutionalized persons, fifteen to fifty-four years of age, from forty-eight states. Close to 50 percent of the respondents indicated that they had suffered from at least one psychiatric disorder during their lifetime, and nearly 30 percent reported having one or more disorders during the twelve-month period directly prior to the study. The most frequently reported disorders during the previous twelve months were depressive disorders, alcohol dependence, social phobia, and simple phobia. With regard to comorbidity, 56 percent of the respondents with a history of at least one psychiatric disorder, reported having two or more disorders. Rural Americans are less likely when compared to their urban counterparts to suffer from three or more disorders during the previous twelve-month period. A surprising finding was that blacks reported much lower prevalence rates of affective and substance abuse disorders than whites, despite the fact that the black respondents had much lower levels of both education and income than whites. Unfortunately, fewer than 40 percent of the respondents with a lifetime disorder had ever received treatment from a mental health professional, and less than 20 percent of those persons reporting a recent disorder had received crisis intervention, psychotherapy, or other clinical treatment during the past twelve months (Kessler, et al., 1994).

In view of the millions of people encountering acute crises as well as psychiatric disorders each year, the need for crisis intervention and brief treatment is vital. As society-at-large begins to recognize the huge number and impact of acute crisis events, an enormous number of social workers and psychologists will be needed to help people to cope with and resolve social impairments.

ROBERTS' SEVEN-STAGE CRISIS INTERVENTION MODEL

Clinicians working in private practices, at community mental health centers, or in hospital settings are often charged with responding to a wide array of mass emergencies, disasters, and victims of violent crimes and other traumatic events. Various practice models have been developed to assist clinicians in working with persons in crisis.

Roberts' seven-stage crisis intervention model (figure 2.1) can be applied to clients presenting with acute psychological crises, acute situational crises, and acute stress disorders. This model can facilitate early identification of crisis precipitants, problem solving, and effective crisis resolution.

Effective intervention and brief treatment with persons in crisis (e.g., adolescent suicidal patients, survivors of incest, alcoholic clients, parents of abducted children, etc.) always should begin with a thorough intake assessment or collection of background information by the therapist. Subsequent crisis interventions should be based on this initial assessment. A critical part of any assessment with depressed, suicidal, sexually assaulted, or battered women survivors is a lethality or level of danger assessment; in addition to using published lethality scales (see chapter 4 for a detailed discussion of assessing lethality by clinical psychologists David Jobes and Alan L. Berman) and determining if the patient is in danger (e.g., battered women who recently received death threats from their batterers). In addition to determining

26

Figure 2.1
Roberts' Seven-Stage Crisis Intervention Model

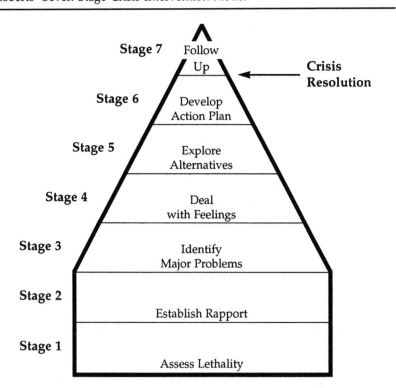

lethality and the need for emergency intervention, it is useful for the clinician to have immediate access to emergency phone numbers for the police, twenty-four-hour crisis intervention unit, addiction treatment centers, emergency rescue squad, hospital emergency rooms, and poison control centers. First and foremost, it is crucial to maintain active communication (by phone or in person) with the client while these procedures are being activated.

The seven stages of the crisis intervention model are as follows:

1. Plan and conduct a thorough assessment (including lethality, dangerousness to self or others, and immediate psychosocial needs).
2. Establish rapport and rapidly establish the relationship (con-

veying genuine respect for and acceptance of the client, while also offering reassurance and reinforcement that the client, like hundreds of previous clients, can be helped by the therapist).

3. Identify major problem(s). This step includes identifying the ''last straw'' or precipitating event that led the client to seek help at this time. The clinician should help the client to focus on the most important problem by helping the client to rank order and prioritize several problems and the harmful or potentially threatening aspect of the number one problem. It is important and most productive to help the client to ventilate about the precipitating event or events; this will lead to problem identification. Sometimes clients are in a state of denial. Other times clients have an all-consuming need to ventilate and talk about their symptoms. Catharsis and ventilation of feelings are important as long as the therapist gradually returns to the central focus: the crisis precipitant or actual crisis event.

4. Deal with feelings and emotions. This stage involves active listening, communicating with warmth and reassurance, nonjudgmental statements and validation, and accurate empathetic statements. The person in crisis may well have multiple mood swings throughout the crisis intervention. As a result, nonverbal gestures such as smiling and nodding might be distracting and annoying to the person in acute crisis. Therefore, the author suggests the use of verbal counseling skills when helping the client to explore his or her emotions. These verbal responses include reflecting feelings, restating content, using open-ended questions, summarizing, giving advice, reassurance, interpreting statements, confronting, and using silence.

5. Generate and explore alternatives. Many clients, especially college graduates, have personal insights and problem-solving skills as well as the ability to anticipate the outcomes of certain deliberate actions. However, the client is emotionally distressed and consumed by the aftermath of the crisis episode. It is therefore very useful to have an objective and trained clinician assist the client in conceptualizing and discussing adaptive coping responses to the crisis. ''In cases where the client has little or no introspection or personal insights, the clinician needs to take the initiative and suggest more adaptive coping methods'' (Roberts, 1990, p.13). During this potentially highly productive stage, the therapist/crisis intervenor and client collaboratively agree upon appropriate alternative coping methods.

6. Develop and formulate an action plan. Developing and imple-

menting an action plan will ultimately restore cognitive functioning for the client. This active stage may involve the client agreeing to search for an apartment in a low-crime suburban area, for example, or it may involve the client making an appointment with an attorney who specializes in divorce mediation, or agreeing to go to a support group for widows or persons with sexually transmitted diseases (STDs). Many clients have great difficulty mobilizing themselves and following through on an action plan. It is imperative that the client be encouraged and bolstered so that he or she will follow through. Clients in crisis need to hear that you have had other clients who have failed and have been lethargic, yet have made an all-out effort to overcome the obstacle and were successful in resolving the crisis.

7. Follow up. Stage seven in crisis intervention should involve an informal agreement or formal appointment between the therapist and client to have another meeting at a designated time, either in person or on the phone, to gauge the client's success in crisis resolution and daily functioning one week, two weeks, or one month later.

BRIEF TREATMENT AND COGNITIVE THERAPY WITH PERSONS IN CRISIS

Brief and cognitive-oriented therapy are more than packages of techniques. They provide models for understanding individuals, based on the assumption that persons' perceptions determine their feelings and behaviors. Time-limited cognitive therapy is excellent for conceptualizing crises, since a crisis is a crisis when the individual *perceives* it as such.

Cognitive therapy was developed by Beck and his colleagues (1979, 1985, 1990, 1993). The basic assumption is that individuals' basic beliefs, thoughts, ideas, etc., impact how they feel and act. For example:

1. In *depression*, the individual perceives self as inadequate, unlovable, or suffering unrecoverable loss.
2. In *anxiety*, the individual perceives self as being vulnerable to some threat.
3. In *addiction*, the individual perceives self as needing a substance in order to have fun or deal with pain.

29

4. In a *personality disorder*, the individual has some chronic, overdeveloped, maladaptive beliefs about self, world, or future. For example, a person with borderline personality disorder perceives self as inevitably being abandoned. Hence these people are extremely vulnerable to crises.

In a crisis, some "dangerous" situation has activated an individual's basic beliefs about self. It is useful for the therapist to ask the client to describe a critical incident indicative of his or her problems. According to cognitive therapy, a person's early life experiences provide him or her with basic beliefs. These basic beliefs tend to lie dormant until an individual encounters critical incidents. *This is the pivotal point of crisis theory:* Critical incidents (which are situational variables) activate personal variables (including basic beliefs, automatic thoughts, emotions, behaviors, and physiologic responses) in a crisis. Thus, it is easy to understand why the same situation does not necessarily produce a crisis in two different people. Depending on a person's early life experiences, he or she may or may not experience an event as a crisis.

CASE STUDY

When reviewing the case of Dominic and his thirteen-year-old son (the cocaine incident discussed earlier), we see the influence of early life experiences on adult beliefs and cognitions. Dominic experiences chest pains when his wife telephones to tell him about the drug incident and their son's suspension. Early in his life, Dominic learned that "deviant behaviors are *intolerable*" and that "children are a reflection of their parents." He also learned that "it is extremely shameful when a family is in legal trouble." Thus, when his son engaged in illegal behavior, he experienced a crisis (the symptoms were consistent with a panic attack).

On the other hand, individuals with different life experiences and resulting beliefs from Dominic's might believe that it is useful to use denial and ignore a major problem. This type of person was socialized to believe that if you ignore problems sometimes they do go away, and other times they get worse. Because of some individuals' early life experiences they opt for denial as their coping mechanism.

The cognitive case conceptualization and triage assessment are applied in many of the chapters in this text. The basic premises are:

(1) crises are determined by situational and personal variables; (2) personal variables relate to individuals' thought processes, which determine emotional and behavioral patterns; (3) these variables must be systematically assessed prior to providing crisis intervention, in order to define the exact nature of the crisis; (4) cognitive therapy provides a systematic method for assessing personal and situational variables, the *cognitive case conceptualization*; (5) *triage* logically follows the case conceptualization.

CONCLUSION

All of the data and national trends cited in this chapter reflect the continued refinement of sampling procedures, data collection methods, and special tabulation methods by federal agencies such as the National Institute on Drug Abuse (Division of Epidemiology and Prevention Research), the Department of Justice (Bureau of Justice Statistics), the National Institute of Mental Health (Division of Epidemiology and Services Research and the Center for Mental Health Services, Substance Abuse, and Mental Health Services Administration), the Center for Disease Control (C.D.C.) of the U.S. Public Health Service, the National Cancer Institute, and the American Cancer Society.

A major obstacle to finding the most accurate estimates of crisis episodes lies in differences from state to state and city to city in how information about specific types of crisis events is collected and reported. Whether we focus on suicide attempts, crises in the aftermath of violent crime victimization, drug overdoses, or abducted children, the agency reporting the statistics and the agencies collecting the data vary tremendously in how much information they provide.

Future research and epidemiological studies are needed to provide nationally standardized data on base rates of diagnoses for psychiatric, medical, crime-related, and family crisis. In addition, research is needed to determine the extent of each type of prevalent acute crisis, the characteristics of persons in crisis, and the most cost-effective time-limited treatment methods. Although several hundred thousand clinicians are intervening on behalf of patients in acute crisis, numerous different time-limited treatment strategies are being utilized. Each of the chapter authors has met with considerable success in the use of the seven-stage crisis intervention model. We all hope that readers will send us brief reports on the effectiveness of their use of the crisis intervention model.

Persons in crisis may only need a sympathetic ear, reassurance, and social support. Other persons in crisis may need crisis intervention for three to twelve sessions. The third and least popular treatment for persons in crisis is long-term psychotherapy. However, after the crisis episode is resolved, long-term psychotherapy is very appropriate for persons diagnosed with personality disorders, chronic depression, and/or post-traumatic stress disorder (PTSD).

REFERENCES

American Cancer Society. (1993). *Cancer facts and figures—1993*. Atlanta, GA: American Cancer Society.

American Hospital Association. (1992). *American Hospital Association hospital statistics 1992–93*. Chicago, IL: American Hospital Association.

American Psychiatric Association. (1994). *Diagnostic and Statistical Manual of Mental Disorders*. 4th ed. Washington, DC: American Psychiatric Association Press.

Beck, A. T. and Emery, G. (1985). *Anxiety disorders and phobias: A cognitive perspective*. New York: Basic Books.

Beck. A. T., Rush, A. J., and Emery, G. (1979). *Cognitive therapy of depression*. New York: Guilford.

Beck, A. T., and Freeman, A. (1990). *Cognitive therapy or personality disorders*. New York: Guilford.

Beck, A. T., Wright, F., Newman, C., and Liese, B. (1993). *Cognitive therapy of substance abuse*. New York: Guilford.

Bureau of Justice Statistics. (1992). *BJS national update, April 1992*. Washington, DC: U.S. Department of Justice, Bureau of Justice Statistics.

Burgess, A.W., and Lazare, A. (1976). *Community mental health* (p. 6). Englewood Cliffs, NJ: Prentice-Hall.

Centers for Disease Control. (Jan. 1993). *AIDS information: statistical projections/trends*. Atlanta, GA: Centers for Disease Control.

Centers for Disease Control. (April 1993). *CDC quarterly HIV/AIDS surveillance report*. Atlanta, GA: Centers for Disease Control.

Daro, D. (Feb. 15, 1993). Personal communication. Chicago, IL: National Committee for the Prevention of Child Abuse.

Federal Bureau of Investigation. (1977). *Uniform crime reports in the United States*. Washington, DC: U.S. Department of Justice.

Federal Bureau of Investigation. ((1993). *Uniform crime reports in the United States*. Washington, DC: U.S. Department of Justice.

Freeman, A., and Dattilio, F.M. (Eds.). (1992). *Comprehensive casebook of cognitive therapy*. New York: Plenum Press.

Foy, D.W. (1992). *Introduction and description of the disorder.* In D.W. Foy (Ed.), *Treating PTSD: Cognitive-behavioral strategies.* New York: Guilford Press, 1-12.

Gilliland, B.E., and James, R.K. (1993). *Crisis intervention strategies.* Belmont, CA: Wadsworth.

Kessler, R.C., et al. (1994). Lifetime and 12-month prevalence of DSM-IIIR psychiatric disorders in the United States. *Archives of General Psychiatry, 51* 8-19.

Klingbeil, K., and Boyd, V. (1984). Emergency room intervention: Detection, assessment, and treatment. In A.R. Roberts (Ed.), *Battered women and their families: Intervention, strategies and treatment programs.* New York: Springer, 7-32.

Manderscheid, R. W., Rae, D.S., Narrow, W., Locke, B.Z., and Reiger, D. (1993). Congruence of service utilization estimates from the epidemiologic catchment area project and other sources. *Archives of General Psychiatry, 50,* 108-114.

Maris, R. W., Berman, A.L., Maltsberger, J.T., and Yufit, R.I. (Eds.). (1992). *Assessment and prediction of suicide.* New York: Guilford.

Mechanic, D. (1989). *Mental health and social policy.* 3d ed. Englewood Cliffs, NJ: Prentice-Hall.

Narrow, W. E., Reiger, D. A., Rae, D. S., Maderscheid, R. W. and Locke, B.Z. (1993). Use of services by persons with mental and addictive disorders. *Archives of General Psychiatry, 50,* 95-107.

National Institute on Drug Abuse. (1991). *Annual medical examiner data 1990.* Rockville, MD: National Institute on Drug Abuse, Division of Epidemiology and Prevention Research.

National Institute on Drug Abuse. (1991). *National household survey on drug abuse, population estimates 1991.* Rockville, MD: National Institute on Drug Abuse, Division of Epidemiology and Prevention Research.

Reber, A. S. (1985). *Dictionary of psychology.* New York: Penguin.

Reiger, D. A., Narrow, W. E., Rae, D. S., Manderscheid, R., Locke, B.Z., and Goodwin, F.K. (1993). The defacto U.S. mental and addictive disorders service system. *Archives of General Psychiatry, 50* 85-94.

Roberts, A. R. (1991). *Contemporary perspectives on crisis intervention and prevention.* Englewood Cliffs, NJ: Prentice-Hall.

Roberts, A. R. (1990). *Crisis intervention handbook: Assessment, treatment and research.* Belmont, CA: Wadsworth.

Straus, M. and Gelles, R.J. (1990). *Physical violence in American families.* New Brunswick, NJ: Transaction.

Acute Psychological Crisis, Crisis Intervention, and Brief Therapy Applications

CHAPTER 3

Working in Hospital Emergency Departments: Guidelines for Crisis Intervention Workers

RICK A. MYER and
FRED J. HANNA

Mr. Allen Lewis was brought to the emergency room following an automobile accident. He had suffered several broken ribs, a punctured lung, a broken leg, lacerations to the face and arms, and a concussion. Although his injuries were not life threatening, they were serious and would involve a prolonged hospital stay and some rehabilitation. However, a passenger in Mr. Lewis's vehicle and the driver of the other automobile had not fared as well. Both were in critical condition and might not survive their injuries.

Upon his arrival in the emergency room, Mr. Lewis began inquiring into the condition of the others involved in the accident. Initially, the staff deferred answering his questions by treating his physical injuries. After two hours this tactic became ineffective and they attempted to shift the focus to the fact that his injuries were not life threatening and in a few weeks he would be well enough to be discharged. Mr. Lewis continued questioning, however, leaving the staff somewhat perplexed as to how to deal with his persistence. They were simply seeking to avoid distressing him with the details of the injuries suffered by others in the accident. As Mr. Lewis's questioning became more determined and vehement, the staff requested that the chaplain talk with Mr. Lewis regarding the accident.

Jennifer was brought to the emergency room by her husband, Donald, due to a suspected overdose of valium. When the nurse questioned Jennifer, she discovered that Jennifer had taken ten to twelve valium tablets in reaction to her husband's disclosure that he was having an affair with a coworker. Jennifer stated that she would rather die than suffer the embarrassment of her friends learning of her husband's infidelity. Once the physical concerns were addressed, the physician requested a consultation with the psychiatric nurse assigned to respond to emotional/physical crises in the emergency room.

After conferring with the attending physician, the psychiatric nurse asked to talk with Jennifer alone in a quiet room so that she could assess Jennifer's suicidal risk. The psychiatric nurse found that Jennifer had a history of impulsive behavior, poor coping skills in stressful situations, and suicidal threats. While this was the first time she had ever acted upon a threat, the psychiatric nurse was convinced that Jennifer should not be left alone for the next twenty-four to forty-eight hours. Given her poor relationship with her husband throughout his affair, the nurse recommended that Jennifer be admitted for observation and a more thorough evaluation.

The wife and two daughters of Mr. Anderson waited silently and patiently for information. Mr. Anderson had collapsed while doing some yard work that morning. He had grabbed his chest and complained of pain just prior to falling. The paramedics had arrived quickly and the family had overheard them say something about a myocardial infarction. When questioned about what that was and how serious, the paramedics explained that Mr. Anderson had experienced a heart attack but that at this time no one could determine the seriousness of his condition. The paramedics quickly placed Mr. Anderson in the ambulance and suggested the family follow in their car. Since that time, the family had been waiting in the public area of the emergency room for over one and one-half hours.

One of the nurses had taken time to talk with the Anderson family to get some basic information. The nurse discovered that Mr. Anderson had no history of heart problems and that one child, a son, lived out of town and could not be reached. The nurse reassured the Andersons that everything was being done to make Mr. Anderson comfortable. When the family inquired about his condition, however, the nurse did not respond directly and stated that when the physician had time, she would talk with them. The nurse recognized that the family was becoming increasingly distraught and called the hospital social worker to talk with them.

These three cases represent typical situations in hospital emergency rooms. Crisis intervention workers would likely encounter similar situations. They might also confront a combination of these three. One of the inherent problems of such situations is that the patients and their family members are usually unfamiliar with hospitals or their routine. In addition, the circumstances in which patients and family members find themselves may require changes in their assumptions about themselves (Viney et al., 1985). Whether patients are physically ill, acutely emotionally disturbed, or the families of these patients, crisis workers are asked to help these people mobilize their coping mechanisms in a setting that may isolate them from support systems and limit their independence (Viney et al., 1985). This chapter presents a model for working with patients and families. Along with this model, some practical suggestions will be provided that define the role of crisis intervention workers, delineate the goals of crisis intervention, and describe a practice framework for crisis intervention in the emergency room.

SCOPE OF THE PROBLEM

Visits to the emergency departments of hospitals increased from 30 million in 1965 to 92 million in 1990 (Staff, 1992). This staggering increase has stretched the capacity of emergency departments and staffs almost beyond their limits. The resulting overcrowding often translates into waiting periods of over four hours to receive services (Staff, 1992). As staff are being asked to provide services to increasing numbers of patients, nonmedical issues can often be neglected. Researchers have found that nonmedical issues can be quite severe (Hess and Ruster, 1990) and may influence recovery from the medical issues (Cohen, 1983).

At the same time, emergency department staff are being faced with new challenges of differentiating accidental injuries due to abuse. Making these judgments requires knowledge and takes time. With an already overworked staff, these types of patients can be easily overlooked. For example, elderly persons are increasingly the victims of abuse. The Yale–New Haven Hospital found that during a six-month period of 1991, 6.3 percent of elderly patients seen in the emergency department were victims of elderly abuse (Fulmer, et al., 1992). Victims of domestic violence (Hadley, 1992) and child abuse also are groups that can go undetected due to the volume of patients seen in emergency departments. Some hospitals have developed special in-service training to instruct staff to identify these types of problems (Lazzaro and McFarlane, 1991). Other hospitals have established working relationships with programs developed to work with these types of populations (Hadley, 1992). Crisis workers can be integral in helping hospitals develop programs that minimize the chance that victims of abuse are overlooked.

Increased violence is also illustrative of the scope of the problem (Staff, 1992). The psychological trauma of suffering violent crime should be addressed early to minimize any long-term effects. Research has demonstrated that timely treatment of such emotional issues decreases the chances of the development of post-traumatic stress disorder (Gilliland and James, 1993). The potential for natural disaster is also suggested as a reason for hospitals to develop crisis intervention services (Wood and Cowan, 1991). Plans to address the psychological impact as well as the physical trauma of natural disasters are needed to promote a stable recovery.

Cohen (1983) noted that consumer awareness is another basis for crisis intervention in the health care system. This movement has helped medical personnel become aware that nonmedical issues are essential factors to be reckoned with in patient care (Cohen, 1983). Thus, the demand for crisis services in emergency departments is clear. Of course, this demand necessitates the training of staff in the theory and practice of crisis intervention.

REVIEW OF THE LITERATURE

Research has demonstrated that crisis intervention in hospital emergency departments has beneficial effects on patients, family members of patients, and staff (Ayers and Janosik, 1984). However, Siegel, Slaikeu, and Kimbrell (1984) noted that training, unfortunately, has not kept pace with increased awareness of the psychological and emotional well-being of patients in recovery. They further observed that even though some medical personnel receive minimal instruction in crisis theory, most hospital staff simply do not feel comfortable dealing with patients in psychological or emotional crisis. Nevertheless, many hospitals do recognize the value of trained crisis intervention workers in the emergency department. A primary example is found in the Boston City Hospital, which has employed psychiatric nurses since 1969 (Pisarick, Zigmun, Summerfield, Mian, Johansen, and Deveraux, 1979).

It is important to note in this regard that many hospitals employ chaplains to provide crisis intervention in emergency departments. As Cohen (1983) observed, medical personnel have become more receptive to services that address these psychological and emotional factors in recognition of the impact that treatment of these issues has on physical recovery.

Inclusion of crisis intervention services in hospital emergency departments has at least four advantages, resting upon the at-risk nature of the population being served (Ayers and Janosik, 1984). Together these advantages facilitate the speedy recovery of patients and assist families in making changes that might be precipitated by illness and/or injury. First, crisis intervention services help prevent additional psychological problems and complications that may accompany hospitalization (Cohen, 1983). If not addressed, crisis reactions can develop into more severe affective, cognitive, and/or behavioral impairments (Gilliland and James, 1993). Recognition of and intervention in crisis situations in emergency departments create an environment and expectation for patients and families that relieves a portion of the overall shock.

Second, crisis intervention in emergency departments may serve to alleviate possible exacerbation of physical trauma. In emergency departments, situations occur in which the emotional trauma of patients causes them to resist medical treatment. Patients can become so distressed that they are unable to remain immobile, causing their injuries to be aggravated. In situations such as these, crisis intervention can permit patients a catharsis, thereby calming them and preventing physical injuries from being worsened.

Third, crisis intervention may serve to make patients more responsive to treatment. Cohen (1983) argued that psychological problems can interfere with patients' ability or desire to perform the behaviors necessary to control a medical problem. For example, a person who has received extensive burns will undoubtedly need to address the psychological effect of the injury (Croushore, 1979a). This advantage is also important for families. Families are involved in the recovery of patients by virtue of their relationships. If, for example, a family has not addressed the emotional impact of the burn victim described above, their communications with the patient may result in the patient not feeling supported in the effort to recover from the injury. Crisis workers can facilitate patients and their families to examine and eventually resolve the psychological and emotional effect of an injury.

Fourth, crisis intervention in emergency departments can identify abuse victims. The number of reported abuse cases increases signif-

41

icantly each year as the public becomes more sensitive to this problem. For example, records indicate that 22–35 percent of women who present at emergency departments do so because of symptoms related to physical abuse (McLeer and Anwar, 1987; 1989). Emergency departments have a unique opportunity to identify these victims and interrupt the abuse cycle. As an entry point into the health care system, the recognition of abuse by emergency departments can provide intervention and possible prevention of the exacerbation of the crisis (Hankoff, et al., 1974).

CRISIS THEORY

Roberts' (1990) seven-step model for crisis intervention provides an excellent guide for crisis workers in hospital emergency departments. Crisis workers, however, should recognize that this model is not set up to be rigidly followed in a step-by-step fashion. Instead, the model should be viewed as fluid and adaptable for work in emergency departments. For example, as new information is made available, such as a patient's condition unexpectedly deteriorating, the patient, family members, and even staff may experience further reactions. Crisis workers, therefore, must be attentive to changes in clients and the environment that might influence reactions to the crisis event. As changes occur, crisis workers must be flexible in moving to that part of the model that best corresponds with current circumstances.

Before reviewing Roberts' (1990) model, it is important to understand that a key element in crisis intervention is rapid, accurate assessment. This assessment should be holistic, taking into account affective, cognitive, and behavioral reactions (Myer et al., 1992). Affective reactions to crises fall into three primary types: (a) anger/hostility; (b) fear/anxiety; and (c) sadness/melancholy. Cognitive perceptions of crisis events are experienced as these impact four areas: (a) physical—food, water, shelter; (b) psychological—identity, emotional well-being; (c) relationship—family, friends, coworkers; and (d) moral/spiritual—personal integrity, values, and belief system aspects of patients and their family. Cognitive reactions to crises are: (a) transgression, which occurs when patients' or their families' rights have been violated; (b) threat, which occurs when a person judges the event as having potential harm or damage to themselves or others; and (c) loss, which involves the belief that an irretrievable loss has occurred. Behavioral reactions to crises are: (a) approach, in which individuals make overt or covert attempts to address the crisis; (b) avoidance, in which active attempts are made to ignore, evade, or escape the crisis event; and (c) immobility, in which nonproductive, disorganized, or self-canceling coping behaviors are displayed.

Assessment also should be continuous, providing workers with information that will facilitate sound clinical judgments (Gilliland and James, 1993). Ongoing assessment is essential in determining the needs of patients and their families at that moment. As stated previously, new information may result in crisis workers adjusting their approach to match the current state of patients and their families.

The seven steps in Roberts' (1990) model are:

1. *Make psychological contact and rapidly establish the relationship.* Establishing rapport with a client in the hospital emergency setting involves active listening skills, including attentiveness, reflection of feelings, restatements of content, asking open and closed questions, and use of minimal encouragers (Gilliland and James, 1993). When combined, these skills communicate both respect for a client and an interest in his or her well-being. Researchers have found that for patients and families to feel satisfied with emergency services, they must perceive a sense of caring by the staff of emergency departments (Staff, 1992).

In establishing rapport with patients and their families, workers will gather information important to the assessment process. This information will help crisis workers to judge the affective, cognitive, and behavioral reaction along with the severity of these reactions. To gauge the reactions, three basic questions need to be answered. First, what are the feelings that patients and their families have about the crisis event? Second, how have they perceived the crisis event affecting their lives? And third, what have they done to overcome the impact of the crisis event?

2. *Examine the dimensions of the problem.* In practice, steps 1 and 2 frequently blend together. While working in hospital emergency departments, crisis workers should not automatically assume that the crisis reaction is concerned with medical issues (Croushore, 1979a). For example, a patient comes to the emergency department with a broken leg. The patient discovers that he will be off his feet for the next five weeks as he recovers from his injury. His family is also at the hospital, clearly anxious about the recovery time. While the injury is neither life threatening nor serious, the crisis worker learns that the patient works in construction and will not collect a paycheck for the time he is unable to work. The family as well as the patient are worried about having enough money to pay bills, buy groceries, etc. As can

43

be seen from this example, even though the precipitating event was a medical issue, the crisis reaction originated from a financial concern.

Again, assessment is integral in developing insight into the dimensions of the problem. Crisis workers should pattern questions to gather relevant information with respect to affective, cognitive, and behavioral reactions. The pattern of these questions should help crisis workers understand the effect the crisis is having or will likely have on day-to-day functioning of patients and families. Crisis workers should ask themselves: ''Will the affective, cognitive, and/or behavioral reaction interfere with the day-to-day activities and if so, how and to what degree?''

Also important during step 2 is to assess patients' and families' potential to harm themselves or others (Roberts, 1990). Recently, this aspect has become particularly important due to increased concern over aggressive and violent outbursts among patients and their families (Martin et al., 1991). Appropriate precautions should be taken if patients or their families manifest warning signs associated with suicide or other aggressive acts.

3. *Encourage an exploration of feelings and emotions.* Crisis workers' sensitivity to the need for expressing emotions is critical in emergency departments. At times, this step can be overlooked as crisis workers attempt to focus more on the crisis event rather than the reaction to that event (Roberts, 1990). Active listening skills along with the demonstration of a nonjudgmental attitude, empathy, and genuineness are invaluable in this step (Gilliland and James, 1993). As patients and their families perceive they are being supported, they will be more open to expressing their feelings. This catharsis is therapeutic and can lead to a healthy resolution of the crisis.

Crisis workers should use this step to develop an accurate assessment of patients' and their families' affective reactions to the crisis event. This assessment will determine the primary affective reaction and the severity of the reaction.

Crisis workers also should be alert for the staff's affective responses to individual and cumulative crisis situations. Croushore (1979b) suggested that a leading cause of burnout among nurses is the pressures that build while working with patients and their families unless this pressure is relieved. The staff should be allowed to debrief from particularly stressful situations.

4. *Explore and assess past coping attempts.* The shock of an unexpected visit to a hospital emergency department may result in the inability of patients and families to mobilize otherwise effective coping mechanisms. Simply exploring coping skills used in the past may be

all that is needed. Merely asking some patients and families how they have coped in the past with similar situations may serve to activate these mechanisms. However, in other situations, uncovering and triggering coping skills may be more complicated. The success of previous coping skills in conjunction with the suddenness and perceived severity of the crisis event combine to determine how easy it will be to activate appropriate, helpful coping skills.

5. *Generate and explore alternatives and specific solutions.* Generating and exploring alternatives and solutions to crisis events depend on the severity of patients' and their families' reactions. The more severe the reaction, the more directive the intervention needed (Gilliland and James, 1993). Mild types of crisis generally require a more *non-direct* level of intervention. This intervention level uses active listening skills to support and demonstrate caring. Moderately severe crises necessitate a *collaborative* intervention level. In this level of intervention, crisis workers, patients, and their families work together as a team. Crisis workers are compelled to use a *direct* level of intervention for patients and families who have suffered a severe crisis. This intervention level requires crisis workers to use directives with patients and their families. Care must be taken with intervention levels not to foster undue dependence on crisis workers. After the initial shock of the crisis is over, crisis workers might then retreat to a more collaborative rather than a direct intervention level.

6. *Restore cognitive functioning through implementation of action plan.* Roberts (1990) proposes a three-step process to restore cognitive functioning. First, patients and their families must have a realistic understanding of the crisis event. A realistic understanding is critical for patients and their families. For example, if the patient has just suffered a massive stroke, it is unrealistic to believe that he/she will return to work in a short period of time. Second, patients and their families should understand the meaning of the event and its likely effect on their lives. Patients and their families should consider how the injury will influence their lives on a short- and long-term basis. The example used above illustrates this well. In the short-term scenario, the family will have to visit the hospital to see the patient. Hospitalization will most likely involve spending time in rehabilitation, possibly at another hospital, again causing disruption in the family's functioning. In the long-term scenario, the patient may suffer physical and mental disability resulting in changes within the family. It is important to note that crisis intervention in emergency departments may not involve exploration of the long-term effect. However, sensitivity to this issue is necessary.

7. *Follow up*. Follow-up crisis intervention is twofold. First, follow-up is important to ensure the well-being of patients and their families. If patients or their families are regaining a sense of equilibrium in their lives, additional interventions may be required. Second, follow up is useful to evaluate the effectiveness of the services, and subsequently, to improve those services. In hospital emergency departments, follow up may involve visits to the hospital room if the patient is admitted. If the patient is not admitted, crisis workers may telephone or correspond with patients and their families.

The following case vignette illustrates the steps of crisis work in hospital emergency departments. Although all cases are unique, requiring crisis workers to tailor their intervention, this case represents a typical situation and describes the basic work of crisis workers.

The evening of the crisis, the Andersons were in the emergency department for a total of five hours. The worker met intermittently with the family over this period for a total of three hours. When the physician finally met with the family, the crisis worker was present to facilitate communication. Throughout the duration of this crisis the worker functioned in several different capacities helping the Andersons cope more effectively with the crisis. Follow up continued for several weeks and after Mr. Anderson's discharge.

GOALS FOR CRISIS INTERVENTION IN EMERGENCY DEPARTMENTS

Having described the model for crisis intervention, it is now appropriate to discuss goals of crisis intervention in emergency departments.

1. *Returning to former level of functioning*. As in most crisis intervention work, a primary goal is to return patients and families to their state of functioning prior to the onset of the crisis. Once this is accomplished, a sense of tolerance of the crisis develops. When this goal is met, the crisis state has diminished to the point of being coped with on a routine basis.

2. *Adapting to the hospital setting*. A medical crisis effectively introduces patients and families to a new environment, one that very few persons would choose willingly. A goal of intervention, therefore, would be to induce or facilitate a tolerance of the hospital environment so that the hospital becomes a familiar place in which functioning can take place. Functioning within this setting

CASE DESCRIPTION

Mr. Anderson is a fifty-two-year-old white male who was transported to the emergency department after complaining of chest pains and collapsing. Shortly after his arrival at the hospital, his wife and two daughters also arrive. The nurse talks with the family to gather insurance and medical information. She discovers that Mr. Anderson has no history of heart problems and has never been admitted into a hospital. During this preliminary discussion, the nurse finds the family extremely anxious and learns that they have little experience with hospital routines. At this time, the nurse makes a referral to the crisis worker.

You discover that the Andersons are new to the area and have no support system. They have moved from out of state one month prior to today. You also learn there is a son who is attending college near their former residence. Mrs. Anderson expresses concern for him and wants to call. Yet, she is not sure what she will say to him.

As you talk with the Andersons, they increasingly express fear and anxiety regarding Mr. Anderson. Although the nurse has reported to the family approximately every thirty minutes regarding Mr. Anderson's condi-

tion, Mrs. Anderson often asks what is taking so long and why the physician has not come to talk with them. You suggest that you talk with the physician to see what is happening with Mr. Anderson.

Upon talking with the attending physician, you find that Mr. Anderson had a myocardial infarction (heart attack) and his condition has stabilized. The physician plans to admit Mr. Anderson into intensive care for observation and also to conduct several tests. The physician also states that she plans to talk with the family after Mr. Anderson has been moved to intensive care but suggests that you relate general information to the family about the admission and that Mr. Anderson is resting comfortably.

You relate the information regarding Mr. Anderson to the family. Mrs. Anderson and her daughters break into tears, stating they are relieved. Upon questioning them you find they thought the reason the physician had not met with them was that Mr. Anderson was going to die.

You suggest Mrs. Anderson call her son. However, before calling, you have her practice what she will say to him. After she makes the phone call, you tell her that you will meet with the family tomorrow. You recommend that Mrs. Anderson return home to rest this night after talking with the physician. You also tell the family that you will alert the crisis worker on call in case they need someone to talk with.

The following day you go to the intensive care waiting room and meet with the Andersons.

COMMENTARY

Referral. The nurse is the first contact the Anderson family has with hospital personnel. Based on the information the nurse gathers and guidelines for referral to the crisis worker, a referral is made. The referral was made early to support the Andersons, thereby preventing excessive anxiety. The family should also be taken to a quiet room away from the general emergency department waiting area to protect their privacy.

Establishing rapport. Active listening skills are used to help establish rapport during the initial stages of the crisis. Use of these skills facilitates achieving two goals. First, the family perceives they are being supported. In this situation, the family is not familiar with hospital routines, and therefore can benefit from this support. Second, using these skills also permits crisis workers to assess the affective, cognitive, and behavioral reactions. Although as-

sessment is continuous, the information gathered early in the process often sets the mode for the intervention.

Dimensions of the problem. What are the facets of the crisis? How is the crisis affecting their ability to function as a family? What are the major issues that should be addressed to restore a sense of equilibrium?

In this situation, the Andersons are struggling with two predominant concerns. The first is contacting their son. Timing is the key issue for making this contact. At this point, contacting the son may be premature because the family has only tentative information. The crisis worker is directive and suggests delaying the call until they have more specific information. The second issue is concerned with getting information from the physician. Although they have received regular reports, often families prefer information directly from the physician. The crisis worker in this case can serve as a facilitator of this communication. The crisis worker can suggest that the family use a small spiral-ring notebook to record questions they have for the physician. In this way, the family can concentrate on listening to the physician rather than trying to remember what their other questions were.

Exploration of affect. This process is repeated throughout each of the steps in the intervention. Again, active listening skills will promote exploration and disclosure of relevant affective reactions. Empathy, genuineness, and unconditional positive regard are fundamental to this process. Crisis workers can help in identifying and expressing their feelings. The crisis worker should be prepared for and comfortable with intense affective reactions.

Explore past coping skills. A good question the crisis worker can ask is how similar experiences have been handled in the past. In this situation, the Andersons have no background for this type of situation. Therefore, the crisis worker will be more directive in the development of coping strategies and help to orient them to hospital routines.

Generate alternate solutions. The crisis worker is direc-tive in assisting Mrs. Anderson to make rational decisions. This process is based on sound theoretical understanding of crisis theory and the worker's previous experience. In this situation, the worker utilized role play and cognitive rehearsal to help Mrs. Anderson plan her conversation with her son.

Restore cognitive functioning. Realizing the family would not be allowed to see the patient until the following day, the worker advised the family to get as much rest as possible. In addition, the worker provided further support by assuring the family that the on-call crisis worker would be available throughout the night.

Follow up. Follow up helps to bolster the action plan. This step also provides an evaluation of the crisis worker's effectiveness.

would be without automatic thoughts associated with a hospital, such as those of catastrophe, illness, or death.

3. *Setting up a referral network.* Patients and families are provided with a list of support sources and groups that can ease the sense of isolation accompanying the emergency. Crisis workers provide information about the nature of each resource, from support groups to community based services, and show how these can be contacted and utilized.

4. *Mobilizing coping skills.* When a trauma occurs, established coping

skills are often inadequate to the task of dealing with the chaos of the crisis. A goal of crisis workers is to adapt patients' and families' inherent coping skills to a point that allows them to tolerate and respond to the demands of the new situation.

5. *Providing psychoeducation.* There can be some serious psychological ramifications associated with crisis events of a medical nature. These can often manifest after the initial shock has passed. Part of the crisis worker's duty is to inform patients and families to expect certain psychological consequences such as depression, despair, and anxiety as appropriate to the situation.

6. *Establishing lines of communication.* A smoothly operating communication network should be established between crisis worker(s), staff, patients, and, families. This minimizes confusion for all concerned and provides a sense of order and organization. This network can be structured in such a way as to allow a policy of who talks to whom, when, and under what circumstances.

GUIDELINES FOR WORKING IN EMERGENCY DEPARTMENTS

An essential part of translating crisis theory into practice is an understanding of crisis workers' role within hospital emergency departments. This is a largely intuitive and situational understanding that dictates the modes in which crisis theory is actually applied. This section will describe the role and functions of crisis workers in putting theory into practice in hospital emergency departments. In addition, the training needs of crisis workers will be summarized.

Role of Crisis Workers

The role of crisis workers in hospital emergency departments is best understood in the context of a multidisciplinary team. In emergency departments, many professionals typically interact to assist in the overall care of patients and their families (Leff-Simon, Slaikeu, and Hansen, 1984). While specific members of such a team differ among various hospitals, the team generally includes various medical personnel (e.g., physicians, nurses, x-ray technicians, phlebotomists, respiratory therapists), and support staff (e.g., receptionists, clerks, chaplains, social

50

workers). The team may operate informally with a loose association of professionals or formally with recognized guidelines and tightly defined relationships among members.

Crisis workers thus find themselves functioning within the particular boundaries of the team of which they are a part. To function effectively multidisciplinary teams should demonstrate a sense of mutual trust, collaboration, and willingness to compromise when needed (Gibson, Mitchell, and Higgins, 1983). The crisis worker's primary role is that of mental health specialist. Within the multidisciplinary team, crisis workers specifically address the psychological and emotional effects of trauma on patients and their families. In light of this, part of their role is also to enlighten other team members regarding such phenomena.

Functions of Crisis Workers

Crisis workers, of course, function within guidelines established by the hospital. Some hospitals may have vague guidelines while others may have precise rules about contact with patients and their families. These rules may be written or unwritten and typically involve procedures and/or lines of authority to be followed. A knowledge and understanding of these guidelines promote the effective performance of crisis workers.

Hess and Ruster (1990) suggest that the role of the crisis worker can be divided into five distinct functions. First, crisis workers function as advocates. This function may occur with patients' family members, community resources, or medical staff. It can involve facilitating communication among the medical staff, patients, families, and hospital administration. Second, crisis workers function as case coordinators. Case coordination occurs when patients and their families need assistance in managing the environmental complexity of emergency departments. This includes subsequent hospitalization and rehabilitation if needed. It also includes managing interruptions in daily activities and adjustment to changes in lifestyle in cases of debilitating injuries or illnesses. Crisis workers may also be asked to assist in the development of a treatment plan that will facilitate the speedy recovery of patients and the return to normalcy for their families. Third, crisis workers function as counselors. Crisis workers are often called upon to provide an environment that permits patients and their families to express reactions to the crisis event. This expression serves to provide psycho-

51

logical and emotional support. Of course, a sense of caring is also part of this work and is an intrinsic part of delivering proper service to patients and their families. Fourth, crisis workers function as educators. As educators, crisis workers function to help patients and their families learn about the hospital environment and to learn skills that will equip them to endure their difficult experience. Crisis workers may also educate the hospital administration and community about the needs of patients and their families. Through this process, hospitals and communities can become sensitive to their needs and better able to meet them. Fifth, crisis workers serve to mobilize resources and provide referrals. Linking patients and their families to resources such as self-help groups, social service agencies, and so on, is a primary function of crisis workers. A current list of community and state resources should be maintained.

Crisis workers will seldom perform all of these functions with any one case. Instead, functions are performed on the basis of the needs, both immediate and necessary, of patients and their families.

Training Crisis Workers

A variety of persons provide crisis intervention services in hospital emergency departments. Regardless of their status as professional or paraprofessional, knowledge of crisis theory and techniques is essential for effective functioning. This knowledge enables crisis workers to assess situations accurately and apply appropriate techniques. Knowledge of this nature is gained through two interrelated methods. Through the first method, didactic training, crisis workers can develop the requisite theoretical knowledge. This knowledge will permit crisis workers to identify patients' and families' distress and select suitable interventions. However, academic instruction is not enough. Crisis workers also need to have supervised experience putting theoretical knowledge into practice. Supervised practice allows crisis workers to make the shift from the classroom to real life.

Crisis workers in emergency departments also benefit from knowledge of medical terms and procedures. While they will never achieve the information level of medical personnel, elementary understanding of medical terms and procedures is useful to help patients and families comprehend these. This knowledge serves to facilitate communication between patients and families with medical staff as well as with crisis workers and other members of the interdisciplinary team. In many cases, simply explaining the meaning of a term or the nature of a procedure can reduce the overall crisis.

Study of the local and state laws that affect emergency departments is also important for crisis workers. For example, in some states, if a patient is transported to the emergency department with certain types of injuries or dies in transit, local police are required to conduct an investigation. Although the purpose of this procedure is to detect foul play, the routine can severely upset innocent families. Crisis workers can be helpful by informing families that this policy is to distinguish criminal activity from legitimate injuries and that the investigation is done with all cases fitting a certain description. This disclosure generally minimizes discomfort and helps families recognize that they are not being singled out.

As with everyone who works in the field of mental health, periodic updating of skills and knowledge is important. However, with crisis workers this instruction is especially meaningful. Because of the intensity of the situations in which this group works, routine attendance at training sessions can prevent burnout through encouraging workers to expand their skills, share their experiences, and learn from others in the field. In addition, continuous supervision or consultation is highly beneficial. Regular supervision or consultation is generally required by professional organizations such as the American Counseling Association and the American Psychological Association.

PRACTICE FRAMEWORK

A clear practice framework should be developed for crisis workers in hospital emergency departments. Special attention should be given to this element as both the volume and intensity of work in emergency departments can lead to confusion, overlap of services, and inadvertently overlooking psychological and emotional trauma of patients and families. Attention should also be given to the process of referral, qualities of crisis workers, and work environments.

Referrals to Crisis Workers

Developing protocols for referring patients and families to crisis workers is important in emergency departments. These protocols serve to avoid unnecessary referrals and expedite appropriate ones. For example, an appropriate referral might involve a family from out of town who needs a room to spend the night and a meal because their patient will be kept overnight. In this situation, crisis workers can help arrange lodging and a meal in the hospital cafeteria. An unwarranted referral might involve patients who come to the emergency department during the day with a minor illness. At times, these types of patients are using the emergency department as a substitute for a personal physician and for insurance purposes. While these patients may have a variety of valid concerns due to socioeconomic problems, crisis workers unfortunately do not typically attend to these kinds of problems. For these patients, referral to appropriate social agencies is indicated.

Two issues to consider in developing referral protocols include timing of the referral and contacting the crisis worker. Timing the referral is critical in emergency departments. We suggest that a referral be made prior to the situation becoming extreme. Making referrals in this manner increases the chances that patients and families will be more receptive to intervention. With respect to patients, however, crisis workers will most often see them after the physical trauma has been stabilized (Getz, Fujita, and Allen, 1975). With families, a referral may be made prior to families arriving in the emergency departments. This method anticipates the need for crisis intervention by considering the magnitude of the physical trauma suffered by patients. For example, in situations involving severe injury or illness, this method would have crisis workers meeting the family upon their arrival. Being able to contact crisis workers is also vital. We suggest that hospitals use a paging system that can contact crisis workers twenty-four hours a day. This system would ensure patients and families of having assistance available no matter what time of day or night a crisis occurs.

A final consideration for making referrals is social history information. Although at times minimal, this information can be invaluable and help crisis workers structure their interventions and medical staff provide services to patients and families. For example, religious information might prove useful in certain circumstances, as different religions have distinct procedures for treatment, dismemberment, and handling death (Sharer, 1979). A related issue is completing business after a patient's death. We suggest that crisis workers assist hospitals in developing guidelines for these circumstances. Hospitals should recognize families may need assistance in this situation or are not likely to want to sign forms and pay bills. Crisis workers can assist hospital administrators to develop a strategy that respects the sensitivity of this situation while safeguarding their interest.

Eleven Desirable Qualities of Crisis Workers

1. *Quick Thinking.* As part of working in an emergency department, crisis workers will be faced with an amazing array of varying circumstances and human reactions. Confronting these requires the ability to think quickly, to assess the relative severity of situations in a short time, and to accurately determine the coping limits of patients, families, and staff.
2. *Creativity and Flexibility.* Due to the tremendous range and combination of symptoms of problems presented in emergency departments, crisis workers must be able to deal with these on a situational basis. Innovation and flexibility are therefore required to be able to work with the variables that each case presents.
3. *Parallel Process.* The sheer numbers of patients in emergency departments demand that crisis workers regularly deal with more than one serious situation at once. It is also important that workers feel reasonably comfortable with the idea that several situations may be occurring simultaneously, and that each of these are deserving of their full attention.
4. *Quick and Easy Rapport Building.* As in the previous point, the number of patients that the emergency department serves make it necessary to inspire trust and develop an empathic relationship in a relatively short time. When patients and families perceive that someone is there and attending to their psychological needs, the situation will usually begin to subside.
5. *Tolerance of Medical Trauma.* An emergency department routinely handles serious physical injuries. Some may find these so disturbing that one's performance could be adversely affected. Crisis workers who can become desensitized to such trauma will be able to focus on crisis intervention without being impaired or preoccupied by the nature of the crisis itself.
6. *The Ability to Maintain Calm and Inspire It in Others.* Unlike many crisis intervention settings, emergency departments provide an in vivo setting where the crisis is often occurring and developing in the worker's presence. The ability to cultivate and maintain a sense of calm is an invaluable attribute. To be able to inspire quietness in others allows rapport to be established with patients and families, and eventually staff will look to crisis workers for this kind of support as well.
7. *Self-Awareness.* Crisis intervention workers should be aware of their strengths and weaknesses. What kinds of emergencies are

most disturbing? Which kinds of clients are more difficult for one to deal with? Does a particular kind of trauma affect one in certain ways? Ready answers to such questions will help crisis workers to get through situations more smoothly without unnecessary complications.

8. *A Sense of Reconciliation with Death*. When one has found the inevitability of one's own death existentially, one will not be quite so disturbed by the prospect of it occurring to others. The existential anxiety that is associated with death is ever present in hospital emergency departments, where injuries are often judged according to life threatening potential. When crisis workers are reasonably comfortable with death and dying, they will be far more capable of working with those who are facing it due to the severity of their injuries.

9. *Ability to Maintain Objectivity and Derole*. The intensity of emotion, heartbreak, and tragedy that accompanies work in emergency departments can pull crisis workers into individual situations to the point of worrying and obsessing about the case well past the end of the shift. Although part of this issue is a result of genuine, empathic contact with a patient and family, the ability to leave such problems at work is essential in order to avoid burnout and general job dissatisfaction. In other words, crisis workers must be able to attend to their own needs as well as those of patients and families.

10. *A Sense of Humor as Appropriate*. Having mentioned the importance of inspiring calm and building rapport, few qualities in crisis workers can be so conducive to such conditions as a sense of humor. The ability to get patients or families to genuinely laugh in the face of possible tragedy can be a remarkably effective aid to recovering equilibrium and the sense of perspective that comes with the mobilization of coping skills.

11. *Space Allocation*. Space for private consultation of patients and families should be provided in emergency departments. Ideally this space should be adjacent to the emergency department and sound insulated. The space should be adequate to accommodate families. Local building codes may provide data for how much square footage is needed for rooms of this nature. The decor and furnishing of this space should facilitate self-disclosure and/or emotional expression. In addition, we suggest that the furniture be sturdy, use a durable fabric, and be comfortable. Furnishing of this type will stand up to the abuse of many people using it while also enabling families to be comfortable during a prolonged

visit. Furnishings may include several chairs, a couch, tables, and several lamps. A phone should also be installed in this room, allowing families to make calls in private. This space should not be crisis workers' offices. Instead, separate space should be allocated. This will allow crisis workers to retreat to a place for rest.

SUMMARY

The number of people requiring services provided in hospital emergency departments has increased drastically during the past decade (Staff, 1992). The type of services has also expanded as we have become more sensitive to issues such as domestic violence and child abuse. Services provided by crisis workers are useful in addressing these needs by assisting patients and their families in confronting and managing the psychological and emotional effects of physical trauma. They help to mobilize effective coping strategies and return patients and families to a sense of equilibrium. In addition, crisis workers serve to expedite communication between patients, their families, and medical personnel and support staff.

Crisis workers are an invaluable component of the hospital emergency department, serving as versatile, effective troubleshooters for an entire range of problems. The short-term benefit of crisis intervention in emergency departments has been demonstrated, yet more research is needed to fully understand the long-term impact of these services (Viney, et al., 1985). This research should continue to establish and unfold the value of this type of professional services in treatment and public relations.

REFERENCES

Ayers, A., and Janosik, E. H. (1984). Crisis of trauma: Multiple trauma and sexual assault. In E. H. Janosik (Ed.). *Crisis counseling: A contemporary approach* (pp. 241–274). Monterey, CA: Wadsworth.

Cohen, R. Y. (1983). Crisis intervention for medical problems. In L. H. Cohen, W. L. Claiborn, and G. A. Spencer (Eds.). *Crisis intervention: Vol. IV. Community-Clinical Psychology Series* (pp. 127–146). New York: Human Sciences Press.

Croushore, T. (1979a). Helping the patient overcome a distorted body image. In J. Robinson, T. Croushore, and B. F. McVan (Eds.). *Using crisis inter-*

vention wisely (pp. 43–56). Horsham, Psychotherapeutic: Intermed Communications, Inc.

Croushore, T. (1979b). Recognizing and dealing with unit crisis. In J. Robinson, T. Croushore, and B. F. McVane (Eds.). *Using crisis intervention wisely* (pp. 163–176). Horsham, Psychotherapeutic: Intermed Communications, Inc.

Fulmer, T., McMahon, D. J., Baer-Hines, M., and Forge, B. (1992). Abuse, neglect, and exploitation: An analysis of all elderly patients seen in one emergency department during a six-month period. *Journal of Emergency Nursing, 18,* 505–510.

Getz, W. L., Fujita, B. N., and Allen, D. (1975). The use of paraprofessionals in crisis intervention: Evaluation of an innovative program. *American Journal of Community Psychology, 3,* 135–144.

Gibson, R. L., Mitchell, M. H., and Higgins, R. E. (1983). *Development and management of counseling programs and guidance services.* New York: Macmillan.

Gilliland, B. E., and James, R. K. (1993). *Crisis intervention strategies.* Monterey, CA: Brooks/Cole.

Hadley, S. M. (1992). Working with battered women in the emergency department: A model program. *Journal of Emergency Nursing, 18,* 18–23.

Hankoff, L. D., Mischorr, M. T., Tomelson, K. E., and Joyce, S. A. (1974). A program of crisis intervention in the emergency medical setting. *Journal of Psychiatry, 131,* 47–50.

Hess, H. J., and Ruster, P. L. (1990). Assessment and crisis intervention with clients in a hospital emergency room. In A. R. Roberts (Ed.). *Crisis intervention handbook: Assessment, treatment, and research* (pp. 197–220). Belmont, CA: Wadsworth.

Lazzaro, M. V., and McFarlane, J. (1991). Establishing a screening program for abused women. *Journal of Nursing Administration, 21,* 24–29.

Leff-Simon, S. I., Slaikeu, K. A., and Hansen, K. (1984). Crisis intervention in hospital emergency rooms. In K. A. Slaikeu (Ed.). *Crisis intervention: A handbook for practice and research* (pp. 229–237). Boston, MA: Allyn and Bacon.

Martin, L., Francisco, E., Nicol, C., and Schweiger, J. L. (1991). A hospital-wide approach to crisis control: One inner-city hospital's experience. *Journal of Emergency Nursing, 17,* 395–401.

McLeer, S., and Anwar, R. (1987). The role of the emergency physician in the prevention of domestic violence. *Annual of Emergency Medicine, 79,* 1155–1161.

McLeer, S., and Anwar, R. (1989). A study of battered women presenting in an emergency department. *American Journal of Public Health, 79,* 65–66.

Myer, R. A., Williams, R. C., Ottens, A. J., and Schmidt, A. E. (1992). Crisis assessment: A three-dimensional model for triage. *Journal of Mental Health Counseling, 14,* 137–148.

Pisarick, G., Zigmund, D., Summerfield, R., Mian, P., Johansen, P., and Devereaux, P. (1979, July) Psychiatric nurses in the emergency room. *American Journal of Nursing*, pp. 1264–1266.

Roberts, A. R. (1990). An overview of crisis theory and crisis intervention. In A. R. Roberts (Ed.), *Crisis intervention handbook: Assessment, treatment and research* (pp. 3–16). Belmont, CA: Wadsworth.

Sharer, P. S. (1979). Supporting survivors of unexpected death. In J. Robinson, T. Croushore, and B. F. McVan (Eds.). *Using crisis intervention wisely* (pp. 57–70). Horsham, PA: Intermed Communications, Inc.

Siegal, D. S., Slaikeu, K. A., and Kimbrell, G. M. (1984). Crisis intervention by health care professionals. In K. A. Slaikeu (Ed.), *Crisis intervention: A handbook for practice and research* (pp. 205–228). Boston, MA: Allyn and Bacon.

Staff. (1992). The sagging: Emergency departments on the brink of crisis. *Hospital: The Magazine for Health Care Executives*, pp. 36–40.

Viney, L. L., Clarke, A. M., Bunn, T. A., and Benjamin, Y. N. (1985). Crisis intervention counseling: An evaluation of long- and short-term effects. *Journal of Counseling Psychology, 32*, 29–39.

Wood, D. P., and Cowan, M. L. (1991). Crisis intervention following disasters: Are we doing enough? (A second look). *American Journal of Emergency Medicine, 9*, 598–602.

CHAPTER 4

Crisis Assessment and Time-Limited Intervention with High Risk Suicidal Youth

DAVID A. JOBES and
ALAN L. BERMAN

Tom is a troubled seventeen-year-old high school senior. Since the divorce of his parents the previous year, and a recent break up with his girlfriend of three years, Tom has become increasingly depressed and reckless in his behavior. His attendance at school has become irregular, and his increased use of alcohol, marijuana, and LSD has alarmed some of his close friends. At a recent high school dance Tom was arrested for being drunk and disorderly and for carrying a concealed weapon. Friends reported that Tom had been waving a loaded handgun at his head and placing the muzzle of the gun in his mouth.

Lisa is a twelve-year-old seventh grader who was referred by her school guidance counselor to a psychologist for an evaluation. Lisa had become quite despondent since the recent death of her beloved grandfather. One of her teachers contacted the guidance counselor after Lisa had turned in a five-page poem entitled ''Grandpa and Me in Heaven.'' The poem depicted a fantastic journey into ''sweet death'' that culminated in a ''heavenly reunion'' with her grandfather. When her parents were contacted, they reported that they recently found a shoe box full of pills and pictures of her grandfather in her bedroom closet.

Bill, a twenty-year-old college junior, was found by a roommate hanging by a belt in their dorm room closet. The roommate (who was supposed to be away for the weekend) entered the room only moments after Bill had begun to hang from the belt—his immediate intervention probably saved Bill's life. The roommate reported that Bill had become increasingly depressed since he had recently "come out" to his parents about being gay. Bill's parents were enraged by this news, and threatened to disown him if he "did not get such a silly notion out of his head."

The acute suicidal crisis is produced by a unique synergy of intrapersonal, environmental, social, and situational variables. As a response to life crises, suicide and self-destructive behaviors are seen among people of every age, sex, race, religion, and economic and social class. As patients may respond to life crises with suicidal behaviors, clinicians must be prepared to face the immediate tasks of assessing possible self-harm behavior while concurrently protecting against that possibility. These tasks must often be accomplished under conditions of incongruent expectations and goals. Suicidal people tend to defy the health professional's expectation that fostering and maintaining life is a shared goal of patient and doctor (Hoff, 1984). Suicidal individuals typically are brought to treatment by others under conditions of acute and volitional threat to life. These are not characteristics of the "good patient"; instead, these qualities bring tension and instability to (and potentially impede) the necessary working alliance with the caregiver (Vlasak, 1975). Thus, working with depressed and suicidal people can be a scary and difficult undertaking. Indeed, the assessment, treatment, and general management of an acute sucidal crisis is perhaps one of the most difficult challenges faced by any mental health professional, despite its being one of the most frequently encountered of all mental health emergencies (Roberts, 1991; Schein, 1976).

Completed suicide is a complex and relatively rare (low base-rate) event. Ideally, clinicians would like to be able to "predict" future occurrences of suicidal behavior and thereby make appropriate interventions. Attempts to construct inventories and use psychological tests to predict suicide (in a statistically valid and reliable manner) have thus far failed. Since completed suicide occurs relatively infrequently, most instruments tend to identify a prohibitive number of "false positives" (i.e., the identification of individuals as suicidal who do not complete suicide). Clinicians are therefore forced to make interventions based on inexact and subjective calculations of potential "suicide risk" (refer to Berman and Jobes, 1991).

Nevertheless, clinicians can strengthen their ability to effectively assess and intervene by increasing their understanding of suicidal behaviors. The tragic finality of suicide demands that clinicians develop a knowledge base and a level of competence in suicide risk assessment and intervention. As suicidologists point out, suicidal impulses and behaviors are largely temporal, transient, and situation-specific. Suicide intent is state-dependent and tends to wax and wane, disappear and return (Berman and Jobes, 1991). Empirical research indicates that most people who kill themselves give some form of prior warning (cf. Shafii, et al., 1985) and often desire an outcome other than the termination of their biological existence (Shneidman, 1985). The crisis clinician is thus in a pivotal position. Accurate risk assessment and appropriate interventions can make a life or death difference.

Making a life-saving difference is perhaps all the more poignant when the object of assessment and intervention is a young person. Many hold the view that youthful years should be a carefree time of innocence, play, and exciting exploration. Crisis clinicians must struggle with the incongruity between this commonly held view and direct evidence that for some youngsters, life may be filled with intense turmoil and abject despair.

SCOPE OF THE PROBLEM

In 1990 there were 30,906 certified suicides in the United States (National Center of Health Statistics, 1993). A total of 4,869 of these deaths, approximately 16 percent, were of young people between the ages of fifteen and twenty-four. The age-specific rate of youthful suicide (13.2 per 100,000 for fifteen- to twenty-four-year-olds) was somewhat higher than that for all other ages combined (12.4), but somewhat lower than rates for adults ages twenty-five to forty-four (15.2) and forty-five to sixty-four (15.4). However, between 1950 and 1990 the suicide rate for youth fifteen to twenty-four increased from 4.5 to 13.2 per 100,000 (almost tripled), making suicide the third leading cause of death for young people in this age range.

Over five times more adolescent males than females complete suicide in the United States. In contrast, females are four times as likely to make nonfatal attempts as males. The gender differences in suicidal behaviors observed in adolescents, with some variations, tend to remain fairly consistent across the adult life span. For all ages, completed suicide is a primarily male activity (particularly among the elderly).

While approximately 2,243 American youth under the age of nineteen completed suicide in 1990, as many as 2 million teenagers may make nonfatal attempts at some point in their teenage lives (Smith and Crawford, 1984). One plausible explanation for these observed sex differences lies in the differential choices of methods employed. While the majority of both sexes use guns to complete suicide (in 1990: 67 percent of males and 55 percent of females), the overwhelming majority of nonfatal suicidal behaviors are comprised of ingestion overdoses, better than 80 percent of which are effected by females. The ingestion of poisons, the lethality of which depends on a number of factors including the greater chance of rescue and intervention given the time necessary for toxic action, accounted for only 267 suicide deaths in 1990.

Suicidal death among adolescents also is more common among whites than blacks, with white males comprising the majority (73 percent in 1990) of all youth suicides. However, fifteen- to twenty-four-year-old black youth account for a greater proportion of all black suicides (22 percent) than do white youth (15 percent). For all youth, the highest rates are recorded for youth living in the western, primarily intermountain, states.

CRISIS INTERVENTION:
ROBERTS' SEVEN-STAGE MODEL

Effective intervention and treatment of suicidal people always begins with a thorough assessment and subsequent intervention based on that assessment. Through all phases of working with a suicidal patient, ongoing risk assessment is an imperative. In general practice, clinicians must be prepared to face a range of potential suicidal crisis situations. Suicidal crises may range from a telephone call from a desperate patient who has just ingested a potentially lethal overdose, to one from a borderline personality in an unstable, intense, and dramatically shifting mood state, to that of a patient in session simply stating vague suicidal ideation and hopelessness, in a context of a history of impulsive acting out.

As described by Roberts (1991), clinicians may effectively respond to an individual in crisis by working through seven stages of intervention: (a) assessing lethality and safety needs, (b) establishing rapport and communication, (c) identifying the major problems, (d) dealing with feelings and providing support, (e) exploring possible alternatives, (f) formulating an action plan, and (g) providing follow up. While

Roberts' seven-stage model was developed to apply broadly to a range of crises, it is clearly applicable to specific interventions with suicidal youth.

Stage 1: Assessing Lethality

An assessment of the overall lethality (i.e., dangerousness) of a crisis situation is the starting point for any crisis intervention effort. The assessment of lethality may perhaps be best understood as a process of psychiatric triage which leads to three treatment options: (a) emergency psychiatric treatment, (b) outpatient counseling/psychotherapy, and (c) basic emotional support, validation, reassurance, or education. In the case of suicide lethality assessment, clinicians are faced with two primary scenarios—the imminently dangerous situation and the potentially dangerous situation.

Imminent Danger. In some cases, crisis intervention may need to begin with a suicidal patient who has already initiated a suicide attempt. In the imminently dangerous situation, the clinician must be fully prepared to respond to the individual whose suicide attempt may require prompt first aid and/or medical treatment. The patient's level of consciousness and orientation, rationality, and agitation will affect the level of cooperation he/she may give to the immediate assessment of the need for emergency intervention. With appropriate cooperation, questions need to be raised and answered (by the patient or person making the contact) with regard to the location of the patient, exactly what the patient has done, and the availability of significant others. The clinician's immediate task, to assess the lethality of the attempt, can be aided by the availability of published lethality scales (Smith, Conroy, and Ehler, 1984). Where it is determined that there exists medico-biological danger, or where sufficient data for that determination is available, emergency medical intervention is required. As discussed by Hoff (1984) imminently dangerous situations should be handled by police and rescue squads who can assure rapid transportation to a hospital emergency room—prompt medical evaluation is crucial.

In addition to using lethality scales, potential lethality can be assessed by accessing a hospital that has a poison control center that can be called for specific overdose information. The exact amount of drug needed to effect a fatal overdose may be difficult to ascertain as the effects vary according to the size of the person, the amount and kind of drug taken, and the person's tolerance for a drug. Generally, sleeping pills, major tranquilizers, tricyclic antidepressants, and aspirin/acetaminophen are dangerous overdose drugs (especially in combination with alcohol). One rule of thumb is that a lethal dose is ten times the normal dose; in combination with alcohol only five times the normal dose may result in death (Hoff, 1984). It is useful for the clinician to have ready access to emergency phone numbers for the police, emergency rescue squad, hospital emergency rooms, and poison control centers. Needless to say, it is essential to maintain active contact/communication with the client while these procedures are being effected. As part of this communication, the clinician should begin to structure the client's expectations through clear directives about what will happen, thus increasing the chances that a therapeutic alliance with both paramedics and emergency personnel will be established. Future treatment may be facilitated by the presence of the clinician during the medical crisis. Close contact and follow up after the immediate medical danger is resolved assures that the patient is not simply treated and discharged without a crisis prevention plan in place.

Potential Danger. In contrast to imminently dangerous suicide crises, clinicians more typically encounter suicide crisis situations that are *potentially* dangerous. In these situations clinicians must be prepared to intervene in suicide crises where there is active suicidal ideation but an attempt has not yet been made (but could be made in the near future). In these circumstances, intensive one-to-one clinical contact that fully addresses stages 2 through 6 in Roberts' model is necessary.

Stage 1 lethality assessments of the three initial cases of Tom, Lisa, and Bill reveal three moderately to highly suicidal youth. Bill, who was found hanging in an imminently dangerous situation by his roommate, is obviously the most lethal of the three. However, Tom's depression, reckless behavior, substance abuse, and access to a gun clearly put him at high risk as well. Finally, while Lisa's level of risk is somewhat less extreme, her suicidal preoccupation and her cache of medication for overdosing are distinct causes for concern.

Stage 2: Establishing Rapport and Communication

The importance of the clinical relationship (and the technique used to enhance it) in the suicidal crisis cannot be overestimated. A number of authors have discussed the difficulties inherent in working with a suicidal individual (Farberow, 1970; Shneidman, 1980; Hendin, 1981). As Shneidman (1980) has observed, working with a highly suicidal person demands a more active and directive kind of involvement. Particularly in a crisis, the ability to make interpersonal contact is critical, and a supportive working relationship must be rapidly established. Hipple and Cimbolic (1979) have noted that the suicidal client must know (and feel) that they are talking with a person who is actively interested in their well-being. Any technique or approach that potentially strengthens the relationship and connectedness should therefore be employed. Eye contact, posture, and other nonverbal cues may be used to express a level of interest, concern, and involvement. Empathic listening, mirroring of feelings, emotional availability, honesty, warmth, and caring can help foster a sense of trust and a willingness to examine possibilities other than self-destruction. While empathy and support are crucial, it is important to remember that suicidal adolescents often feel out of control. Accordingly, a more active and directive role than would normally be seen in ongoing individual psychotherapy can provide valuable reassurance and structure in a time of crisis.

There are some unique aspects to developing rapport and communication with a suicidal youth. Young people inherently bring to the suicidal crisis a unique set of developmental and emotional issues that may complicate effective assessment and intervention. Adolescence and young adulthood can be a time of tremendous change and turmoil. As Berman (1984) has discussed, adolescents are developmentally caught between childhood and adulthood, which engenders the conflictual task of separating from the world of parents and family, while simultaneously and paradoxically seeking protection from and inclusion within the family system. Accordingly, potential mistrust of adults further complicates the assessment of the young person's emotional status. An example of youthful distrust can be seen when a young person tells a friend about his/her suicidal thoughts with the clear understanding that the peer is not to betray this confidence to an adult. Youthful distrust of adults has been indirectly substantiated in the empirical literature. One recent study of a youthful sample of completed suicides revealed that 83.3 percent had made suicidal threats in the week prior to their deaths, and, of these, half made their suicidal intention known *only* to a peer or sibling (Brent et al., 1988).

Other developmental forces also increase the assessment challenge. With limited life experience, youth tend to be more focused on the present rather than the future. When a young person experiences stress, there may be a limited view of future possibilities—momentary and immediate solutions may become appealing (Berman, 1984). Adolescents characteristically have a limited capacity to delay gratification. Plainly stated, if something is wrong, the adolescent may want it fixed immediately. As Cantor (1976) has pointed out, the situation is further complicated by suicidal fantasies that may be common among adolescents. This combination of adolescent impulsivity, poor problem-solving skills, and suicidal fantasies (of escape and relief from pain) can become a recipe for lethal action. Additionally, adolescents are highly vulnerable to peer influence and are often eager to imitate role models as they seek to develop their own sense of identity. It is therefore important to assess and intervene in youthful crises with a keen awareness of the unique developmental issues of the population.

Stage 3: Identify the Major Problems

The need to assess the major problems that may underlie a suicidal crisis is best accomplished through a thorough assessment interview. Ideally, an assessment interview should draw upon theory, the strength of the therapeutic relationship, and empirical/clinical knowledge specific to suicidal individuals. Theoretical knowledge provides a conceptual frame and foundation, while the therapeutic relationship (alliance) becomes the vehicle of assessment and treatment. Empirical and clinical knowledge is used to assess key variables that bear on the assessment of suicide risk. In the course of the assessment interview it is essential for the clinician to listen closely, make direct inquiries, and assess/evaluate key variables.

Clues to Suicide. The clinician must listen carefully for signs, symptoms, or clues that may indicate suicidal intent. Often the clinician is alerted by a direct or indirect comment made by a patient or nonverbal behavior. The vast majority of suicidal people provide clues to their self-destructive feelings. Close scrutiny of the patient is essential, as the clinician must determine whether the youth shares some commonality with those who have acted out their suicidal fantasies (Berman and Jobes, 1991). As Hipple and Cimbolic (1979) have discussed, the suicidal individual may make only veiled or disguised verbal references to suicide feelings. The clinician must be alert for veiled threats such as: ''Sometimes it's just not worth it, I feel like giving up''; ''I'm just so tired, I just want to sleep''; ''People would

67

be a lot happier if I weren't around." Often other communications (e.g., diaries, journals, school essays, drawings, poems, etc.) contain valuable nonverbal clues to the adolescent's ideational focus.

Asking about Suicide. The assessment of suicide risk fundamentally requires direct inquiries about suicidal thoughts and feelings. Simply stated, vague suicidal comments should *always* elicit a direct question from the clinician as to whether the patient is thinking about suicide (e.g., "Sometimes when people feel depressed they contemplate suicide, are you thinking about killing yourself?"; "Do you feel like hurting yourself or ending your life?"; "You sound pretty hopeless, have you been considering suicide?").

Even for the experienced clinician, asking directly about suicide can be unsettling. Accordingly, there may be a tendency to underestimate the seriousness of the situation and a strong temptation to avoid directly asking about suicide. Frequently, potential helpers fear that a direct inquiry might introduce a dangerous new option not previously considered by the patient (i.e., planting a seed for suicide in the patient's mind).

While avoidance and fear are understandable reactions to suspicions of suicide, experts in the field strongly support the value of direct inquiry (Hipple and Cimbolic, 1979; Beck, et al., 1979; Pope, 1986; Curran, 1987; Alberts, 1988; Berman & Jobes, 1991). Critically, direct inquiry gives the potentially suicidal individual permission to discuss feelings that may have seemed virtually undiscussable. Direct inquiry can bring great relief to the patient—at last the inner battle of life or death can be openly discussed and explored in a safe, supportive, and accepting climate. Moreover, direct inquiry opens the doors for further assessment, potentially bringing out otherwise veiled resistances. The expression of resistances in the therapeutic context may alert the clinician to the distinct possibility of suicidal urges in the client signaling an interpersonal alienation common to the suicidal character. It is our experience that when clinicians are sensitive and attentive to their suspicions of suicide, they are more often correct than incorrect (i.e., suicide will probably have been at least a consideration for the client).

If suicide is genuinely not being considered by the client, the dyad can easily move on from the topic of suicide to other areas of inquiry. On the other hand, if suicide is being considered by the client and the counselor avoids direct inquiry, the client may interpret the counselor's behavior as clear evidence of a lack of caring, therefore confirming his/her sense of both unlovability and the impossibility of help. Hopelessness may thus be reinforced, and the risk increases accordingly.

Assuming that the clinician has attended to suicidal clues and the client has affirmed some degree of suicidal thoughts or feelings upon direct inquiry, the clinician must determine whether there is an imminent danger of suicidal behavior at potential risk to the life of the client. The degree and immediacy of suicide risk must be evaluated for both clinical and legal/ethical purposes. When voluntary hospitalization is refused in extreme cases, the law often allows involuntary hospitalization (commitment) when there is evidence of clear and imminent danger to self or others (these considerations being defined by statute in each state). Therefore, the clinician must establish whether the risk of suicide is acute and immediate or chronic and long-term. Is this indeed a crisis situation with a risk of a suicide attempt in the immediate or near future? Is there sufficient upsetness, agitation, and emotional energy to create an immediate dangerous situation?

Approximately 80 percent of all suicides occur in a state of acute impulsive crisis. Only a small percentage of suicides are methodical or planned (especially among youthful populations). It can be reassuring to both the client and the clinician to know that most cases are those of *transient* crises. Getting through the crisis phase provides the young person the opportunity to consider more constructive and reversible options for coping. Therefore one of the most important aspects of suicide assessment, the temporal evaluation of imminent versus long-term risk of self-harm, is essential to further assessment, intervention, and treatment.

The final determination of imminent danger depends on the assessment of key variables or "risk factors" that reflect the degree of suicide risk. It is important to assess the following (not necessarily in the following order): (a) psychological intent, (b) the suicide plan, (c) the history of previous suicide behavior, and (d) clinical risk variables.

Assessing Psychological Intent. Many attempts have been made to operationally define the concept of suicide (see Jobes, Berman, and Josselson, 1987; Jobes et al., 1991; Rosenbert et al., 1988; Shneidman, 1985). Most define suicide as a death that is self-inflicted and intended. By definition, an individual who dies by a self-inflicted accidental death does not intentionally seek the end of his or her life, whereas the aim or purpose of one who completes suicide is escape and/or death.

Clearly, the motive of ending one's existence versus the motive of receiving more attention from a loved one reflects very different kinds of suicidal intent. It is therefore critical to assess the psychological intention, purpose, motive, or goal of the suicidal individual—what does the option of suicide *mean* to the youth? As Berman and Jobes (1991) have discussed, the stated intent of a suicidal motive in young people is often interpersonal and instrumental. In general, the intended goals of youthful suicidal behavior involve an effort to escape the experience of pain, helplessness, hopelessness, and the emotions and cognitions associated with the suicidal state. For some this means seeking relief through death; for others, relief may be sought through changes in others' behavior, effected by gambling with life.

Assessing the Suicide Plan. The presence or absence of a plan to attempt suicide is critical to ascertain. The plan reflects both the desired and expected consequences of suicidal behavior and, therefore, provides one of the best indicators of what may actually come to pass (Berman and Jobes, 1991). Again, direct inquiry about a potential suicidal plan is necessary. If a plan is acknowledged, it is important to assess the lethality of the plan. Suicidal plans generally reveal the relative risk in that the degree of intent is typically related to the lethality of the potential method (e.g., using a gun or hanging implies higher intent whereas overdosing or cutting implies lower intent).

Empirical research indicates that there tends to be a relationship between level of intent and the lethality of a method identified in the suicidal plan. Indeed, Brent (1987) found that a robust relationship appeared to exist between medical lethality and suicide intent in a study of youthful attempters. In general, lethal plans tend to be concrete and specific and involve dangerous methods. Risk increases when there is evidence of a carefully thought through and articulated self-harm strategy. Similarly, the availability of lethal means (such as guns or lethal quantities of medications) about which the youngster is knowledgeable also increases the suicide risk.

A plan that minimizes the chance of intervention and rescue reflects a greater suicide risk. Conceptually and empirically, potential for rescue has been found to be central to two well-respected instruments that were specifically constructed to assess the lethality of suicide attempts (see Weissman and Worden, 1972); Smith et al., 1984). Simply put, the less likely that someone is able to intervene, the greater the risk. Under the heading of rescue, the reversibility of a chosen method and the discoverability of an attempt must be differentially evaluated. A much higher level of suicide intent and lethality is reflected in an attempter who plans to use an irreversible method (e.g., a gun) in a place with little likelihood of discovery (e.g., a remote wooded area). For example, suicide risk may be assessed as low in a case of a vague plan involving the ingestion of pills in front of parents versus high in a case where an individual has access to a large quantity of barbiturates and plans to ingest them after the parents leave the house.

In summarizing various elements of the assessment of a suicide plan, the clinician must evaluate the lethality and availability of the proposed method and the specificity of the self-harm strategy. Moreover, the clinician must evaluate the probability of post-attempt discovery and whether efforts could be made to reverse the impact of the potential suicide act (e.g., pumping the stomach after an overdose). Assessment of the various aspects of a potential plan is perhaps the best means of evaluating suicidal intent and imminent risk of self-harm.

It should be noted that perhaps the majority of suicidal acts by youth are impulsive and unplanned. That does not in any way decrease their potential lethality, particularly if the youth has available a lethal weapon accessible at the time of urge and impulse. In the context of the other levels of assessment, the absence of a plan simply means the clinician is absent only one significant source of information.

Assessing Suicide History. Another variable that bears significantly on suicide risk is the presence or absence of a suicidal history. The risk and dangerousness increase significantly when there is *any* previous history of suicidal ideation, gestures, and particularly previous attempts. Risk increases if a previous attempt was recent, if a potentially lethal method was used, or if an effort was made to avoid rescue. Multiple past attempts, particularly if these occurred within the last twelve months and if one or more was potentially lethal, significantly increase the risk of further suicide attempt behavior and of ultimate completion. The clinician should note the contingent reinforcers to prior behaviors to determine what was learned by the client in consequence of these events. In addition, the history of suicidal events in the client's family is an important area of inquiry in order to assess the level of exposure to suicide the client has had and its legacies of possible imitation and modelling and/or possible biological causes of suicidal vulnerability.

Assessing Clinical Risk Variables. It is helpful for the clinician to have a working knowledge of additional risk variables for suicide that have been identified in the empirical literature. Research conducted over the past twenty-five years has provided practitioners with

71

valuable information concerning various correlates of increased suicide risk (Garland and Zigler, 1993).

As described by Beck and his colleagues (Beck, Resnik, and Lettieri, 1986; Kovacs, Beck, and Weissman, 1975), for example, hopelessness may be one of the single best indicators of suicide risk. A profound sense of hopelessness and helplessness about oneself, others, and the future has been closely linked to depressive conditions and suicide (Rush and Beck, 1978). Other clinical indicators of suicide may include the following: dramatic and inexplicable affective change; affect that is depressed, flat, or blunted; the experience of recent/multiple negative environmental changes (losses); feelings of isolation, emptiness, experience of extreme stress, free-floating rage, agitation, and fatigue.

Young people can be very sensitive to the various interpersonal pressures and expectations of others, including parents, brothers/sisters, peers, coaches, teachers, and girlfriends/boyfriends. Murray's (1938) construct of "presses" may be applied to suicidal youth to identify a range of additionally experienced pressures that may be less socioculturally bound such as genetic factors, physical danger, chance events, alcohol/substance abuse, and psychopathology. As Berman and Jobes (1991) have noted, it is important to examine predisposing conditions, precipitating factors, and psychopathology in the assessment of those forces that may affect the suicidal youth.

Biological and sociocultural forces create a range of predisposing conditions that impinge upon the suicidal adolescent. The suicidal youth often experiences blows to self-esteem, sense of self, and ability to cope (Berman and Jobes, 1991). These may be the direct result of growing up in stressful families and having conflicted interpersonal relationships. Research has indicated that parents of suicidal adolescents (more often than controls) have conflictual relationships, including threats of separation or divorce, and more frequently, early loss of a parent (Stanley and Barter, 1970; Corder, Shorr, and Corder, 1974; Miller, Chiles, and Barnes, 1982). Further, suicidal youth have more frequent and serious interpersonal problems with peers, are more interpersonally sensitive, and are less likely to have a close confidant (McKenry, Tishler, and Kelley, 1982; Tishler and McKenry, 1982).

Adolescent suicides often are linked to a significant precipitating event, particularly an acute disciplinary crisis or a rejection or humiliation (Shaffer, 1988). It is important to note that these events—for example, a fight with parents, a breakup of a relationship, or being teased—are common to the experience of all adolescents, and thus, must be considered within the broader context of each adolescent's vulnerability to respond with increased suicidality to such stressors.

The crisis clinician must be attentive to evidence of psychopathology, as perhaps as many as 90 percent of adolescent suicide completions are by youth with retrospectively diagnosable mental disorders (cf. Berman and Jobes, 1991; Shaffer, 1988). Empirical research has confirmed that certain types of psychopathology are correlated with suicidal behavior; in particular, mood disorders, particularly manic-depressive illness or bipolar spectrum disorders (Garfinkel, Froese, and Hood, 1982; Robbins and Alessi, 1985; Brent et al., 1988), schizophrenia (McIntire et al., 1977), and personality disorders—particularly borderline and antisocial (Alessi et al., 1984; Berman and Jobes, 1991). Substance abuse disorders (both alcohol and drugs), as in adults, are often implicated in adolescent suicides and may be comorbid with the preceding disorders (Brent et al., 1988; Garfinkel, Froese, and Hood, 1982). The clinician must therefore be particularly sensitive to young people with any evidence of psychopathology who may be in distress but may not reveal suicidal intention.

Imminent risk for self-harm behavior appears most reactive to conditions that threaten a breakdown in usual coping mechanisms and, consequently, that increase loss of behavioral control. In addition to a variety of psychopathological disorders, as noted above, the clinician needs to be alert for significant changes in behavior, particularly if they involve increased reliance on alcohol or drugs. Level of rage and anxiety, as well, are good measures of the adolescent's ability to maintain control. In addition, behavioral change and/or loss of control often alienate the adolescent from significant others who, otherwise, could serve to buffer or protect the youth from untoward consequences of thinking designed simply to impulsively end painful affect. Again, hopelessness tends to get increased and/or reinforced under these interactional conditions.

Stage 4: Dealing with Feelings and Providing Support

As Shneidman (1985) has discussed, the suicidal person fundamentally seeks to escape unendurable psychological pain. Critically, the feeling of pain that drives the suicidal situation must be understood idiosyncratically—what is painful to one person may not be to the next. Therefore, it is essential that the clinician be empathically connected to the

73

youth's subjective experience of pain. Connecting with the pain can be achieved through careful and thoughtful listening, emotional availability, and warmth, and may be shown by eye contact, posture, and nonverbal cues that communicate genuine interest, concern, and caring. However, as Curran (1987) has discussed, a suicidal youth may be unwilling or unable to communicate painful feelings. This, of course, is a formidable problem for the accurate assessment of risk. It may be necessary in emergency situations to confer with friends and family who may be aware of the youth's recent emotional status. A teacher or best friend may be able to provide critical information concerning recent behaviors, changes in mood, and potential losses in the young person's life. Whether the information comes directly from the young person, a friend, parent, or teacher, it is important to try to infer an accurate assessment of the subjective pain experienced by the young person. It should be noted, however, that such contacts may adversely affect a therapeutic relationship after the crisis is resolved.

Even though emotional pain is difficult at any age, young people may experience it especially intensely. It is critical that the clinician respect the depth and degree of pain reported by a youth. Self-reports of extreme emotional pain and trauma should not be dismissed as adolescent melodrama. The experience of pain is acute and real to adolescents and potentially life threatening. As discussed earlier, young people tend to be present-oriented and lack the years of life experience that may provide the perspective needed to endure a painful period. It is therefore critical that the clinician appreciate this perhaps limited world view.

Simply stated, the risk of suicide increases as subjectively perceived psychological pain increases. Accordingly, it may be useful to have the suicidal youth actually rate their pain or hopelessness (e.g., ranging from 0, absolutely no pain, to 10, absolutely unendurable pain). Subjective ratings can be especially useful in helping to understand the young person's degree of pain. The rating can also help make the suicidal experience more concrete and less abstract for both the youth and the counselor. Moreover, the subjective rating can provide an ongoing barometer of suicide risk as changes and improvements can be tracked beyond the initial crisis and throughout the course of treatment.

Stage 5: Exploring Possible Alternatives

In the course of crisis work it is important to explore possible options and alternative ways of coping (other than suicide). The exploration of possible alternatives typically requires a thorough evaluation of negative forces in the young person's life, as well as positive influences—what are the relative strengths and weaknesses of the individual? Various expectations and pressures can become overwhelming to the young person in the midst of a suicidal crisis, making effective problem solving difficult, if not impossible. The intensity of one particularly salient pressure can potentially outweigh other objective strengths, resources, and abilities. For example, among adolescents who complete suicide, there is a subgroup of seemingly outstanding victims who "seemed to have it all." In such cases various abilities, skills, and strengths may be irrelevant when the individual's self-worth is rigidly defined by extraordinarily high standards and an expectation of continued success or perfection. Such a compulsive demand may defend against an underlying fragile sense of self. Accordingly, an unacceptable performance such as a C grade on an exam, easily interpreted as the equivalent of an F, could actually precipitate a suicide attempt to thwart the experience of unacceptable feelings. Operationally, the clinician needs to directly ask a youth about pressures and worries he or she is experiencing and perhaps rank order them to better ascertain their relative importance to the youth. Among these pressures to be considered is the adolescent's perceived "fit" within his or her family. Suicidal adolescents often talk of feeling responsible for family problems and conflicts. Some even consider their expendability as a way of freeing their family to move beyond current impasses. Conversely, it is critical to identify and assess the potential strengths, coping skills, and resources available to the young person. Reflecting back strengths and resources to the youth may provide some comfort in the midst of a crisis and underscore alternative means of coping. The risk of suicide is significantly lessened when there is evidence of internal (e.g., cognitive) and external (e.g., interpersonal) resources for coping with conflict and stress (Berman and Jobes, 1991).

The need to explore alternatives in the cases of Tom, Lisa, and Bill is abundantly clear. Tom, a troubled youth reeling out of control, is a suicide waiting to happen. At the time of his arrest, Tom was primarily dealing with his losses and depression by abusing substances and acting out. As an intelligent and generally popular teenager, with friends and family willing to support him, Tom had notable personal and interpersonal resources at his disposal but seemed unable to ask for help. Lisa, struggling to overcome the loss of her beloved grandfather, seems to be living in a romanticized fantasy world of death and reunion. Her concerned parents were at a loss as to how to help their daughter work through her grief. Bill, overwhelmed by his parents' hostile reaction to his homosexuality, sought escape from his unbearable feelings. In hindsight, it would seem that Bill perhaps came out to his parents prematurely in that he had only just begun to explore his sexual identity in a gay support group on campus and in psychotherapy at the college counseling center. In each of these three cases we see individuals suffering through painful losses and debilitating feelings, yet in each case there are resources and potentials for alternative ways of coping.

Stage 6: Formulating an Action Plan

Having thoroughly assessed the risk of suicide, the clinician is in a position to formulate an action (treatment) plan of intervention. As described by Hoff (1984) and others, a series of strategic steps needs to be initiated to insure the patient's immediate safety and shift the patient's focus from crisis to resolution.

Removing the Means. The first goal should be to immediately reduce the lethality of the situation. This is best accomplished by literally removing the means from the client's access or, at a minimum, delaying access to available means. Pills should be flushed down the toilet or given to others to monitor and dispense; guns and/or other weapons should be removed from the home. Where available, parents or significant others need to be involved in all efforts to safeguard the environment.

Negotiating Safety. One of the clinician's most effective interventive tools involves the negotiation of the patient's safety. Generally, the concrete goal of these negotiations is to insure the patient's physical safety by establishing that the patient will not hurt him- or herself for a specific period of time. The more concrete and specific the understanding, the better. Typically, the patient will agree to maintain his or her safety until the next clinical contact, at which point a new understanding can be negotiated. The clinician must remember to keep these agreements time-limited and renewable. The clinician should also remember that a "contract" with a psychologically wounded (narcissistically injured) teenager does not necessarily guarantee the patient's safety, in that early wounds may have severely affected the youth's trust and trustability.

Future Linkage. The clinician and the patient must create a crisis game plan that orients the patient toward the future. Long-term goals should be established and operationalized with the patient in short-term steps. This may be accomplished by identifying when the next clinical contacts will occur. Plans for activities and social contacts may be made as well. Scheduling phone contacts to touch base can also be planned. It is critical that suicidal patients have something to which they can look forward. Future linkage helps orient the patient to a different and hopefully better future, creating a distance from the immediate crisis.

Decreasing Anxiety and Sleep Loss. If the suicidal youth is acutely anxious and/or not able to sleep, the suicidal crisis may become worse. Medication may be indicated as an emergency intervention. However, dosages must be closely monitored and linked to ongoing psychotherapy such that the medication is not used for an overdose. Other symptoms that may exacerbate the patient's ability to benefit from verbal intervention and/or threaten the patient's ability to maintain control must be continuously monitored and treated accordingly.

Decreasing Isolation. The patient must not be left alone in the midst of a suicidal crisis. It is critical that a trustworthy friend or family member be with the patient through the crisis phase. Efforts must be made to mobilize friends, family, and neighbors, making them aware of the importance of ongoing contact with the suicidal youth. In cases where friends or family are unavailable (or unwilling), hospitalization may be necessary.

Hospitalization. When the risk of suicide remains unabated and high, and patients are unable to negotiate their safety, hospitalization becomes the necessary intervention. Simply stated, stabilization through hospitalization can provide the patient with a safe environment and a chance to remove him/herself from the environment that produced the suicidal crisis.

Stage 7: Providing Follow Up

Beyond emergency medical treatment and crisis intervention, after crisis resolution, ongoing counseling and psychotherapy follow-up is essential. The absence or amelioration of an immediate crisis is not synonymous with the decision to not provide ongoing psychotherapy. It is important for the clinician to remember that people who have used suicidal behavior to respond to life crises in the past are prone to use such behaviors in future life crises. As the final phase of crisis resolution, the clinician must insure that follow-up evaluation and treatment is arranged and that a strategic, preventive treatment plan is in place to circumvent potential future suicidal crises.

Various treatment modalities with suicidal clients have been discussed in the literature (refer to Berman and Jobes, 1991). The modalities range from longer-term individual treatment (Hendin, 1981; Jobes, 1995; Toolin, 1962), to shorter-term individual models (Beck and Beck, 1978; Getz et al., 1983), to group treatment (Comstock and McDermott, 1975; Farberow, 1976; Hipple, 1982). Family therapy may be particularly helpful with youthful populations (Alanen, Rinne, and Paukkonen, 1981; Richman, 1979, 1986). In addition, ongoing pharmacotherapy may be helpful in stabilizing mood and intrusive psychopathological symptoms.

It is beyond the scope of this chapter to delineate the many aspects and variants of ongoing inpatient and outpatient psychotherapy with the suicidal adolescent. However, it is imperative that the clinician familiarize himself or herself with the increasing array of effective short- and long- term intervention strategies available to treat the depressed and suicidal adolescent, if the alarming increase in suicide among adolescents is to be halted and reversed.

CASE STUDY OUTCOMES

Tom, Lisa, and Bill were three high-risk youth in serious suicidal crises that could have had tragic outcomes. Thankfully, each case received appropriate and effective crisis intervention.

Following his arrest, Tom's high school guidance counselor, with the support of Tom's parents, arranged to have him psychiatrically hospitalized. He received intensive treatment for his depression and substance abuse, and after four weeks he was discharged to the care of an outpatient psychotherapist. After six months of therapy and regular attendance at AA and NA meetings, Tom finished his remaining semester of high school and was accepted to a local community college.

After the poem episode, Lisa began to meet with a psychologist in both individual and family meetings. Recognizing her creativity, her therapist used art therapy and encouraged her to continue to write poetry about her feelings. Family therapy was helpful in working through the mourning of the grandfather, since the family had not really dealt with his death. In addition, family work led to an improved relationship between Lisa and her father, who had long been jealous of her special relationship with her grandfather (his father).

Bill was hospitalized for three days after his aborted hanging. After discharge, Bill continued to pursue therapy in the counseling center and also continued to attend the gay support group. Bill's parents were horrified by, and felt intensely guilty about, his suicide attempt. While they continued to disapprove of his lifestyle, they nevertheless refrained from threatening to disown him and avoided discussing the topic with him. About three months after his suicide attempt, Bill began dating someone from his support group, and he was markedly less depressed by the end of the school year.

SUMMARY

This chapter has examined the complexities of youthful suicide, a phenomenon that has increased dramatically over the past forty years. While accurate clinical prediction of suicide is virtually impossible, practitioners can nevertheless optimize the capacity to effectively respond to youthful suicide crises by informing themselves of, and developing skills in, suicide risk assessment and interventive strategies.

Roberts' (1991) seven-stage model of crisis intervention has been used to illustrate one approach to working with a suicidal youth in crisis. By assessing lethality, establishing rapport, identifying major problems, dealing with feelings, exploring alternatives, formulating an action plan, and providing follow up, a crisis clinician can make an intervention that may help save the life of a young person in a suicidal crisis.

REFERENCES

Alberts, F. L. (1988). Psychological assessment. In D. Capuzzi, and L. Golden (Eds.), *Preventing adolescent suicide*. Muncie, IN: Accelerated Development Inc.

Alanen, Y. O., Rinne, R., and Paukkonen, P. (1981). On family dynamics and family therapy in suicidal attempts. *Crisis, 2,* 20–26.

Alessi, N. E., McManus, M., Brickman, A., and Grapentine, L. (1984). Suicidal behavior among serious juvenile offenders. *American Journal of Psychotherapy, 141,* 286–287.

Beck, A. J., and Beck, A. T. (1978). Cognitive therapy of depression and suicide. *American Journal of Psychotherapy, 32*, 201–219.

Beck, A. T., Resnick, H. L. P., and Lettieri, D. J. (Eds.). (1986). *The prediction of suicide*. Philadelphia, PA: Charles Press.

Beck, A. T., Rush, A. J., Shaw, B. F., and Emery, G. (1979). *Cognitive therapy of depression*. New York: Guilford.

Berman, A. L. (1984). The problem of teenage suicide. Testimony presented to the U.S. Senate Committee on the Judiciary Subcommittee on Juvenile Justice.

————— (1986). Adolescent suicide: Issues and challenges. *Seminars in Adolescent Medicine, 2*, 269–277.

—————, and Jobes, D. A. (1991). *Adolescent suicide: Assessment and intervention*. Washington, DC: American Psychological Association.

Brent, D. A. (1987). Correlates of the medical lethality of suicide attempts in children and adolescents. *Journal of the American Academy of Child and Adolescent Psychiatry, 26*, 87–91.

—————, Perper, J. A., Goldstein, C. E., Kolko, D. J., Allan, M. J., Allman, C. J., and Zelenak, J. P. (1988). Risk factors for adolescent suicide. *Archives of General Psychiatry, 45*, 581–588.

Cantor, P. (1976). Personality characteristics among youthful female suicide attempters. *Journal of Abnormal Psychology, 85*, 324–329.

Comstock, B., and McDermott, M. (1975). Group therapy for patients who attempt suicide. *International Journal of Group Psychotherapy, 25*, 44–49.

Corder, B. F., Shorr, W., and Corder, R. F. (1974). A study of social and psychological characteristics of adolescent suicide attempters in an urban, disadvantaged area. *Adolescence, 9*, 1–16.

Curran, D. K. (1987). *Adolescent Suicidal Behavior*. Washington, DC: Hemisphere.

Farberow, N. L. (1970). The suicidal crisis in psychotherapy. In E. Shneidman, N. Farberow, and R. Litman (Eds.), *The Psychology of Suicide*. New York: Science House.

————— (1976). Group therapy for self-destructive persons. In J. J. Parad, H. L. P. Resnik, and L. G. Parad (Eds.), *Emergency and disaster management: A mental health sourcebook*. Bowie, MD: Charles Press.

Garfinkel, B. D., Froese, A., and Hood, J. (1982). Suicide attempts in children and adolescents. *American Journal of Psychiatry, 139*, 1257–1261.

Garland, A. F., and Zigler, E. (1993). Adolescent suicide prevention: Current research and social policy implications. *American Psychologist, 48*, 169–182.

Getz, W. L., Allen, D. B., Myers, R. K., and Linder, K. C. (1983). *Brief counseling with suicidal persons*. Lexington, MA: Lexington Books.

Hendin, H. (1981). Psychotherapy and suicide. *American Journal of Psychotherapy, 35*, 469–480.

Hipple, J. (1982). Group treatment of suicidal clients. *Journal of Specialists in Group Work, 7,* 245–250.

Hipple, J., and Cimbolic, P. (1979). *The counselor and suicidal crisis.* Springfield, IL: Charles C. Thomas.

Hoff, L. A. (1984). *People in crisis.* Menlow Park, CA: Addison-Wesley.

Jobes, D. A. (1995). Psychodynamic treatment of adolescent suicide attempters. In J. Zimmerman and G. Asnis (Eds.), *Treatment approaches with suicidal adolescents.* New York: Wiley.

Jobes, D. A., Berman, A. L., and Josselson, A. R. (1987). Improving the validity and reliability of medicolegal certifications of suicide. *Suicide and Life-Threatening Behavior, 17,* 310–325.

Jobes, D. A., Casey, J. O., Berman, A. L., and Wright, D. G. (1991). Empirical criteria for the determination of suicide manner of death. *Journal of Forensic Science, 36,* 244–256.

Kovacs, M., Beck, A. T., and Weissman, A. (1975). The use of suicidal motives in the psychotherapy of attempted suicides. *American Journal of Psychotherapy, 29,* 363–368.

McIntire, M. S., Angle, C. R., Wikoff, R. L., and Schlicht, M. L. (1977). Recurrent adolescent suicidal behavior. *Pediatrics, 60,* 605–608.

McKenry, D., Tishler, C., and Kelley, C. (1982). Adolescent suicide: A comparison of attempters and non-attempters in an emergency room population. *Clinical Pediatrics, 21,* 266–270.

Miller, M. L., Chiles, J. A., and Barnes, V. E. (1982). Suicide attempters within a delinquent population. *Journal of Consulting and Clinical Psychology, 50,* 491–498.

Murray, H. A. (1938). *Exploration in Personality.* New York: Oxford University Press.

National Center for Health Statistics. (1993). *Vital statistics of the United States,* Vol. II—*Mortality,* Part A. Washington, DC: U.S. Government Printing Office.

Pope, K. S. (1986). Assessment and management of suicidal risk: Clinical and legal standards of care. *The Independent Practitioner, 6,* 17–23.

Richman, J. (1979). Family therapy of attempted suicide. *Family Process, 18,* 131–142.

——— (1986). *Family therapy for suicidal people.* New York: Springer.

Robbins, D., and Alessi, N. (1985). Depressive symptoms and suicidal behavior in adolescents. *American Journal of Psychiatry, 142,* 588–592.

Roberts, A. R. (1991). *Contemporary perspectives on crisis intervention and prevention.* Englewood Cliffs, NJ: Prentice-Hall.

Rosenberg, M. L., Smith, J. C., Davidson, L. E., and Conn, J. M. (1987). The emergence of youth suicide: An epidemiological analysis and public health perspective. *Annual Review of Public Health, 8,* 417–440.

Rosenberg, M. L., Davidson, L. E., Smith, J. C., Berman, A. L., Buzbee, H., Gantner, G., Gay, G. A., Moore-Lewis, B., Mills, D. H., Murray, D.,

O'Carroll, P. W., and Jobes, D. (1988). Operational criteria for the determination of suicide. *Journal of Forensic Sciences, 32,* 1445–1455.

Rush, A. J., and Beck, A. T. (1978). Cognitive therapy of depression and suicide. *American Journal of Psychotherapy, 32,* 201–219.

Schein, H. M. (1976). Suicide care: Obstacles in the education of psychiatric residents. *Omega, 7,* 75–82.

Shaffer, D. (1988). The epidemiology of teen suicide: An examination of risk factors. *Journal of Clinical Psychiatry, 49,* 36–41.

Shafii, M., Carrigan, S., Whittinghill, J.R., and Derrick, A. (1985). A psychological autopsy of completed suicide in children and adolescents. *American Journal of Psychiatry, 142,* 1061–1064.

Shneidman, E. S. (1980). Psychotherapy with suicidal patients. In T. B. Karasu and L. Bellak (Eds.), *Specialized techniques in individual psychotherapy.* New York: Brunner/Mazel.

Shneidman, E. S. (1985). *Definition of suicide.* New York: Wiley.

Smith, K., Conroy, R. W., and Ehler, B. D. (1984). Lethality of suicide attempt rating scale. *Suicide and Life-Threatening Behavior, 14,* 215–242.

Smith, K., and Crawford, S. (1984). Suicidal behavior among "normal" high school students. *Suicide and Life-Threatening Behavior, 16,* 313–325.

Stanley, E. J., and Barter, J. J. (1970). Adolescent suicidal behavior. *American Journal of Orthopsychiatry, 40,* 87–96.

Tishler, C., and McKenry, P. (1982). Parental negative self and adolescent suicide attempters. *Journal of the American Academy of Child Psychiatry, 21,* 404–408.

Toolin, J. M. (1962). Suicide and suicide attempts in children and adolescents. *American Journal of Psychiatry, 118,* 719–724.

Vlasak, G. J. (1975). Medical sociology. In S. Perlin (Ed.), *A handbook for the study of suicide* (pp. 131–146). New York: Oxford.

Weissman, A., and Worden, W. (1972). Risk-rescue rating in suicide assessment. *Archives of General Psychiatry, 26,* 553–560.

CHAPTER 5

Assessment and Crisis Intervention with Adult Survivors of Incest

SOPHIA F. DZIEGIELEWSKI and
CHERYL RESNICK

Joan is a well-groomed, intelligent thirty-year-old woman who has sought social work counseling services with her main complaint being, "I don't know what's wrong with me; I am starting to remember things and I am not sure whether they are real or dreams that I have had." Joan states that she is currently under extreme stress and is now in the process of a divorce. When asked what she remembers that is troubling her so, she states that the memories are so sketchy. As she begins to speak the tears run down her face. "I remember my teenage brother coming to my room at night, it was our special secret." When asked when did this happen, she stated, "When I was about nine or ten, he didn't come often but I think it was real. How could I let this happen, or am I just making it up in my mind?"

Don is a highly respected professional. He speaks very clearly of his academic accomplishments, but grows more subdued as he discusses his family of origin. Recently, Don's sister has "come out" and reported that she was molested by their father. After bringing out this point Don states clearly, "God, this would be easier if I had a drink. My father denies it, and I do not believe he could have done it; I am so angry with my sister. How could she lie like that?"

After weeks of work with a counselor, Don was able to leave his anger for his sister and address the anger he was feeling toward himself. Don had also been molested by his father. "Just thinking about it makes me sick. I touched him, he said mom was cold and could not care for him the way he needed. He needed me to help him be strong. I never told. How do you tell something like that anyway. It was better left for me to deal with. I couldn't stand for my wife or family to know. But my sister, I think she may be lying but now I am not so sure."

Jill is a forty-year-old woman who came in for services, requesting help stating, "I feel as though I am losing control of my life." After the counselor talked with her, it became evident that her current fear centered around an expected visit from her father. As Jill became more relaxed she began to tell of her mother's death when she was fourteen. After her mother's death she became caretaker for her younger brother and sister. Her father worked long hours and was always very tired. After the death of her mother his drinking began to increase. According to Jill, this is where it all began. Jill was expected to cook, clean, and care for her siblings. She doesn't remember exactly when or how the relationship changed with her father. He began to belittle her and tell her she was useless; when things did not go his way he often blamed the children. Since Jill was the oldest she was held responsible for everything her siblings did, and her father demanded that she correct all mistakes by "doing things for him." These "things" she was expected to perform were often sexual in nature. When Jill was sixteen, she ran away from home. She met a man and immediately moved in with him. He also had an alcohol problem, and they often quarreled. Eventually, she left him and went home to her father. Her father never forgot this and often used her brief affair as testimony to her "cheap, worthless identity." Jill was frightened and shocked when she became pregnant several months later. Her father told relatives and other family members that he had no idea who the father was and that, with her past history, who could really be sure? When the Department of Health and Human Services questioned her about who the father was and her living arrangements, she hung her head in shame, stating, "I don't know who the father is." In describing this incident the tears still come as Jill talks about giving up her baby for adoption. "How could I ever tell the truth? I had my father's child. Who would ever believe me? How can I ever forgive myself for allowing this to happen? If my father had beaten me, I might have had a reason to do what I did, but he never hit me—and I still stayed."

The situations described in the three case examples are not un-usual when dealing with the adult survivors of incest. Nor is the power-lessness these adult survivors experienced first as children and now, even though years have passed, still feel as adults. In general, the vulnerability of the child in our society can create and perpetuate cir-cumstances conducive to victimization. In a culture and society that deems a multitude of groups "powerless" through racial, religious, ethnic, and gender identifications, perhaps the most defenseless group of all are those involved in the three case examples described above—society's children.

Historically, children were considered the property of their par-ents, and the introduction of child labor laws, as well as child protection laws, is astonishingly recent. Children rely upon significant adults in their lives, particularly parents, for their sustenance, protection, affection, and affiliation. When parental protection and affection be-come intricately tied to sexuality and sexual behaviors, the child be-comes vulnerable to victimization.

SCOPE OF THE PROBLEM

Definition of Child Sexual Abuse

There are many definitions of incest but primarily it is when a child of any age is exploited by an older person (i.e., generally an ineligible partner because of blood and/or social ties) for that person's own grati-fication while there is disregard for the child's own developmental immaturity and inability to understand the sexual behavior (Courtois, 1988). Dinsmore (1991) defines incest as sexual seduction, molestation, and/or rape of a child by an older relative or trusted friend of the family. Russell (1986) expands the definition to any kind of exploitative sexual contact or attempted contact between relatives, no matter how distant, when the child is under the age of eighteen. Sgroi (1982) ex-plains sexual abuse as "a sexual act imposed on a child who lacks emotional, maturational and cognitive development" (p. 9).

Cross-generational incest is always abusive due to the gross power differential between adult and child (Courtois, 1988). In recent years the educational, media, and health care systems have focused attention on teaching children the peril of interactions with strangers, yet the fact that they can be in danger in their own homes is rarely discussed (Burgess, et al., 1978). Generally, in defining the concept of incest, it is important to remember that incest is always an infringement upon the rights of the child (Justice and Justice, 1979). Many adults survivors of incest, similar to those in the case examples described earlier, do not recognize this power differential, often blaming themselves for what has taken place.

Victims of Abuse

Statistics in regard to the incidence and rate of sexual exploitation now abound. Although there has been some suggestion that child sexual abuse has increased, this may be a function of expanded public awareness and reporting. According to the National Resource Center on Child Sexual Abuse, which is a subsidiary of the National Center on Child Abuse and Neglect (U.S. Department of Health and Human Services, 1993), 2.7 million children were abused and neglected in the United States in 1991. Fifteen percent of those, or 404,100, were sexually abused. In 1992, the proportion of sexually abused children rose from 15 percent to 18 percent; in other words, from 404,100 to 486,000.

In 1986, the American Association for the Protection of Children and the American Humane Association reported 82, 325 cases of childhood incest. Parental sexual abuse comprised 42 percent of these cases, other relatives comprised 22.8 percent, and 35.2 percent were attributed to unrelated persons (U.S. Department of Health and Human Services, 1993). In the Kinseys' study the reported incidence of female child molestation was as much as 25 percent prior to age twelve (Finkelhor, 1979; Herman, Russell and Trocki, 1986; Herman, 1992). Specifically, Russell (1986) reported that the percentage of females who have experienced some form of incestuous abuse at some point in their lives was as high as 20 percent.

Females overwhelmingly represent the primary victims, with 97–98 percent of perpetrators being male (Gelinas, 1983; Russell, 1986). In Finkelhor's (1979) study 19 percent of females had been sexually victimized as children, none of the respondents were glad the experience had occurred, and 66 percent remembered the experience as being negative. Russell (1986), who completed a randomized survey of nine hundred homes in the San Francisco area found that 38 percent of the women surveyed experienced incestuous childhood sexual contact. Sixteen percent had been abused by a relative prior to reaching age eighteen, 4.5 percent had been abused by their fathers prior to age eighteen. Only 4 cases out of 187 found sexual abuse to have any positive elements. Not a single case of father/daughter incest was reported to be positive to any degree. Wyatt's 1985 study (Russell, 1986) of 248 women found 62 percent experienced sexual abuse at least once prior to age eighteen. Extra-familial cases accounted for 32 percent of reported cases, and incest accounted for 21 percent of reported cases.

Blume (1986) suggests that at least 27 million women have been sexually abused by persons known to them. Meiselman (1990) postulates a 10–20 percent incidence of female childhood sexual abuse. Both Finkelhor (1979) and Russell (1986) report increased child victimization in the presence of stepfathers.

In a recent study of sexual addiction Carnes found that out of 233 men and 57 women, 81 percent reported childhood sexual abuse (1991). Briere (1992) indicates childhood sexual contact ranging from fondling to intercourse occurs 20–30 percent of the time for females and 10–15 percent for males. Molestation frequently begins when the victim is under eight years of age. Thirty-six to fifty-one percent of female psychiatric inpatients reported a history of child sexual abuse; 70 percent of females who were nonpsychotic emergency room psychiatric patients reported childhood sexual abuse (Briere, 1992).

In reporting the statistics on abuse victims, it must be noted that males are also sexually victimized within families. However, the rate appears to be less than that for female children (Finkelhor, 1984). The reasons for this differentiation remain unclear, but suggestions include: the incidence actually is smaller; males have more difficulty in verbalizing what has happened; males are even less likely than females to seek treatment; and/or, the adult male incest survivor (as in the second case) actively refuses to recognize what has occurred, and even after the event is acknowledged, may continue to deny its happening due to embarrassment. Females are also more likely to be abused within the family system and males outside of the family (Courtois, 1988).

Incidence and Type of Abuse

The bulk of child sexual abuse is perpetrated by someone known to the child, generally a family member. There are many different types of family incest to include: father and/or stepfather toward child, mother and/or stepmother toward child, sibling incest, and other types of "relative" incest (grandparents, uncles, aunts, cousins). Taking into account the many different forms of incest, the most common form is parent to child, and of that father and stepfather toward daughter incest is clearly recognized as the most commonly occurring (Courtois, 1988).

The average duration of abuse within the family is four years, whereas abuse outside the family unit is generally short-term. Often family-related incestuous abuse is repeated and progressive. According to Russell (1986) this pattern of repeated long-term abuse seems to have more serious consequences than that of sexual abuse perpetrated by a stranger. In incestuous families there is often more than one perpetrator, and the patterns of transmission can cross generations. Male children who have been abused also tend to be more likely to continue this cycle of abuse and perpetuate abuse in adolescence and adulthood.

As in the third case example, adult survivors can blame themselves for what happened and for not resisting the incidents (Courtois, 1988; Shapiro, 1987; Herman, Russell and Trocki, 1986). It is not uncommon to be told by a female client that she blames herself—that she could have stopped the abuse because it was not "physical." Many times victims confuse the seriousness of emotional abuse with the actual results of physical force as in rape.

Characteristics of Incestuous Families

It is believed that child sexual abuse is not an exclusively individual or family problem. Incest does not occur in a vacuum and remains a family affair. Challenging the perpetuation of abuse in society compels the comprehension of family dynamics. There are many different characteristics that have been linked to incestuous families (e.g., social isolation, part-time or absent parents, shared secrets, duplicity and deceit between family members, unwanted children, inadequate parenting, intermittent reinforcement, violence or fear of it, few touches except bad touches [Courtois, 1988]).

The isolation factor that is characteristic of so many of these families is a very important consideration in understanding family dynamics. Finkelhor (1979) and Carnes (1991) implicate societal fragmentation and social isolation of families, kin, and community networks as contributing to the pervasive seclusion common among incestuous families. The average executive changes jobs once every eighteen months, and the average family moves once every three years. Studies indicate that it takes up to three years to build a secure, supportive community (Carnes, 1991). Social isolation, which is generally reinforced by the parents, often is a precursor of the occurrence of incest in families.

APPLICATION OF CRISIS INTERVENTION: ROBERTS' SEVEN-STAGE MODEL

Effective intervention with survivors of incest requires careful assessment of individual, family, and environmental factors. A crisis by definition is short-term and overwhelming. According to Roberts (1991) a crisis is described as an emotionally distressing change. The crisis can cause a disruption of an individual's normal and stable state so that the usual methods of coping and problem solving do not work. Thus, denial becomes a common form of coping used by victims of incest. Disassociation frequently occurs, in which the child develops a "not me" persona who can split off from the overwhelming experience (Friedrich, 1990). It is not uncommon for survivors to have little if any memory of the abusive events; and fewer than 7 percent of the victims of child sexual abuse disclose the abuse during childhood (Rhea, 1992), while many keep this secret well into the adult years.

Psychological trauma can be understood as an "affliction of the powerless" (Herman, 1992:33). Threat of life and bodily integrity overwhelm normal adaptive capabilities, producing extensive symptomatology. Adopting a pathological view of symptomatology is not helpful; it is more beneficial when clients can comprehend their symptoms as signs of strength. Symptoms that are understood as coping techniques developed by the survivor in order to adapt to a toxic environment can enhance self-esteem.

There is increasing evidence that trauma significantly alters the biochemistry of the brain, particularly the production of adrenaline and the natural opiates (Herman, 1992; Waits, 1993). Waits (1993) postulates that adaptations such as hypervigilance prepare the victim for fight or flight responses and may become biochemically ingrained when triggered again and again. Studies of inescapable shock have demonstrated neurochemical transformations (Waits, 1993). It is not unlikely that biochemical alterations are involved in post-traumatic stress disorder symptoms (e.g., flashbacks, panic attacks, etc.).

When pain is isolated from awareness, ingrained patterns of self-regulation may be generated. In fact revictimization may be seen as a means of removing pain, thus creating an addiction to trauma. As knowledge regarding neurochemistry increases, adaptations such as hypervigilance, depression, immunological alterations, eating disorders, dissociative states, and post-traumatic stress syndromes may be better understood. In conclusion, current research continues to support the similarities between post-traumatic stress symptomology victims (e.g., Vietnam era veterans) and survivors of incest (Patten, et al., 1989; McNew and Abel, 1995).

Roberts (1991) describes seven stages of working through crisis: (1) assessing lethality and safety needs; (2) establishing rapport and communication; (3) identifying the major problems; (4) dealing with feelings and providing support; (5) exploring possible alternatives; (6) formulating an action plan; and (7) providing follow up. Roberts' seven-stage model applies to a broad range of crises and is clearly applicable in the case of intervention with survivors of incest. In the application of this crisis intervention model for practice, the therapeutic environment is characterized by the following: (1) a here-and-now orientation; (2) a time-limited course (typically six to twelve sessions); (3) a view of the adult survivor's behavior as an understandable (rather than a pathological) reaction to stress; (4) the assumption by the social worker of an active and directive role; and (5) an overall strategy aimed at increasing the individual's remobilization and return to the previous level of functioning.

Stage 1: Assessing Lethality

Incest is unlikely to be clearly evidenced in the initial phase of therapy. In fact, nearly 50 percent of survivors who present for treatment do not disclose their histories of abuse (Courtois, 1988). Since denial is a major coping mechanism for survivors, memories of victimization, and/or recognition of sexual abuse may be triggered by catalysts (process of therapy, sights, sounds, situations). Most victims of incest do not seek treatment for the identified problem of having survived incest. In fact, many of these clients begin to recall and recognize the abuse when its subtleties are identified by the social worker, who then skillfully helps the client work through the memories, feelings, and cognitions.

Listed below are some of the hazardous events or circumstances that can be linked to the recognition of sexual abuse by the adult survivor of incest. These events can have the likelihood of triggering anxious responses from clients so that they seek help, even if the sexual abuse is not immediately identified as the crisis issue: (1) a growing public awareness of the prevalence of sexual abuse/incest; (2) the acknowledgment by a loved one or someone that the client respects that he/she has been the victim of sexual abuse; (3) an act of violence being committed against them or someone they love such as rape and/or sexual assault; (4) the client committing to a serious or permanent relationship; (5) the issue of pregnancy, birth, and preparing for child-rearing; and (6) the sights, sounds, or smells that trigger memories of events from the client's past (these can be highly specific to individuals).

Immediate Danger. Intervention may require careful assessment of suicidal ideation, and the potential for initial and subsequent hospitalization/medication may be required. Questions to elicit pervasive symptomatology should be asked (e.g., depression, suicidal ideation, sexual dysfunction, instances of promiscuity, substance abuse, psychological numbing, self-mutilation, flashbacks, and panic attacks). Self-mutilation and/or suicidal behaviors can be considered common occurrences. If there is a high probability of any such symptoms, the social worker should be alerted to the likelihood that the risk of a history of childhood sexual abuse probably exists. Since revictimization is common, the social worker must be aware that the stress of sexual assault can reactivate previous anxieties, fears, and behaviors, frequently recreating the crisis situation. Based on the age and the circumstances of the client's living situation, assessment must also be made to assure that the client is not still in immediate danger of continued abuse. Several structured and goal oriented sessions may be needed to help the client move past denial into an acknowledgment that the incest actually occurred.

In these initial sessions of therapy (session 1–3) the goal of the therapeutic intervention is recognizing the hazardous event and acknowledging what has actually happened. For some reason (based on the triggering catalyst) the survivor is currently being subjected to periods of stress that disturb his/her sense of equilibrium. (It is assumed that the individual wants to maintain homeostatic balance, and physically and emotionally the body will seek to regain equilibrium.) Often, as stated earlier, the survivor may not present with the actual crisis event, and the social worker may have to help the survivor get to the root of the problem (i.e., the real reason for the visit). During these initial sessions the survivor becomes aware and acknowledges the fact that incest has occurred. Once this happens the survivor is in a vulnerable state. The impact of this event disturbs the survivor, and traditional problem solving and coping methods are attempted. When these do not work, tension and anxiety continue to rise, and the individual becomes unable to function effectively. In the initial sessions the assessment of both past and present coping behaviors of the survivor are important; however, the focus of intervention clearly must remain in the "here and now." The social worker must attempt to stay away from past issues or unresolved issues unless they relate directly to the handling of the incestuous abuse.

Stage 2: Establishing Rapport and Communication

Incest victims commonly blame themselves for the occurrence of child molestation. The socialized obedience to adults that has transpired results in the victim's fear of: being hurt or not being believed, the consequences of betraying the family secret, the loss of love and affection, being abandoned, being punished, and feeling overwhelming guilt. The capacity for trust has been shattered and is reflected in negative self-image and poor self-esteem.

In addition to the inability to trust, incest survivors do not have adequate skills in interpreting the trustworthiness of others. This increases the potential for further victimization. These women understand their own vulnerability and know "once you have been abused, you live knowing it can happen—therefore, it can happen again" (Russell, 1986).

When working with survivors of incest, it is important to go slowly and whenever possible let the survivor set the pace of treatment. Let the client lead, since he or she has a negative history of being coerced, and forcing confrontation on issues may not be helpful. Allowing the client to set the pace creates a trusting atmosphere that gives the message "You will not be hurt here." The society in general, and crisis counselors in particular, can view the youthful years as a time of carefree innocence and exploration. This may cause clients to feel they must not only defend what has happened to them but further justify their role in the abuse. Survivors need to be reminded that their symptoms are a healthy response to an unhealthy environment. They need to recognize that they have survived heinous circumstances and continue to live and cope. Incest victims require a positive future orientation, with an understanding that they can overcome current problems and arrive at a happy, satisfactory tomorrow (Dolan, 1991). Hope that change can occur is crucial to the survivor's well-being.

Women who have lived through trauma need to recognize that victimization represents only one aspect of their lives, and they must focus on other parts of their existence in order to become whole. When therapy focuses solely on the victimization, therapy itself becomes a revictimization.

Perhaps more than anything else, throughout each of the sessions, these clients need unconditional support, positive regard, and concern. These factors are especially crucial to the working relationship since a history of lack of support, "blaming," and breach of loyalty are common. The therapeutic relationship is seen as a vehicle for continued growth, development of coping skills, and the ability to move beyond the abuse (Briere, 1992).

Stage 3: Identify the Major Problems

Once the possibility of denial has been addressed, obsessive focus on the incest may occur. This can precipitate crisis with concomitant flashbacks, nightmares, panic attacks, depressive reactions, withdrawal, and suicide attempts. Support is essential. Group participation has been effective, as well as the use of journal writing, relaxation techniques, physical exercise, and development of an understanding that the victim needs to be good to him/her self at this time (Dinsmore, 1991).

In these next few sessions (sessions 3–6) the social worker needs to assume a very active role. First the major problems to be dealt with and addressed must be identified. These problems must be viewed in terms of how they have affected the survivor's behavior. Education in regard to the effects and consequences of this type of abuse in others is to be discussed. The precipitating factor, especially if the event was in the past, must be clearly identified. Complete acknowledgment of the event can push the person into a state of active crisis marked by disequilibrium, disorganization, and immobility (e.g., the last straw). Once the survivor enters full acknowledgment, the incestuous event can be perceived as a threat, a loss, or a challenge. Whichever reaction is engaged, new energy for problem solving will be generated. This challenge stimulates a moderate degree of anxiety plus a kindling of hope and expectation. This actual state of disequilibrium can last four to eight weekly sessions or until some type of adaptive or maladaptive solution is found.

Stage 4: Dealing with Feelings and Providing Support

The energy generated from the survivor's personal feelings, experiences, and perceptions steers the therapeutic process (Briere, 1992). It is critical that the therapist demonstrate empathy and an anchored understanding of the victim's world. These symptoms are seen as functional, and as a means of avoiding abuse and pain. Even severe symptoms such as dissociative reactions should be viewed as a constructive method of removing one's self from a harmful situation and exploring alternative coping mechanisms. Survivor's experiences should be normalized so that they can recognize being a victim is not their fault. Reframing symptoms are coping techniques that can be helpful. In this stage (sessions 6–8) the survivor begins to reintegrate. The survivor gradually begins to become ready to reach a new state of equilibrium. Each particular crisis situation (i.e., type and duration of incest or rape) may follow a sequence of stages that can generally be predicted and mapped out. One positive result from generating the crisis state in stage three is that in treatment, after reaching a crisis, survivors seem particularly amenable to help.

Once the crisis situation has been obtained, distorted ideas and perceptions regarding abuse need to be corrected and information updated so that the client can better understand what he or she has experienced. Victims eventually need to confront their pain and anger so that they can develop better strategies for coping. Increased awareness helps the survivor of incest face and experience contradicting emotions (anger/love, fear/rage, dampening emotion/intensifying emotion) without the conditioned response of escape (Briere, 1992).

Throughout this process there must be recognition of the client's continued courage in facing and dealing with these issues. Engagement with the anger associated with the violence and out-of-control experience is frequently beneficial. Confrontation of the perpetrator, as well as the survivor's other parent, may be critical to this process. This confrontation, however, does not have to be in reality. Many times survivors can achieve satisfaction by directly confronting the deeds of the perpetrator and significant others in the protected therapeutic environment.

Ripping open the secret requires a safe place with enormous support. The client will need much support and cognizance that direct confrontation with those involved will not necessarily accomplish desired family changes. The social worker needs to help the client recognize that he or she can change even when the family/perpetrator does not. It is crucial that the client acknowledge this (Dinsmore, 1991). The need for continued support through this process is essential.

Most importantly at this stage, therapy cannot recapitulate the violation! Many survivors have been further victimized within therapeutic relationships (Waits, 1993). Clients need to discover their own truth and not perpetuate the fantasy of the "all-powerful other." The teaching of relaxation training techniques becomes essential at this stage in helping the survivor to deal with the strong emotions that are being evoked.

Stage 5: Exploring Possible Alternatives

Moving forward requires traveling through a mourning process (generally in sessions 8–10). Sadness and grief at the loss of a childhood need to be experienced. Grief expressions surrounding betrayal and lack of protection permit the victim to open to an entire spectrum of feelings that have been numbed. Acceptance, letting go, and making peace with the past begins.

It is vital that the survivor forgive him- or herself for not telling, for not making it stop, for responding sexually, and for being a small child. The final perception should be that the abuse was not his or her fault, that there was nothing he or she could have done to stop the abuse from happening, and that even when elements of enjoyment (love, affection, loyalty, and sexuality) were present, the relationship was not one that he or she chose! Consent was never given. If he or she has selected a mutually caring partner, the exploration of possible sexual difficulties and new ways to view these situations must be explored (Maltz, 1988). The survivor can then focus on the role of incest survivor as merely one piece of who he or she is (Faria and Belohlavek, 1984; Dinsmore, 1991).

Stage 6: Formulating an Action Plan

Here the social worker must be very active in helping the survivor to establish how the goals of the therapeutic intervention will be completed. Practice, modeling, and other techniques such as behavioral rehearsal, role play, writing down feelings, and an action plan become essential in addressing intervention planning. Often the survivor has come to the realization that he/she is not at fault or to blame. The doubt and shame of what his/her role was and what part he/she played becomes more clear, and self-fault less pronounced. The survivors begin to acknowledge that they did not have the power to help them-selves or to change things. Often however, these realizations are cou-pled with anger at the perpetrator and what has been done to them. The role of the social worker becomes essential here in helping the client to look at the long-range consequences of acting on their anger and in planning an appropriate course of action. Many times there is a strong desire to openly confront the abuser without regard for the long-term effects that may result from this action. The role of the social worker becomes crucial in helping the client to anticipate problems and solve this confrontation issue, whether it be helping the survivor through confronting the perpetrator in the safety of the therapeutic environment or actually addressing the family system. The main goal of these last few sessions (sessions 10–12) is to help the individual reintegrate the information learned and processed into a homeostatic balance that allows him/her to function adequately once again. Refer-rals for additional therapy should be considered and discussed at this time (i.e., additional individual therapy, group therapy, couples ther-apy, family therapy).

Stage 7: Follow-Up Measures

This area is very important for social work practice in general, but one that is almost always forgotten. In the successful therapeutic exchange, significant changes have been made for the survivor in regard to his/her previous level of functioning and coping. Measures to determine whether these results have remained consistent are essential. Often follow up can be as simple as a phone call to discuss how things are going. Follow up within one month of termination of the sessions is important.

Other measures of follow up are available but require more ad-vanced planning. A pretest/posttest design can be added to the design by simply using a standardized scale at the beginning of treatment and later at the end. Scales to measure depression, trauma, and so on are readily available. See Corcoran and Fischer (1987) for a thorough listing of measurement scales that can be used in the behavioral sci-ences.

Finally, it is important to realize that at follow up many survivors may now realize that they want additional therapeutic help. After they have adapted to the crisis and have learned to function and cope with their incestuous past, they find they want more. After all, returning the survivor to a previous state of equilibrium is the primary purpose for the application of this brief crisis intervention therapy. If this happens, the social worker should be prepared to help the client become aware of the options for continued therapy and emotional growth by giving the appropriate referrals. Referrals for group therapy with other incest victims, individual growth directed therapy, couples therapy to include a significant other, and/or family therapy should be considered.

Supplemental Forms of Treatment for the Crisis Intervention Model

Two additional forms of therapy that can be used to supplement Roberts' Seven-Stage Crisis Intervention Model (1991) when applied to adult survivors of incest are couples therapy and treating the family system.

Maltz (1988) argues that the best therapy or approach for treating adult survivors of incest is not individual therapy alone but rather a couples oriented approach. When incest victims mate with others the level of intimacy that is established between them can make the chosen partners victims of the incest as well, and treatment to help them should be considered (Chauncey, 1994). According to Masters and Johnson (Maltz, 1988), in a committed relationship there can be no uninvolved partner when any form of sexual distress is present. In this view of treatment the therapeutic view centers around the relationship with significant others and not on the incest victim alone (Bergart, 1986; Deighton and McPeek, 1985). Maltz (1988) is clear to point out the varied effects that incest can have on the sexual behavior an individual exhibits; some victims will withdraw from sex, while others may become hypersexual. Many times it is not until a victim establishes a committed relationship that the seriousness of this trauma is recognized (Maltz, 1988).

In order for a couple to achieve a mutually satisfying sex life the process of couples therapy can take months or even years (Maltz, 1988). Both partners must learn to erase the fears and negative feelings and attitudes that are so often associated with the sexual relationship. The four-stage model implemented in this study combines couples therapy, sex therapy, and incest resolution into one format. Here the social worker must not only be versed in each approach but capable of the flexibility required to go back and forth between the concepts of each therapeutic intervention. Individual therapy in conjunction with the couples therapy is considered compatible, and if offered, may contribute to the overall experience.

The second supplemental treatment involves the importance of including the whole family. McCarthy (1990) described a cognitive behavioral model of treatment for accomplishing this. One of the major purposes of this type of intervention was to help individual family members to see themselves as survivors rather than as victims of incest. Actual therapy sessions are considered structured and goal directed, and all members of the family are strongly recommended to attend. This time-limited treatment is expected to last anywhere from three to twelve months with a two-year follow up.

McCarthy (1990) conducted this therapy at three levels: individually, as a couple, and as a family. In the individual sessions the father, mother, and incest survivor are separated. Covert sensitization, an aversive imagery technique, was used to help rid the father of his feelings of sexual arousal for his daughter. Sessions with the mother were designed to help her build her own self-esteem and handle any mood disturbance such as depression. For the incest victim the prime therapeutic intervention was to have her write her own book about the experience. The book covered four areas: (1) a positive view of sexuality; (2) reviewing the incest experience; (3) seeing self as a survivor, not as a victim; and (4) future plans for her sexual self-esteem. At the end of treatment the child could keep the book as a reference. The couples therapy provided focused on building and strengthening the marital relationship and on learning new ways to be intimate. In the family sessions the focus was on creating open yet structured communication.

Need for Treatment

Incest is not a positive experience. The trauma of incest carries the potential for severe long-term effects. These may include: depression, suicidal ideation, anxiety, eating disorders, somatic complaints, sleep disorders, sexual dysfunction, negative attitudes about men and sex, promiscuity, substance abuse, and increased incidence of mental illness (Gelinas, 1983; Herman, 1992; Carnes, 1991; Briere, 1992).

Factors that affect the extent of trauma experienced as a result of sexual abuse include: the degree of the trauma, duration and frequency, multiple perpetrators, penetration and intercourse, the use of physical and/or coercive force, abuse by an adult more than five years older than the victim, concurrent physical abuse, victim's feeling of responsibility, victim's feelings of powerlessness, betrayal, and stigma.

Recent literature correlates dissociative reactions, psychological numbing, self-mutilation, and the development of multiple personality disorder with child sexual abuse (Courtois, 1988; Dinsmore, 1991; Dolan, 1991; Bryant, Kessler, and Shirar, 1992; Briere, 1992). Consequences of post-traumatic stress disorder such as flashbacks, panic attacks, anxiety, and sleeplessness have all been correlated with childhood sexual abuse (Wheeler and Walton, 1987; Briere, 1992; Herman, 1992; Everstine and Everstine, 1993). Approximately 40 percent of sexual abuse victims are so troubled by the incident(s) that they suffer aftereffects that require treatment (Courtois, 1988). In this chapter the need for short-term crisis treatment has been expressed, yet the reality remains that many adult survivors of incest do not seek any treatment at all.

Yet despite the implications and the designated need for this type of treatment, LeRoy Schultz, expert in child sexual abuse, stated, "At best incest could be viewed as a positive, healthy experience and at worst could be viewed as neutral and dull" (Russell, 1986:38–39). Organizations such as the Rene Guyon Society believe incest is mutually beneficial to the adult and child (Dinsmore, 1991). Until incest is recognized as being devastatingly harmful to those who survive such sexual abuse, society risks the preponderance of victims.

In summary, the presented statistics indicate that child sexual abuse and incest are unfortunately present in staggering proportions. In fact incest between an adult and related child is now recognized as the most prevalent form of child abuse (Courtois, 1988). Given the diversity and severity of its long-term effects, crisis intervention treatment for incest and childhood sexual abuse survivors becomes essential.

CONCLUSIONS

When dealing with the adult survivors of incest and applying Roberts' Seven-Stage Model of Crisis Intervention (1991), it is important to remember that victims cannot endure crises for long periods of time. Often when the survivor is able to come to terms with what has happened to him/her and is requesting help, he/she is at the peak of his/her crisis. It is at this peak that treatment gains are most likely and the crisis itself may motivate personal change.

In this model, the social worker must assume an extremely active role in helping the survivor to explore and resolve the crisis. The goals of treatment must be concrete and time-limited (ten to twelve sessions), and the focus of the goals must be clearly related to the crisis situation.

As the social worker, you must be active in instilling hope that this crisis situation can and will be addressed. These survivors need your support and encouragement; often they have been disbelieved for so long. Most have a pattern of seeing themselves as failing. Focusing on the strengths of the survivor becomes essential in building self-reliance. Many times the survivor will need continued help after the crisis therapy sessions to continue improving their self-image, and referrals for this must be made.

This devastating event, which generally occurs in such a formative stage of development and for such long periods of time, is extremely difficult for survivors to overcome. It is important to remember that there is no cure for what has happened, and there is no way to completely erase the pain and suffering that has occurred. In crisis intervention with the adult survivor of incest the goal is to help the person recognize, understand, and learn ways to cope with what has happened. These individuals are survivors; and the use of that term means they have lived through it. The goal now becomes to make the life of the survivor as satisfying as possible and to return to them the chance for a satisfying life—a chance at life they so deserve.

REFERENCES

Bergart, A.M. (1986, May). Isolation to intimacy: Incest survivors in group therapy. *Social Casework*, 266–275.

Blume, E.S. (1986, Sept.). The walking wounded: Post-incest syndrome. *Siecus Report*.

Briere, J.N. (1992). *Child abuse trauma: Theory and treatment of the lasting effects.* Newbury Park, CA: Sage.

Bryant, D., Kessler, J. and Shirar, L. (1992). *The Family Inside.* New York: Norton.

Burgess, A., Wolbert, A., Groth, N., Holmstrom, L.L., and Sgroi, S.M. (1978). *Sexual assault of children and adolescents.* Lexington, MA: Lexington Books.

Carnes, P. (1991). *Don't call it love: Recovery from sexual addiction*. New York: Bantam.

Chauncey, S. (1994, Nov.). Emotional concerns and treatment of male partners of female sexual abuse survivors. *Social Work, 3*, 669–676.

Corcoran, K., and Fischer, J. (1987). *Measures for clinical practice: A source book*. New York: Free Press.

Courtois, C.A., (1988). *Healing the incest wound*. New York: Norton.

Deighton, J., and McPeek, P. (1985 Sept.). *Group treatment: Adult victims of child sexual abuse*. *Social Casework*, 403–410.

Dinsmore, C. (1991). *From surviving to thriving: Incest feminism and recovery*. Albany: State University of New York Press.

Dolan, Y. M. (1991). *Resolving sexual abuse*. New York: Norton.

Everstine, D. S., and Everstine, L. (1989). *Sexual trauma in children and adolescents*. New York: Brunner/Mazel.

————— and Evertsine, L. (1993). *The trauma response*. New York: Norton.

Faria, G., and Belohlavek, N. (1984). *Treating female adult survivors of childhood incest*. *Social Casework*, 465–472.

Finkelhor, D. (1979). *Sexually victimized children*. New York: Macmillan.

—————. (1984). *Child sexual abuse: New theory and research*. New York: Free Press.

Finkelhor, D., and Brown, A. (1985). *The traumatic impact of child sexual abuse*. *American Journal of Orthopsychiatry, 55* (4), 530–541.

Friedrich, W. N. (1990). *Psychotherapy of sexually abused children and their families*. New York: Norton.

Gelinas, D. J., (1983). The persisting negative effects of incest. *Psychiatry, 46*, 312–332.

Herman, J., Russell, D., and Trocki, K. (1986). Long-term effects of incestuous abuse in childhood. *American Journal of Psychiatry, 143* (10), 1293–1296.

Herman, J.L. (1992). *Trauma and Recovery*. New York: Basic Books.

James, K., and MacKinnon, L. (1990, Jan.). The ''incestuous family'' revisited: A critical analysis of family therapy myths. *Journal of Marital and Family Therapy*, 71–88.

Justice, B., and Justice, R. (1979). *The broken taboo: Sex in the family*. New York: Human Sciences Press.

Maltz, W. (1988, Summer). Identifying and treating the sexual repercussions of incest: A couples therapy approach. *Journal of Sex and Marital Therapy, 14*, 2, 142–168.

McCarthy, B. (1990). Treatment of incest families: A cognitive-behavioral model. *Journal of Sex Education and Therapy, 16*, 2, 101–114.

McNew, J.A., and Abell, N. (1995). Post-traumatic stress symptomology: Similarities and differences between Vietnam veterans and adult survivors of childhood sexual abuse. *Social Work, 40* (1), 115–126.

Meiselman, K. C. (1990). *Resolving the trauma of incest*. San Francisco, CA: Jossey-Bass.

Patten, S.B., Gatz, Y., Jones, B., and Thomas, D.L. (1989, May). Post-traumatic stress disorder and the treatment of sexual abuse. *Social Work*, 197–201.

Rhea, G. (1992). *Promise not to tell*. Video. Santa Monica, CA: Direct Cinema Ltd.

Roberts, A.R. (1991). *Contemporary perspectives on crisis intervention and prevention*. Englewood Cliffs, NJ: Prentice-Hall.

Russell, D.E.. (1986). *The secret trauma: Incest in the lives of girls and women*. New York: Basic Books.

Sgroi, S.M. (1982). *Handbook of clinical intervention in child sexual abuse*. Lexington, MA: Lexington Books.

Shapiro, S. (1987). Self-mutilation and self blame in incest victims. *American Journal of Psychotherapy, 41* (1), 46–54.

Silver, R.L., Boon, C., and Stones, M.H. (1983). Searching for meaning in misfortune: Making sense of incest. *Journal of Social Issues, 39* (2), 81–102.

U.S. Department of Health and Human Services. (1993). Interview with the National Resource Center on Child Sexual Abuse, which is a subsidiary of the National Center on Child Abuse and Neglect, Representative Sandra Connaway. Statistics reported for 1990–1993.

Waits, E.A. (1993). *Trauma and survival*. New York: Norton.

Wheeler, B., and Walton, E. (1987, Dec.). Personality disturbances of adult incest victims. *Social Casework*, 597–602.

SECTION III

Acute Situational Crisis, Crisis Management, and Brief Treatment Applications

CHAPTER 6

Coping with the Crisis of a Parentally Abducted Child: A Crisis Intervention and Brief Treatment Perspective

GEOFFREY L. GREIF

When Vera's four-year-old son, Dick, was abducted by her ex-husband, Todd, she was shocked, though not surprised. Todd had abducted him a year before for a week but had been easily located. For Vera, a thirty-year-old white woman who was working toward an advanced degree in architecture, as well as for her live-in boyfriend, Dave, a thirty-two-year-old white community planner, the crisis began after a few days when it became clear that Dick was not going to be immediately returned. The couple reacted differently. Vera, perhaps repeating a pattern of being taken advantage of during the marriage, and in the initial phases of the marital separation, refused to get angry at her ex-husband. She described herself as naive when it came to understanding Todd (he was thirty-two, born in South America, and had been employed as a clerk prior to the abduction) and as easily manipulated. Dave, on the other hand, had a great deal of anger. He had entered this relationship with Vera knowing full well the potential for Todd's obstructing their relationship and the danger he posed to Dick. In addition, he had become quite attached to Dick during the time the three of them lived together. Vera and Dave had custody the bulk of the time with Todd visiting every other weekend.

As a result of these differences in reaction (which are common), the threat to the couple was of a double loss. Not only might Vera and Dave lose the supportive relationship they were developing, they were already suffering in the extreme from the absence of and worry about Dick. Vera in particular worried about what Dick was experiencing and how he would respond to her upon recovery. When I interviewed Vera and Dave six months after the abduction, they wanted to know how a four-year-old might adapt to being in hiding, whether he would retain his resilience, and whether he would even remember them. The unspoken question also was how they could arrange their lives to incorporate the drain of searching. While these could be answered in the broadest sense, that is, children are likely to have difficulty upon recovery if they are gone for longer periods of time, are not living with the parent they have the strongest bond with, and are traumatized physically and emotionally while missing (Greif and Hegar, 1993), the questions could not be answered specifically. It was not known what Dick was experiencing or how long he would be away from Vera and Dave. How could I help them?

Ava's situation was different. She dealt with the pain of abduction and the struggles of recovery after her young children were missing for four years. The children were taken by their father after a series of snatches, first by her and then by him. When the last and longest abduction occurred, Ava, a thirty-five-year-old white woman who had worked as a store manager before becoming a housewife in her second marriage, went into a deep depression and began abusing alcohol. As she put it, "I just couldn't stand the pain of not having my babies, and I had to drink to take it away. Finally, I realized I was not doing myself or anyone any good" (Greif and Hegar, 1993, p. 116). The tears did continue, even through a second marriage and a new baby. But turning to God helped her enormously to put things into perspective as the months that they were missing turned to years.

When the children were finally located, it was learned they had been living in foster care after their father, an occasional construction worker, had been incarcerated. Neither of the children (both of whom had been under five when they were snatched) remembered Ava at first. One of the children had been sexually abused by a baby-sitter, exposed to a great deal of pornography, and propelled through the windshield of a car his father was driving after it crashed during a high-speed chase. Whereas the other child had a relatively easy adjustment to being back with Ava, this child exhibited extreme behavior problems. He rocked incessantly, banged his head against the wall, and was verbally and physically abusive. Crisis management was needed immediately for the whole family—the two recovered children, Ava, her new husband, and their child. Currently they are in hiding with the court's permission and quite fearful that when the father is released from prison he will harm them.

The problems that surface for all parties when parents kidnap their children are enormous. As represented in the two case examples, parental kidnapping affects the children, the searching parents, as well as their significant others and any new children who have entered the family. Even though their voices are not heard in the above example, the abductors could also be included as in need of crisis treatment before or after the abduction. In broadening our consideration of crisis, we could include the motivating factors that compel someone to kidnap—family breakdown, miscommunication, hurt feelings, bungled court interventions or the perception that the courts are not fair, and/or selfish attempts to hurt the other parent and the children. Further, we could add relatives, friends, neighbors, and even personnel at missing children's organizations who become involved in the search for the children.

THE PROBLEM OF
PARENTALLY ABDUCTED CHILDREN

Whereas there is some disagreement about the number of children parentally abducted in any one year, the most recent and comprehensive survey of the problem places the number at approximately 350,000 (Finkelhor, Hotaling, and Sedlak, 1990). (Finkelhor et al.'s research also found that approximately 3,500 children were abducted by strangers during the same time period studied.) The figure of 350,000 encompasses two definitions of abduction. In the broadest sense it includes children who were not returned within twenty-four hours following court-arranged visitation, where there may have been no attempt to hide the child. In these cases where a parent did not honor a custody arrangement, the other parent may call the police or a lawyer and the visiting parent may then adhere to the arrangement. In a more narrow sense, the definition also includes the more commonly thought of occurrence where a parent takes the child with the express purpose of concealing the child's whereabouts. In some of these cases the abductor may leave the state or even the country. The vast majority of abductions are resolved within a week, according to Finkelhor et al. (1990).

It is important to note that what could be considered an abduction is not just the taking of a child by a visiting or noncustodial parent. Frequently, a parent may leave a marriage and take a child at the same time, before any custody has been legally established by a court in a custody proceeding. In addition, a child may be taken by a custodial parent and denied contact with the visiting parent. Thus abduction can refer in the broadest sense to either parent's denial of contact between the child and the other parent.

The United States is not the only country that struggles with the issue of parental abduction, as evidenced by the Hague Convention. The Hague Convention on the Civil Aspects of International Child Abduction is specifically designed to deal with parents crossing international borders for the purposes of abduction. First drafted in 1980 (Dyer, 1991) and signed by 1992 by over twenty-four nations, it calls for the return of an abducted child fifteen years old or younger to the original country. Other countries, like Canada and Great Britain, confront the problem on a much smaller scale than in the United States, with various reports placing the number of abductions in those countries at well under 1,000 in any given year (Greif and Hegar, 1993).

With the rise in divorce over the last twenty years, increasing numbers of parents are likely to be unhappy with custody arrangements. One by-product of this unhappiness is that more people are likely to take custody matters into their own hands. A related by-product of the "divorce revolution" is the increase in noncustodial mothers. Many of these women feel stigmatized by society if they do not have custody (Greif and Pabst, 1988). Whereas it is fathers who traditionally have been more likely to abduct, women are swelling the numbers of parents who are discontented with a custody decision and are willing to take action to right what they perceive to be an injustice. Even though there are no published figures, it is generally agreed that abduction is on the rise (Terr, 1983).

According to the research, parental abductions tend to occur among white, middle- to lower-class families, with younger children the most common target. Custody may not always be determined at the time of the abduction, and some abductions last as long as many years. In Agopian's study of ninety-one California families known to the Los Angeles court system in the 1970s, male abductors were more frequent then female abductors. Children in the three- to five-year-old age group and those who were only children were taken most often (Agopian, 1980, 1981).

108

More recent research tends to confirm the same general patterns. Janvier, McCormick, and Donaldson's (1990) survey of sixty-five parents who contacted a missing children's organization found that perpetrators of domestic abduction were more apt to be female, while international abductors were more apt to be male. The majority of the children hidden in both domestic and international locations were under the age of eight, with females being more apt to be taken domestically and males internationally. The bulk of both domestic and international abductions took place after a separation or divorce, yet custody arrangements tended not to be in effect in almost one quarter of the cases.

Sagatun and Barrett (1990) studied forty-three cases of parental abduction that came before a family court services agency in California. Twenty-five of these involved female abductors, and in half of the total sample a custody order was not in place at the time of the snatching. The length of time of the abductions ranged from a few hours to thirteen years.

Finkelhor, Hotaling, and Sedlak (1991), as part of a larger national telephone survey on missing children, located 104 households where 142 children were reported to have been abducted. The majority of these children were under seven at the time of their abduction, with the gender of the child an insignificant factor. Eighty percent of the sample was white, and the perpetrators were usually in their 30s. Three-quarters of the abductors were male and two-thirds of the responding households had a family income under $30,000 in 1988.

Greif and Hegar (1993; cf. Greif and Hegar, 1991, and Hegar and Greif, 1991) located 371 searching parents through a 1989 survey of missing children's organizations in the United States and Canada. Children ages two and four were the most frequent targets in their predominantly white sample, with three-quarters of the children being under the age of six. Two-thirds of the respondents gave their family income as under $27,500 approximately three years after the abduction occurred. Male abductors slightly outnumbered female abductors and boys were more apt to be taken than girls. The searching parent had custody in half of the cases, with the children living with the abductor in a joint custody arrangement or within a marriage in 29 percent of the cases. The abductor had custody in most of the remaining situations. The length of time the typical abduction in this survey lasted prior to recovery was eighteen months, with nonrecovered children missing an average of four years.

THE IMPACT OF THE ABDUCTION ON THE FAMILY

Survey-based data (Finkelhor, et al., 1991; Greif and Hegar, 1992, 1993; Hatcher, Behrman-Lippert, et al., 1992; Janvier, et al., 1990) as well as anecdotal and clinical reports (Agopian, 1984; Forehand, Long, Zogg, and Parrish, 1989; Schetky and Haller, 1983; Senior, Gladstone, and Nurcombe, 1982; Sagatun and Barrett, 1990; Terr, 1983) paint a sometimes conflicting picture of the impact of the abduction on the family members involved. While acknowledging that trauma also exists for the abductor who may feel compelled to snatch a child, the review here will focus on the child and searching parent during and after recovery.

Abductions occur at two different time periods, at the breaking point in the marriage and months or years after the marriage has ended. In either situation, the child may be caught up in an emotional vortex swirling around the parents as a breakup nears or as post-marital conflict runs high. The parents may be initiating new battles or continuing old ones. Thus a crisis stage may have been reached, with the abduction occurring as the crowning blow. The abduction does not always occur in this type of atmosphere. At times, there is a calm before the storm, with the searching parent caught completely off guard. While most abductions occur during visitation with the abductor, (Greif and Hegar, 1993) and are not dramatic by nature, there are instances where it can be upsetting when children are taken following a physical fight (Greif and Hegar, 1993) or at gunpoint (Senior et al., 1982).

Some of the experiences of children while on the run include being physically, sexually, and emotionally abused or neglected (Finkelhor et al., 1991; Greif and Hegar, 1993; Janvier et al., 1990; Sagatun and Barrett 1990). Research differs as to the incidence of abuse with figures ranging from 8 percent for physical and/or sexual abuse and 16 percent for serious emotional abuse (Finkelhor et al., 1991) to 35 percent for physical and/or sexual abuse (Greif and Hegar, 1993) and two-thirds for "general abuse" (Janvier et al., 1990).

Other traumatic events experienced by children on the run include being trained to be secretive by having a name changed or avoiding authorities (Agopian, 1980; Greif and Hegar, 1993; Sagatun and Barrett, 1990), questioning the abductor about the whereabouts of the other parent and being given false information (Greif and Hegar, 1993; Sagatun and Barrett, 1990), being placed in a foster home (Greif and Hegar, 1993; Sagatun and Barrett, 1990), and taking an either

110

overly protective role of the abductor who may appear emotionally needy (Greif and Hegar, 1993) or severely over-identifying with the abductor (Sagatun and Barrett, 1990). In addition, the child may perceive he or she was abandoned by the searching parent (Hatcher, Behrman-Lippert, et al., 1992).

After an abduction, the searching parent may experience any or all of the following: ''rage, sense of loss, anxiety, depression, guilt, lack of sleep, health problems'' (Greif and Hegar, 1993, 198). Sometimes parents are angry at themselves for not having anticipated the event and preventing it or for becoming involved with the abductor in the first place. For some, a feeling similar to post-traumatic stress has been noted where there may be hyperalertness or a numbing reaction (Greif and Hegar, 1993). These reactions may be stronger or weaker based on whether the searching parent anticipated the event and the sense of blame he or she assumes.

The potential reaction of the significant other if the marriage has already ended also needs consideration. Some join the searching parent in his or her feelings of rage or loss if a strong bond has been formed with the missing child. Others may feel angrier than the searching parent as the searching parent may be still attached in some way to the abductor and not allow him or herself to experience rage. If both react similarly a bond may be formed that will help the couple to cope. On the other hand, when the couple reacts in different ways or assigns different meanings to the abduction, severe stress can be placed on the couple, which impedes their ability to cope with the crisis.

After the Recovery

Upon recovery (it should be noted that location does not always result in reunification), the child confronts a variety of new issues, including concerns about safety and reabduction (Greif and Hegar, 1993; Hatcher, Behrman-Lippert, et al., 1992), guilt and shame (Hatcher, Behrman-Lippert, et al., 1992), confusion following a name change (Hatcher, Behrman-Lippert et al., 1992), and loyalty conflicts (Greif and Hegar, 1993; Hatcher, Behrman-Lippert, et al., 1992). In addition, the child may experience specific problems like problematic dreams (Hatcher, Behrman-Lippert, et al., 1992), bedwetting, thumbsucking, regression, anxiety, depression, and withdrawal (Senior et al., 1982; Schetky and Haller, 1983), and extreme fright (Terr, 1983). The following factors have generally been found to be related to the adjustment of the child after recovery: the child's experiences while on the run; the amount of acrimony between the parents after recovery; the length of time of the abduction and the amount of time that has expired since the recovery; the relationship with both parents; and the experiences of the child during the abduction (Greif and Hegar, 1992). Whereas most researchers found that the abduction had a generally negative effect on the child, one exception is Forehand et al. (1989), who concluded that there were no generally pathological impairments among seventeen abducted children over time.

The recovering parents are faced with trying to pick up the pieces; the longer the child has been gone, the more difficult the transition (Greif and Hegar, 1993). As was true for Ava whose case begins the chapter, there is even the problem of some children not remembering the searching parent. Common issues that may arise and that will vary by the length of the time gone, the age of the child, and the idiosyncratic experiences of the child, include: the parent being angry at the child for not contacting them; dealing with the myth of the perfect or the damaged child; and attempting to incorporate the child into a new family structure (Greif and Hegar, 1993; Hatcher, Behrman-Lippert, et al., 1992).

With the first situation, parents whose children were old enough to know how to dial either locally or long distance are often very hurt that the child did not try to contact them following the kidnapping. If the children are young when kidnapped and are gone for years, the same question arises—why didn't they try to contact me? This can result in residual hurt feelings spilling over into the reunification. In terms of the myth of the perfect child or the damaged child, parents often forget over time what living with a normal child can be like. They not only have missed important developmental stages but also tend to focus on only the positive aspects of their children. The parent has to catch up with where the child is presently without having had prior experience. When the child returns and acts normally (for a formerly missing child), the bubble that the parent has constructed about what the child's behavior should be is burst.

On the other end of the spectrum, there are parents who anticipate the worst behavior from their children and are unprepared for the resilience of which children are capable (Compas, 1987). They wonder, "If the experience has been so terrible for my child, why is he/she not showing more signs of it?" Thus, in some cases, regardless of how the child is coping, the parent may have a difficult time adjusting.

Finally, if the child has been missing for a lengthy time, there is the possibility of remarriage, a step-parent, and even step- or half siblings with whom to get acquainted. The recovered child has to be integrated into a new family with all of its attendant adjustment problems. The parent may be pulled between meeting the needs of the new family members and the needs of the child. As the parent attempts to meet the needs of the recovered child, the others may feel resentment.

Clearly, during the time of abduction in particular, these parents are prone to a wealth of associated problems, as outlined above. These affect crisis intervention and have been noted to include (among a sample of 371 searching parents): feelings of loss (85 percent), rage (77 percent), loss of sleep/nightmares (75 percent), loss of appetite (52 percent), severe depression (49 percent), guilt (49 percent), and health problems (25 percent). Among the same sample, 25 percent were treated for depression, 18 percent for anxiety, and 4 percent for spouse abuse (Greif and Hegar, 1991).

CRISIS THEORY FRAMEWORK

Drawing on the work of Roberts (1990, 1991), how would we look at crisis intervention theory with a family that has experienced an abduction? The first stage is to make psychological contact and establish rapport. In cases of parental abduction, the searching parent is often contacting a cadre of people for assistance. These may include police, the FBI, a lawyer, a private detective, and, later, a mental health practitioner. The role of most of those contacted is to assist in locating the missing child and to "just get the facts." When the mental health practitioner is called it is usually because of an emotional crisis in relation to the abduction. Thus, time can be spent on building trust and communication. The role of mental health professional and legal professional are clearly separate.

With both Vera and Dave (the couple described at the beginning of this chapter), establishing rapport was easy as they were voluntarily seeking help. They had made the necessary contacts with services that could assist with recovery. Now they were seeking help for their own emotional well-being and for related couples' issues. Ava (whom this author did not see in treatment but whom this author interviewed extensively over a four-year period) would present a slightly different clinical picture. Her desire would have been, initially, for treatment of depression related to the loss of her children, her continued pattern of victimization, and some episodic alcohol abuse. If she did not enter treatment until after her children were located, the focus would be on reunification issues with the whole family, with a particular focus on behavior management on her acting out son.

Stage One

This initial stage is particularly crucial when working with families buffeted by parental abduction. Many of these families feel ignored by the "system." With law enforcement frequently overwhelmed, the police and FBI are often absorbed with pursuing murderers, rapists, and other violent criminals. Whereas finding their missing child is vitally crucial to the searching parents, they quickly learn that, within the law enforcement realm, the abduction of a child by another parent is not considered a serious crime (Greif and Hegar, 1993). Ignorance of the issues related to parental abduction on the part of the mental health practitioner may be perceived by the family as further neglect. Telling the parent and family members that their situation is important and that their concerns will be addressed is one specific way of combatting this.

Stage Two

The second stage in the Roberts model is to examine the dimensions of the problem and assess lethality. This would include learning how dangerous the searching parent might be to him- or herself or to others. The potential for suicidal behavior is usually low, though; substance abuse as a way of medicating for pain needs to be explored. In these high conflict situations where there is always a specific person to blame, assessing danger to others (the abducting parent) is key. Parental abduction often occurs after months or years of marital conflict, perceived and actual victimization, and abuse. As men tend to be more violent than women in these relationships (Hegar and Greif, 1991), as well as in the method used to abduct (Sagatun and Barrett, 1990), the male searching parent may be especially at risk for harming the abductor once she is located. It is not uncommon for there to be a number of snatchings back and forth and for threats of violence or actual violence to occur. In fact, some women flee with their children to avoid a violent husband (Greif and Hegar, 1993).

114

Working with the searching parent, then, must include an initial focus on the potential reaction of that parent when the missing parent and child are located. Being told of plans to "kill that bitch or bastard when I find her/him" is not uncommon. Sometimes those feelings may be expressed by significant others in the searching parent's lives.

In Vera and Dave's situation, it was Dave who was expressing the most anger at the abductor. Vera tended to repress her anger, perhaps in a continuation of a pattern established during the marriage. Was Dave potentially violent? My assessment was that he was not, but that conclusion had to be established after spending a few hours with him and after asking him directly about it. Ava's marital relationship included multiple snatchings as well as violent behavior on the part of her ex-husband. If *he* had been seen in treatment at some point during the time that Ava had the children (he is not a likely prospect for voluntary treatment, though he could have been court-referred), this issue could have been explored with him. Ava's second husband could also be asked about his intentions, as her ex-husband will pose a threat to the family when he is released from prison. He has threatened to harm Ava on numerous occasions.

Stage Three

Once rapport has been established and lethality ascertained, the mental health practitioner encourages an exploration of feelings and emotions. In this third stage, the chance to vent is optimized. Assessment needs to be made with an eye toward post-traumatic stress disorder, a reaction that is similar to what some parents appear to experience after the abduction. Severely stressful events sometimes produce reactions ranging from numbness, sleep difficulties, and physical symptoms, to feelings of shame and guilt (e.g., see Stone, 1992). Within this context, the searching parent should be guided into a number of areas of discussion by the practitioner.

The discussion can be framed with some of the following statements (depending upon their applicability to the specific situation): "Having a child taken can be a very unsetting event. It is common for parents to feel a range of emotions, including anger, guilt, betrayal, numbness, and perhaps even relief. Some parents react by losing sleep, feeling depressed and anxious, and having thoughts of revenge that they were not aware they were capable of. A lot of parents blame themselves for either not seeing the warning signs or for getting involved with someone in the first place who would abduct. Others see the kidnapping as a replay of other issues in the relationship and this can be upsetting." Then, later on, the practitioner can say: "A major question for many parents in the situation is how much time to spend searching. Do you search all of the time? Do you allow yourself to have any pleasurable time when you are not thinking about finding your child?"

Making these types of statements can let the parent know that a range of feelings in reaction to a kidnapping is normal and that the practitioner is willing to listen to a discussion of them. These statements also put their finger on the key issue of future work—how to arrange your life both to include the child and also have something left when the child remains missing.

Questions specific to the abduction and the searching parent's reactions can include: "Do you blame yourself for the abduction? Do you think you could/should have prevented it? How has this affected other relationships with family members and friends? How is it affecting your work? What has been your relationship with the legal authorities helping you in the search? Do you feel that people have been helpful in the search process?"

Another series of questions should center on the child's well-being. Even though the child is with a parent, searching parents often fear that neglect or abuse may be taking place. The parent can be asked: "How do you think your child is doing? How close was he to you and to the abducting parent? How has the child coped with separations from you in the past? Searching parents who believe their child was taken to get back at them would tend to have more fears about the child's well-being than parents who see the abductor as very invested in the child.

In working with Vera and Dave, discussion of how they were each coping with the abduction and how their styles differed was important not only in building rapport but in opening up the area of accepting each other. I began this part of the inquiry by asking them if they allowed themselves, six months after the abduction, to have any fun. Could they go to the movies for a few hours and not think about Dick? Could they have a romantic dinner? Was it okay with Vera if Dave was more angry at Todd than she was? Was Vera's lack of anger acceptable to Dave?

These questions and supportive statements opened up a new level of discussion for them. Dave talked about having trepidation about coming home after a hard day at work because he was unsure how Vera was going to be reacting. He joked that they saw a lot of double feature movies as a means of escape. Vera kept repeating that she believed *she* was going to recover Dick, as Dave interjected, "*We* are going to recover Dick." Each was supported in their varying approaches to dealing with the crisis and asked to accept the other's.

With Ava's situation, the focus would center to a greater degree on her feelings about continued victimization. Does she see the abduction as another attempt to victimize her? Is it making her feel helpless? How are her reactions and her (second) husband's reactions the same and how are they different?

Stage Four

Exploration of these types of issues leads easily into the next stage of the crisis theory—exploring and assessing past coping attempts, both adaptive and maladaptive. This is beneficial in terms of both assessment and tapping into potential reservoirs of strength that the searching parent may have utilized in the past. The questions here can be guided in two directions: how have you coped in general with crises in the past, and how have you coped with similar actions from the abducting parent?

Questions about general crises can center on past issues of loss, feeling out of control, feeling unsupported by the "system" that is supposed to help with locating the missing child, and feeling betrayed by a loved one. Exploration about prior interactions with the abducting parent can often reveal emblematic information about how the searching parent will cope as well as the types of attempts the parent may make to locate the missing child. For example, if a parent was accustomed to being controlled or victimized by the abducting parent, the chances of that parent suddenly feeling empowered enough to reverse that continued pattern are slim. In Ava's situation, she had recovered her children once before prior to the final and longest snatching. Thus, she maintained a high level of hope that she would find them again as she had in the past.

Vera and Dave perceived Dick's abductor as being very controlling and, in Dave's words, "diabolical." Their previous attempts at dealing with him had not been totally successful, so they were less optimistic about the outcome of their current attempts to find him.

This is often the case with a parental abduction where, as mentioned earlier, previous patterns in the couple's interaction come into play and may hamstring present attempts at coping. Consider the scenario where one spouse has finally decided to maritally separate from the other spouse after many years of wrangling over a wealth of issues. If the first spouse felt mired in the relationship and has finally freed him- or herself only to have their child taken, the first spouse may feel dragged back into a situation and continually harassed. He or she may not have the strength to continue to battle.

Stage Five and Stage Six

Alternative methods need to be offered to these family members. In this fifth stage of Roberts' (1990, 1991) model, the mental health practitioner focuses on new ways of coping and also helps predict potential impediments to success. This is closely connected to the sixth stage, which includes restoring cognitive functioning while developing a short-term action plan. The first step with searching parents is to normalize the experience for them. I tell them that they are experiencing a normal reaction to an abnormal situation. Having previously laid out a normal range of reactions, I have spoken to some parents' fears that they are going crazy. For searching parents, the goal is to mobilize them to the point they feel is appropriate to search for their children, to help them cope with the continued demands of a search, and to ask them to consider how to find pleasure in their lives while they search.

Standard ways of helping searching parents to cope cover the range from emphasizing the importance of exercise and connecting with support systems, like missing children organizations, to talking specifically about how much time they should devote to searching. One parent said he spent hundreds of hours searching the first weeks when his daughter was missing. He would contact every police officer, missing children's organization, and women's shelter he though might be of assistance. As the weeks wore on to months, though, he had to scale back, as every other aspect of his life was being affected and he was in jeopardy of being fired from his job. He promised himself instead that he would spend one hour a day either in searching for his own child or in helping other parents search for theirs (Greif and Hegar, 1993).

Another issue that should be explored with searching parents is to prepare them for the ups and downs (impediments) of the search. Parents often get phantom leads as to their children's whereabouts,

118

or they arrive at a location only hours after the abductor and their child have left and the trail becomes cold again. Predicting for a searching parent that there will be such disappointments is one way of helping them cope when those disappointments occur.

For Vera and Dave, a specific action plan that was put into place and that was related to the stress of the search centered on their concern for Dick's well-being. They were asked the following: ''What fantasy can the two of you construct together as to Dick's well-being that will allow you both to continue to search and to find pleasure in your life while you search? The purpose of this intervention was two-fold—it enabled them to work together; and it put them in control in a situation in which they had no control.

Vera and Dave could also be asked to negotiate how many hours a week to spend searching, who should be primarily responsible for the search (usually the biological parent), and what steps to take to continue to prepare for Dick's return. They, in fact, were already keeping a videotape of their searching attempts and of other events in their life that they planned to show Dick upon his recovery. In that way they were going on with their lives while keeping him abreast of any changes. Finally, they could be asked to anticipate short-term ups and downs in their relationship as normal. When those occurred they could remember that the nature of their situation was such that differences should be addressed but within a context that permitted different styles. Essentially, they should recognize at times of crisis that they are locked in to the circumstances around the abduction but do not have to agree on how to deal with it. With this cognitive reconstruction, they would each be given permission to cope individually and as part of a couple.

Work with Ava after the recovery could focus on reunifying the family and getting assertiveness training as a parent. She could be given specific suggestions about boundary making within the family. When her recovered son was acting out in the extreme, she needed to assert control as a way of providing the structure that he had lacked for so many years. The crisis of his behavior, while ameliorated somewhat by the joy of having him back home, posed a threat to her new husband and child. She needed to be helped to also deal with her son's request to return to his father where life was a lot more exciting due to the illicit lifestyle they were maintaining. She tried first to clarify that her ex-husband was not a bad person but that he just did bad things from time to time. That gave the son, who identified with his father, permission to act out while not fearing the loss of Ava's love. There was a place for him to be accepted. With the father in jail, Ava had time to establish a rapport with her son that could be used to deal with any future eventualities if there were continued requests by her son to return to his father. In addition, Ava needed support in not putting herself in a one-down position with her children and her second husband. The more competent she became in various aspects of her life, the more she would be able to cope with the continuing threat of harm to her family from her ex-husband. Over time (four years after recovery), the threat continued, but the bond between mother and son strengthened. Her ability to cope with the telephoned threats also improved.

Ava's son's reaction, while somewhat extreme for abducted children, is not unusual. As noted, the majority of children are seen for counseling at some point after an abduction. Crisis intervention services must also be available to meet the individual needs of children, particularly those who have been physically or sexually abused.

Stage Seven

In the seventh stage of crisis intervention, the mental health practitioner either follows up with the client or refers elsewhere. With searching parents, both are advisable. It must be recognized that out of the array of assistance sought by the searching family members, mental health services are usually of secondary concern, with recovery of the child primary. Some follow up may occur naturally as the practitioner comes across potential new resources for the family to tap into for the search. New support groups may be developed in the area and new methods of advertising for missing children may come up, all of which can be conveyed to the searching parent. The practitioner both in the role of providing follow-up and as part of the referral process can hook up those resources with the searching parent. This would be construed as extremely helpful as it would be helping not only with the search but with the provision of emotional support as well.

Finally, another way to think about the referral process is to get searching or recovering parents involved in public speaking engagements or press interviews. Parents often want to help others in similar situations and believe that by doing so they may in turn be helped in the future. Recovering parents often feel they can pay back a debt or help prevent future abductions by speaking out about their own experiences. For some parents, this can assist in their coping with the abduction crisis.

CONCLUSION

Mental health practitioners may be called in to assist with a crisis at a number of different stages following a parental abduction, from the time of the actual snatching to the period of adjustment following reunification. Unlike many other crises that people sustain, interventions with these families (while the child is missing) must be undertaken in a context that is cognizant of the parent's need to continue an active search. Thus the foci of crisis interventions are often on both preserving mental health and the actual stages of a search process, from the development of posters to the on-going telephone contact with FBI and police. Sound and consistent intervention will help the parent not only to cope with an abduction but to be better prepared for the child's return. Ultimately such interventions will help everyone.

REFERENCES

Agopian, M. (1980). Parental child stealing: Participants and the victimization process. *Victimology: An International Journal, 5,* 263–273.

———— (1981). *Parental child-stealing.* Lexington, MA: Lexington Books.

———— (1984). The impact on children of abduction by parents. *Child Welfare, 63,* 511–519.

Compas, B.E. (1987). Coping with stress during childhood and adolescence. *Psychological Bulletin, 101,* 393–403.

Dyer, A. (1991). Children's rights in private international law. *Australian Journal of Family Law, 5* (1), 103–109.

Finkelhor, D., Hotaling, G., and Sedlak, A. (1990). *Missing, abducted, runaway and throwaway children in America. First Report: Numbers and characteristics.* Washington, DC: U.S. Department of Justice.

————, Hotaling, G., and Sedlak, A. (1991). Children abducted by family members: A national household survey of incidence and episode characteristics. *Journal of Marriage and the Family, 53* , 805–817.

Forehand, R., Long, N., Zogg, C., and Parrish, E. (1989). Child abduction: Parent and child functioning following return. *Clinical Pediatrics, 28,* 311–316.

Greif, G. L. and Hegar, R.L. (1991). Parents whose children are abducted by the other parent: Implications for treatment. *American Journal of Family Therapy, 19,* 215–225.

————, and Hegar, R.L. (1992). Impact on children of abduction by a parent: A review of the literature. *American Journal of Orthopsychiatry, 62* (4), 599–604.

————, and Hegar, R.L. (1993). *When parents kidnap: The families behind the headlines*. New York: Free Press.

————, and Pabst, M. (1988). *Mothers without custody*. New York: Lexington/Macmillan.

Hatcher, C., Barton, C., and Brooks, L. (1992). *Families of missing children: Psychological consequences*. Washington, DC: Office of Juvenile Justice and Delinquency Prevention, U.S. Department of Justice.

Hatcher, C., Behrman-Lippert, J., Barton, C., and Brooks, L. (1992). *Reunification of missing children manual*. Washington, DC: Office of Juvenile Justice and Delinquency Prevention, U.S. Department of Justice.

Hegar, R.L., and Greif, G.L. (1991). Parental kidnapping: A survey of the problem. *Social Work, 36,* 421–426.

Janvier, R.F., McCormick, K., and Donaldson, R. (1990). Parental kidnapping: A survey of left-behind parents. *Juvenile and Family Court Journal, 41,* 1–8.

Roberts, A.R. (1990). *Crisis intervention handbook: Assessment, treatment and research* (pp. 3–16). Belmont, CA: Wadsworth.

Roberts, A.R. (1991). Introduction and overview. In A.R. Roberts (Ed.), *Contemporary perspectives on crisis intervention and prevention* (pp. 1–17). Englewood Cliffs, NJ: Prentice-Hall.

Sagatun, I.J., and Barrett, L. (1990). Parental child abduction: The law, family dynamics, and legal system responses. *Journal of Criminal Justice, 18,* 433–442.

Schetky, D.H., and Haller, L.H. (1983). Parental kidnapping. *Journal of the American Academy of Child Psychiatry, 22,* 279–285.

Senior, N., Gladstone, T., and Nurcombe, B. (1982). Child snatching: A case report. *Journal of the American Academy of Psychiatry, 21,* 579–583.

Stone, A. M. (1992). The toll of shame in post-traumatic stress disorder. *American Journal of Orthopsychiatry, 62,* 131–136.

Terr, L.C. (1983). Child snatching: A new epidemic of an ancient malady. *Journal of Pediatrics, 103,* 151–156.

CHAPTER 7

Crisis Assessment and Intervention: Abused Women in the Shelter Setting

SOPHIA F. DZIEGIELEWSKI and
CHERYL RESNICK

Susan is a well-groomed, intelligent thirty-five-year-old woman who was brought to the Domestic Abuse Shelter by a hotline volunteer. Susan was picked up at a safe place by the volunteer and admitted to the shelter at 3:30 in the morning. Upon interview it was evident she had been beaten, with a blackened eye and multiple bruises to her arms and head. When asked by the social worker what had brought her to the shelter, she responded tearfully.

> I don't understand what is happening to me, to us. We get along so well on the weekends but when I have to go to work on Monday, he goes crazy. He accuses me of terrible things, he won't let me bathe, and he even checks my underwear. He is looking for evidence that I have been with another man. I haven't been, actually I am so sick of him I really can't even imagine trying with someone else. We have no money; and, he blames me because he cannot hold a job. If I don't work we will have no way to pay the rent. But when I am just a few minutes late coming home from work he is convinced I was with another man. I love him so much but he is making me crazy. I have to get away from him before we kill each other.

When she finished talking she put her head in her hands and sobbed angrily, shaking her head in sheer frustration.

Later in the day, it was reported by another resident that Susan's boyfriend called the pay phone at the shelter (it is unclear how he got the number, which is not listed). That night Susan asked the housekeeper to leave and go to the store; however, she did not return.

Approximately two weeks later Susan was readmitted to the shelter. This time the emergency room staff called the shelter and she was picked up at the hospital emergency room. Susan's arm was in a cast and she had a large reddened area on her face. When asked by the social worker what had transpired resulting in her readmission, the client stated the following.

> He was drinking again, he hit me for laughing at him. He accused me of cheating and he was the one that had the woman's phone number he refused to explain. So I knocked him one. I was drinking too—but not as much as him. I guess I didn't see it coming but he picked up a baseball bat and hit me hard. I guess that's how my arm got broke. I am never going back. I can't. He will kill me if I do.

After two days, Susan went back to work while still residing in the shelter setting. She refused to give up her job, arguing that it was the only stable thing she had. She did, however, call her boss (at the urging of the social worker) and requested that her boyfriend be banned from her place of employment. Her employer was quite angry to hear what happened to her and agreed to have her boyfriend removed if he came on the premises. After approximately one week in the shelter Susan did not return as expected from work. The social worker called her work to verify that she was all right. The employer reported that Susan had reportedly been seen talking through a car window with a man similar to her boyfriend. After approximately twenty minutes the two left together in the car.

Two months later Susan called the shelter herself, asking for admission. She was admitted to the shelter via the emergency room. Susan was four months pregnant and reportedly had a miscarriage due to trauma from a fall. Upon readmission to the shelter Susan sat quietly showing little emotion. She did not make direct eye contact with the worker and stared intently at the floor.

> So what do I do now? I told the emergency room I fell over a shoe. I think they knew but no one said anything. He didn't mean to kick the baby, he was trying to hit me, and I turned to avoid getting hit. He lies, he says he will change, but he never does. Damn it, can't this be stopped? I feel so lost and alone, my mother doesn't call anymore and we [Susan and her boyfriend] fight whenever I even talk with my friends. I have

no one to turn to. I really appreciate the help and I do not think I would have made it if it was not for the support of the shelter counselors. If I could just control when we are together, something other than him, me and this craziness.

After this last admission Susan seemed more determined than ever to stay away. She began a plan of intervention that included attending groups and getting individual treatment. After her first group Susan was able to address her anger with her boyfriend and herself. The other members of the group openly expressed their concern for Susan and fear for her life. Susan cried and stated she knew that the women in the groups were right. Three days later Susan left the shelter without following proper discharge procedure; however, three months later Susan called the counselor and said she was living with her mother in another state. She stated that her boyfriend did not know where she was staying.

The case situation described here is not that unusual when dealing with abused women; nor is the powerlessness these women, as well as the social workers that seek to help them, feel in trying to gain back control of the client's life. Current estimates of victims of spouse abuse indicate that two million women are battered each year (Roberts and Roberts, 1990; Novella, 1992; Council on Scientific Affairs, 1992) with more than one million women annually seeking help for medical injuries due to battering (Schecter, 1987; Wodarski, 1987); and 22 to 33 percent of all emergency room visits for women were for symptoms related directly to partner abuse. No matter how extreme the violence is, Lenore Walker (1984) estimated that 50 percent of women didn't get the medical and psychological help that they needed. While the term spouse abuse has been redefined by some researchers to include incidents of females abusing males, research shows that 95 percent of assaults are directed against females (Schecter, 1987). For the purposes of this chapter, the term spouse abuse will include only women who are assaulted by a male partner, regardless of whether or not the relationship is legally defined.

The diagnostic assessment and treatment of women abused by partners is a fairly recent area of interest for researchers and clinicians. Actually, the 1939 through 1969 issues of the *Journal of Marriage and the Family* made literally no reference to violence (Schecter, 1982); and in the twenty-five years following this only about thirty articles were published in the area of family violence, with the majority of them (twenty-one articles) being between the years 1986 and the present (Dziegielewski et al., in press).

In order to understand the plight of the battered woman and subsequently set up effective interventions, it is crucial to remember the importance of viewing this problem from a feminist perspective. In societies the beliefs that what happens within the family is a private matter; that the male should "rule" his partner; and that women want to be dominated and men need to keep their women in line—all can prove a hindrance in helping a woman to leave an abusive situation (Schecter, 1982). The fact that treatment of the abused partner must consider these cultural influences remains obvious. Furthermore, the rigidity of these cultural influences combined with the unresponsiveness of institutions and the ingrained beliefs of the support system can often limit treatment options for abused women (Dziegielewski et al., in Press).

SHELTERS AND SAFE HOUSES

Today, many women receive treatment through the use of shelter programs that offer a wide range of services. Originally, Erin Pizzy, who is credited with establishing one of the first women's shelters, began the Women's Aid Project in England by setting up a *refuge home* for women with personal problems. Within three years this refuge was filled to capacity with battered wives. Currently, the shelter setting still remains the primary recourse available to women and children fleeing abusive situations. It is important to note that one to two thirds of women who actually stay at a shelter for a period of time do not return to their abusive partners. These women also report decreased depression and increased independence (Dziegielewski et al., in Press).

Unfortunately, however, the safety and security of the shelter is only temporary. Upon discharge, working class women frequently have few options available to them. They are presented with the alternatives of poorly paid jobs, welfare, living off the kindness of families and friends, finding another relationship, or depending once again upon the abuser. Davidson and Jenkins (1989) call upon us to "recognize that a woman might not find that her partner's violence is her first concern nor her worst oppressor" (p. 494). The shelter provides a haven from domestic violence; however, it is important to be sure that the structure of the shelter experience does not contribute to the battering experience of women. Programs set up to help women escape abuse must in no way revictimize those they seek to serve (Srinivasan and Davis, 1991); this makes building and running ethnically, racially, and socioeconomically equitable shelters a necessity (Coley and Beckett, 1988). The role of the social worker becomes crucial in seeking to establish equality for all involved.

TREATMENT IN THE SHELTER SETTING

When treatment is provided within the shelter setting, research supports that once a woman has received the help and support of the shelter, she is less likely to return to her abuser. According to McDonald (1989), empirical support of the shelter's role in ending battering does exist. However, as Schecter (1982) explains, "the issues facing many battered women are so overwhelming, medical problems, loneliness, children with emotional scars, poor housing and jobs, that they may decide to go back to their husbands. Many women want to reunite with their husbands for emotional, as well as, economic reasons and they hope the violence will cease" (p.283).

There also appears to be a patterned style of living that emerges within the battering relationship, which is characterized by intense love-hate interactions (Dziegielewski et al., in press). Once a woman must force herself to survive in this chaotic relationship, it is a difficult task to just let go of this survival mechanism. The characteristic intense lows and highs cease to exist once the client is no longer in the household. This makes the transition to the shelter environment difficult because the old patterns of "survival" coping still remain. Often this relationship dynamic is not considered, and the woman feels lost in her emotions. It is during these first critical days that she is most likely to return to the environment from which she came. Many times there is comfort in the familiarity of the situation, and the previous coping styles are allowed to resume.

In addition, the time a qualified counselor has to spend with the client and the number of sessions available may also be limited by the client's decision to return to her spouse. This makes the need for an effective model of short-term treatment essential to help bring her out of a crisis state, establish a safety plan, and provide her with needed referrals.

In working with victims of spouse abuse, denial runs rampant in the client's presentation (Geffner and Pagelow, 1990; Walker, 1984). Bolton and Bolton (1987) describe victims as wanting direction and information and typically not being "verbal," and the traditional in-

127

sight therapies do not meet the needs of these individuals. Treatment must therefore be highly structured and short-term oriented, avoiding long-term introspective efforts. Constantino (1981) asserts that counselling is most effective when it is short-term and focuses on solving immediate problems. It is important to note that many times these women leave their homes in a rush and arrive with few resources of their own. They need a great deal of help and assistance; however, neither victim nor shelter generally has enough time and money to undertake any type of a prolonged treatment process. Unfortunately, the abusive situation is generally multi-problematic and there is not going to be a simple solution. To further understand the dynamic characteristics of the abused and the abuser, high correlations between substance abuse and domestic violence have been established (Sigler, 1989; Tolman and Bennett, 1991; Stith, Williams and Rosen, 1990). These additional factors support the need for professional comprehensive assessment and treatment.

THEORETICAL MODEL

The theoretical base recommended for this form of short-term treatment has two major contributors: crisis intervention and cognitive behavioral techniques.

The major conceptual development of crisis theory is attributed to Dr. Eric Lindemann, Gerald Caplan, Rueben Hill, and Lillian Rappaport. *Crisis* is identified as an upset in a steady state that creates disequilibrium in a system. The occurrence of a hazardous event disturbs the homeostasis of the individual (or family) and creates a vulnerable state, and former effective problem-solving strategies are no longer effective. A crisis generally entails a period of transition or a turning point during which confrontation with an unfamiliar obstacle in life's path occurs. Familiar resources and past experiences come under test and may be found wanting.

In a crisis, the individual responds according to his/her specific personality traits and coping patterns, and crisis intervention therefore focuses on the individual's capacity to restore equilibrium, learn new coping mechanisms, and develop problem-solving skills. Emphasis is placed upon the strong, healthy aspects of the individual and not on pathology. This model suggests that during critical situations people are more open to change, and crisis need not be viewed negatively. Crisis intervention is time-limited, rapid intervention in which the focus is here and now. With an increasing demand for mental health services, crisis theory has gained popularity as an effective, brief method of treatment. The emotional and physical abuse that can occur constitutes battering, which exemplifies a crisis.

Roberts and Roberts (1990) note that the clinician in a shelter must have "an understanding of crisis theory and the techniques of crisis intervention" to effectively address the client's needs. Most spouse abuse victims have encountered sustained abuse with a recent severe attack and, therefore, enter the shelter in a crisis state. The crisis state occurs with a "precipitating or hazardous event" followed by a time of tension and distress. As evidenced by the case illustration, the three most common precipitating events that will bring abused women into the shelter for treatment are: (1) acute battering that results in severe injury; (2) serious injury inflicted upon the woman's child (children); and (3) temporary impairment of hearing, vision, and/or thought processes resulting from battering (Stith et al., 1990). Roberts and Roberts (1990) state that the precipitating event(s) is generally viewed as the last straw. Once the precipitating event has occurred the client generally tries her usual coping methods, and when they fail, the resultant active crisis state follows (Roberts, 1990).

Roberts (1991) describes seven stages of working through crisis: (1) assessing lethality and safety needs; (2) establishing rapport and communications; (3) identifying the major problems; (4) dealing with feelings and providing support; (5) exploring possible alternatives; (6) formulating an action plan; and (7) providing follow up. Roberts' seven-stage model applies to a broad range of crises, and is clearly applicable in the case of intervention with those involved with domestic violence.

In the application of this crisis intervention model to practice, the therapeutic environment is characterized by the following: (1) a here and now orientation; (2) a time-limited course (typically six to twelve sessions); (3) a view of the battered woman's behavior as an understandable (rather than pathological) reaction to stress; (4) the assumption by the social worker of an active and directive role; and (5) an overall strategy of increasing the individual's remobilization and returning to the previous level of functioning.

In crisis theory, it is paramount that the atmosphere underlying the process of therapy must be one of respect for the client. The goal of crisis work is to enable the client to regain the "capacity to deal effectively with the crisis" and "to increase his/her mastery over his/her own behavior and gain greater self awareness" (p.43) (Getz et al., 1974). While interventions based on crisis theory seek to restore

129

the client to a level of functioning that existed prior to the crisis, Roberts and Roberts (1990) see the end result for the domestic violence victim as a "person returning to their pre-crisis state or growing from the crisis intervention so that she learns new coping skills to utilize in the future" (p. 27). This type of crisis intervention usually lasts from one to six sessions (Puryear, 1979) and, due to the time- and goal-limited focus, it can provide an excellent therapeutic milieu for the client living in the shelter.

Another form of short-term treatment that has been shown to be effective in working with victims of domestic violence is cognitive behavior therapy. As Webb (1992) explained, "distorted beliefs interfere with the abused women's ability to manage their lives effectively" (p. 206). These beliefs may arise from efforts to cope with the abusive situation, from an abusive childhood, and/or from societal norms in relation to gender roles and expectations (Webb, 1992).

From a cognitive behavioral perspective the "assumption that maladaptive behaviors are learned and maintained in accordance with principles of conditioning" is emphasized in Getz et al., 1974, (7). In cognitive behavioral therapy the casual relationship between thinking, feeling, and behaving is highlighted, as well as the belief that people experience emotional distress as a result of faulty thinking (Webb, 1992).

Researchers specializing in the treatment of domestic violence victims agree that these women have distorted beliefs about themselves (including their self-worth, ability to survive on their own, and responsibility to an abusive partner) and about others (Webb, 1992; Wodarski, 1987; Bolton and Bolton, 1987). Walker (1984) sees these women as demonstrating Seligman's "learned helplessness" and writes that cognitive behavioral techniques are especially suited to treating phobic responses conditioned during violence. Walker (1984) stated, "cognitive therapy fits with most battered women's need to control their own minds."

Albert Ellis' Rational Emotive Therapy (RET), which is based on cognitive therapy, is a form of short-term treatment that can be employed in work with domestic violence victims. Geffer and Pagelow (1990) describe the use of RET to reduce irrational beliefs such as the idea that "violence, intimacy, love, sex, and affection are intermingled" (p. 129). RET techniques can be useful in conjunction with crisis intervention, for example when a client is "catastrophizing" (Getz et al., 1974). In RET, irrational unrealistic thoughts are identified, and the client is taught how to extinguish them (Ellis and Grieger, 1977). It is a short-term procedure, which "begins to work promptly" in most cases and is "strongly oriented toward homework assignments," as well as to other active-directive techniques, such as role-playing, assertion training, and conditioning and counter-conditioning procedures (Ellis, 1971), (4).

When using RET, the ABCDE format is utilized with abused women: A is the activating experience, B is the belief about A, C is the consequence (emotional, behavioral, or both). It is the irrational or faulty belief that causes C, not the activating experience. Treatment includes D, which is the disputation of distorted beliefs, and E, the new effect or philosophy that evolves out of the rational belief that replaces the faulty belief (Ellis and Grieger, 1977). RET sees behavior as "habituated" (Ellis and Grieger, 1977) and "irrational" thoughts as present in all people. As a treatment model, RET is relatively confrontive, yet respectful of the client, and it works to promote the client's independence and positive self-regard.

IMPLEMENTATION OF TREATMENT

As described earlier, treatment is initiated with the victim in a crisis state, and techniques from a time-limited crisis intervention model (Roberts, 1991) and techniques of cognitive behavioral therapy are applied.

Stages 1 and 2: Assessing Lethality and Establishing Rapport and Communication

In highlighting the focus of the *beginning phase*, it is useful to consider what condition the client will be in upon arrival at the shelter. Often the abuse will have taken one or more forms including physical, emotional, sexual, and economic (Schecter, 1988). There will probably be medical injuries to the victim. Examples of physical abuse run the gamut from pinching to hitting, burning, choking, mutilation, and destroying a beloved pet (Schecter, 1988). Several studies show that pregnant women are more likely to suffer abuse, perhaps because they are most vulnerable while pregnant (Geffner and Pagelow, 1990; Walker, 1984; Wodarski, 1987). The victim is likely to have suffered a sexual assault, and "oversight of rape or sexual assault can lead to serious consequences for victims because of incomplete or inadequate treatment plans" (Geffner and Pagelow, 1990).

The incident of abuse that serves to prompt a victim to go to a shelter averages several hours in length, and physical abuse is coupled with psychological and emotional abuse (Walker, 1984). The victim may also be dealing with psychiatric difficulties and alcohol and/or drug abuse. The victim may be suffering from post-traumatic stress disorder or some dissociative reaction in response to pain (Walker, 1984)(25); Geffner and Pagelow, 1990 (117). Some authors compare the behavioral and emotional reactions of the victim to that of hostages. Those exhibiting symptoms of the "Stockholm Syndrome" react with "frozen fright" and "psychological infantilism." Victims suppress their rage for survival purposes and suffer a "traumatic depression" after escape. The victim takes on the perspective of the victimizer (Graham, Rawlings, and Rimini, 1988). The victim's behavior can be characterized by low self-esteem, denial of the abuse, an inability to trust, and a dependency on the victimizer (Bolton and Bolton, 1987). In these initial sessions of therapy (sessions 1–3) the goal of the therapeutic intervention is recognizing the hazardous event and acknowledging what has actually happened. For some reason (based on the triggering catalyst) the battered woman is currently being subjected to periods of stress that disturb her sense of equilibrium. (It is assumed that the individual wants to maintain homeostatic balance, and physically and emotionally the body will seek to regain equilibrium.)

Based on all the things that may have happened to the client, it is important to assess for the potential of suicide. It has been stated that one-half of all battered women have considered suicide, and one-fourth of all suicide attempts are directly related to abuse (Geffner and Pagelow, 1990). Many times these women may view suicide as a permanent solution to a seemingly unsolvable problem. Principles that need to be included in the first session include: (1) provide immediate intervention (deal with the victim immediately, in the hospital or police station, if needed); (2) be action oriented; (3) set limited goals; (4) provide support to the victim; (5) assist with focused problem solving, (6) begin to assess and help the client improve her self-image; and (7) work with the client to foster as much independence and responsibility for her own actions as possible. Walker (1984) states that the first interview will take one-and-one-half to two hours. The social worker should take a brief history, work to build trust, evaluate the risks of further danger, and assist the client in devising an "escape plan." The victim will be terrified and overwhelmed, and the social worker must focus only on immediate problems and get the client to a point where she can more objectively view her situation. It is important to note, however, that although a great deal of information needs to be obtained and transmitted during this session, the therapeutic time allotted for this session should not be rushed or reduced. Time to establish rapport and elicit the agreement and cooperation of the client in the treatment process is essential. Roberts and Roberts (1990) note that an overriding goal of crisis intervention in this phase of work is to be certain that the woman and her children are safe. The clinician must assess the safety of the victim while in the shelter, reassuring the victim while respecting the victim's fears. Geffner and Pagelow (1990) explain that sometimes battered women have developed a fear so great that they believe their abusers are almost omnipotent. These fears should be addressed and not ignored. Many times the victim may try to deny or minimize the violence and can be helped to attain a more realistic perspective by getting her to acknowledge the particular injuries she has suffered. According to the cognitive behavioral approach, the denial of violence is a learned behavior. Walker (1984) comments that battered women often are not believed when they talk about the details of violence, and thus, when discussing the events, will act as if they don't remember. But if the discussion focuses on the details, as in "tell me how you got the bruises on your arms," the victim is capable of remembering and will feel more comfortable discussing the information in a safe, nonjudgmental environment.

Even if the victim is currently in a "safe" place such as a shelter, treatment must include an evaluation of risk and the joint development of a safety plan. This is a crucial step to take in the first session, given the possibility that the victim will return to her batterer. The clinician can evaluate risk to the victim by asking the victim whether the abuser is suicidal or homicidal, or if he has a weapon and what it is (Schecter, 1987). Questions should also focus on how obsessive the abuser is regarding the victim, his access to the victim, and the presence of rage, depression, and drug and alcohol dependence or abuse in the abuser (Hart, 1988).

The social worker must assess the condition of the victim, ascertaining whether she needs medical care, psychiatric care, or entry into a drug/alcohol treatment program, depending on the policy of the shelter. Tests to assess the possibility of suicide and level of depression can be administered. If the client presents suicidal ideation and has a plan to complete the suicidal act, hospitalization will be required. The development of a safety plan is a crucial portion of the beginning phase, and it can also serve as an intervention that acts to empower the victim by offering her options.

Work with the victim will be immediate and action oriented. The clinician will create an atmosphere where the client feels that the therapist believes her and is capable of helping. As the client begins to gain a level of precrisis functioning, the therapist will begin to outline the treatment program and set the number of sessions (generally six to eight sessions are recommended). At the end of each session the social worker must have the victim verbally review the safety plan.

The safety plan should also be developed through sessions 1–3 of the treatment program. One portion of the plan must deal with the safety of the victim should she return to the abuser or come into contact with him under other circumstances. The plan should focus on how the victim can escape, where she can go, and who can help her. This should be laid out in terms of very specific behaviors, including such items as which phone she would use, where she could keep some clothes and an extra set of car keys, and more.

The second part of the safety plan is accomplished by supplying the victim with information. Hart (1988) wrote that men who batter often engaged in withholding information, or manipulated and distorted it in order to control their battered partners. The clinician must work through several sessions to provide the victim with information about the causes and effects of battering, legal services, government benefits, and treatment programs for *batterers*. Referrals given to the victim may include legal aid, medical care, careers for homemakers, day care programs, low cost housing, shelter in another state, Big Brothers, drug and alcohol treatment programs, GED programs, and more (Roberts and Roberts, 1990). The power and control issues of abuse and Walker's (1984) cycle theory of battering can be taught to the client using handouts that explain the dynamics.

Guidelines for treatment of the domestic violence victim include a focus on what Schecter (1987) terms an "empowerment process." All phases of the counselling experience should involve tasks of validating experiences, exploring options, building on the client's strengths, and respecting her right to self-determination. Questions about the abuse should be direct and concise (Rodenburg and Fantuzzo, 1993). The clinician must emphasize to the victim that it isn't her fault, and needs to "make statements like the following: abuse is criminal and wrong; leaving an abuser is frequently the only way to stop the violence; keeping the family together is not always best" (Follingstad et al., 1991; Schecter, 1987). This is often a delicate dance for the clinician, because the client must make her own decisions. The client is likely to express a sense of ambivalence about her relationship with the victimizer. The clinician must promote the victim's sense of her own strength and at the same time communicate her opinion that the relationship is not healthy.

Stages 3 and 4: Identifying the Major Problems, Establishing Goals, and Dealing with Feelings While Providing Support

The energy generated from the survivor's personal feelings, experiences, and perceptions steers the therapeutic process (Briere, 1992). It is critical that the therapist demonstrate empathy and an anchored understanding of the victim's world. These symptoms are seen as functional, as a means of avoiding abuse and pain. Even severe symptoms such as dissociative reactions should be viewed as a constructive method of removing oneself from a harmful situation and exploring alternative coping mechanisms. The experiences of battered women should be normalized so that they can recognize that being held a captive in this abusive cycle is not their fault. Reframing symptoms as coping techniques can be helpful.

In this *middle phase* of treatment, which may include sessions 4 through 6, both crisis intervention and cognitive behavioral therapy are used. Here the social worker and client set up goals and objectives. Goals must be stated in measurable terms, and a way to evaluate progress must be designed. Goals should include the development and enacting of an action plan for the victim. It is vital that the social worker express the sense of the danger that could result from her returning to her abuser, yet it is important for the victim to participate in the establishment of her own plan of action. Walker (1984) states, "it is crucial for the woman to understand that the purpose of therapy . . .is to help her grow and regain her emotional strength . . ." (p. 122). An overall goal may be simply stated as "the client will regain her sense of self-worth," and one of the objectives to directly address this would be "not returning to the abuser." The victim may need assistance in getting help from various organizations and institutions, including obtaining government benefits and going to court.

In the middle phase of treatment, it is important that the social worker introduce the client to the principles of cognitive behavioral therapy. This could include a simple statement to the client that sometimes we "learn" things that are incorrect and that incorrect thoughts lead to certain unwanted emotional reactions. The therapist takes some time to assess illogical beliefs that the client has and begins to point them out to her. One irrational belief mentioned earlier in this chapter is that violence, intimacy, and love are enmeshed. Another distortion in thinking is that for the victim a task of maintaining a "stress free

135

world for their batterers" is feasible (Walker, 1984). Other irrational or illogical beliefs may include the victim's idea that the abusive situation is her fault, that violence is a normal part of relationships, and that she can't get out of the abusive situation (Finkelhore, 1988). Webb (1992) explains that battered women "learn a host of mistaken beliefs about themselves and others that cause them significant emotional distress and behavioral disorders" (p. 208).

Treatment must include intervention to increase assertiveness and promote self-esteem. This results in a focus on strengths and assets which can help to offset the strong dependency and feelings of worthlessness that have been conditioned as part of the cycle of battering (Geffner and Pagelow, 1990). In teaching assertiveness it is important to note that those who work with victims of domestic violence caution that the possible results in terms of the abuser's responses must also be explored (Geffner and Pagelow, 1990; Walker, 1984).

After introducing the client to the basic premises of RET and beginning to assess the client's illogical beliefs in reference to herself and others, assignments can be given to the client to carry out on a daily basis in the shelter. The client is taught to observe and record irrational thoughts and then to replace distorted thought with ones that are more realistic. Ellis and Grieger (1977) say irrational beliefs fall into categories that include overgeneralizations, should and must ("I must stay in this relationship"), "awfulizing" ("it would be awful if I left him") and "damning" of self.

The client can begin to assess her own thoughts in several ways. She can be asked to keep an "emotional diary" for a few days, noting changes in feelings and what was going on when they occurred (Wessler and Wessler, 1980). In using the triple column technique the client records an event associated with an unpleasant mood on the left side, the middle column is for actual cognitions, and the right side is left blank for the clinician and client to assess the validity of the cognitions while in session (Beck, 1976; Beck, Rush, Shaw and Emery, 1979). Another intervention, rational self-analysis, requires that the client record A—facts and events, and B—self-talk. In the C section, the client asks whether the thinking is factual, will the thinking help the client protect herself, and will the thinking help her feel the emotions that she wants to feel. Next, the client works on D, the debate of B; and E, which is the way she wants to think and act.

Rational-Emotive Imaging (REI) can also be utilized during the middle phase. REI is based on the same principles as RET, but adds the "use of imagination" to "pattern nerve impulses." For ten minutes at a time, four times a day, the client writes out her ABC analysis and then comes up with a rational response. She learns relaxation techniques, including deep breathing with a mental rehearsal of the event with a rational response (Ellis and Grieger, 1977). This is a skill that the victim can learn and generalize to areas of difficulty in her life.

Other cognitive behavioral techniques used with battered women include modeling, thought stopping, cognitive restructuring, reframing, and stress inoculation (Webb, 1992). Retribution techniques (Beck et al, 1979) that challenge the assumption that the victim is responsible for the abuse can be utilized. Alternative techniques (Mancoske, Standifer, and Cauley, 1994; Beck et al., 1979) can be used to generate a range of solutions or interpretations of events. Behavioral change tasks must be small and should increase in difficulty as the client progresses. These might include contacting a lawyer or calling a family member to ask for support.

In working with the client to collect, examine, and replace illogical cognitions, it is important to tread carefully in areas where anger may erupt. In order to survive, abused women will repress their anger toward the batterer and those people or organizations who proved unwilling or unable to help them. Walker (1984) warns that feelings of anger shouldn't be unleashed too quickly. Anger management techniques should be taught while highlighting the victim's right to live without abuse (Geffner and Pagelow, 1990).

An ongoing component of the treatment program should be a group for the victim to attend while at the shelter (Roberts and Roberts, 1990) and perhaps to continue after discharge. The same techniques utilized in the shelter (e.g., RET and REI) can also be used in group work to aid victims in finding options, learning to protect themselves, and keeping away from abusive relationships.

Stages 5 and 6: Exploring Possible Alternatives and Formulating an Action Plan

In the final sessions or the *ending phase* of treatment (sessions seven and eight), overall progress should be summarized at the end of each session with an emphasis on empowerment of the victim. The practical concerns of the client in terms of accessing resources are discussed while an atmosphere is maintained that engenders hope and fosters independence. If in the final stage, progress toward goals has been hampered, a new contract for additional sessions may need to be established.

Roberts (1991) states that there are approximately 1,250 battered women's shelters in the United States and Schecter (1988) reminds us that the shelters that do exist to provide this service have turned away thousands of women. Lack of funding and the possibility of a victim returning to her abuser limit the time of treatment. As treatment is terminated, the social worker and client can measure progress related to the client's goals. A safety plan should be reviewed during the final session, along with a review of progress made toward modifying distorted thoughts. The client should leave treatment with information about resources available to her and the batterer in the community, an understanding of the dynamics of abuse, and a set of techniques that will allow her to assess her unrealistic thinking and explore options.

If the client has elected to leave the abusive relationship, a portion of final sessions should be spent in insuring that the client has been able to access needed services such as housing and government benefits. It is the victim's choice as to whether or not she should return to her abuser. The social worker may be tempted to evaluate treatment in terms of the victim leaving her abuser, but successful treatment can be measured in the client's increased self-esteem and ability to objectively assess her situation. It is crucial to let the client know that, if she returns to the abuser, she will be in danger, and at the same time to convey to the victim that you and your agency will be available to them should they need further help.

STAGE 7: FOLLOW-UP MEASURES

This area is very important for social work practice in general, but one that is almost always forgotten. In the successful therapeutic exchange, significant changes have been made for the abused woman in regard to her previous level of functioning and coping. Measures to determine whether these results have remained consistent are essential. Often follow up can be as simple as a phone call to discuss how things are going. Follow up within one month of termination of the session is important.

In assessing the effectiveness of the treatment method, the social worker will want to consider if the client has been returned to a pre-crisis level of functioning. However, this level of functioning is likely to have been one characterized by low self-esteem and fearfulness.

Effectiveness of treatment should be measured by administering some type of objective measure (i.e., a depression and/or a self-esteem measurement scale). For a listing of such scales in the behavioral sciences, the reader is referred to Corcoran and Fischer (1977). These scales should be given prior to the initiation of treatment and again at termination (Webb, 1992). If treatment has been effective, the client should be able to give to the social worker a basic explanation of the dynamics of abuse and should leave armed with information, including referrals. The victim's experience should have been validated by the shelter. Treatment has also been effective if the victim is able to highlight her own core strengths in a final session.

FUTURE DIRECTIONS

Walker (1984) stated that the "ultimate goal of therapy is to become a survivor, putting the effects of victimization in the past and getting on with life" (p. 128). Treatment in a shelter setting based on a crisis intervention and cognitive behavioral therapy appears to be an effective and efficient way to serve abused women. The abused woman has learned not to act and that trying to escape does not reap rewards; she has accepted the victimizer's distorted perspective. Now she must learn a more stable and healthy view of reality. With the teachings of cognitive behavioral therapy she can learn that she has options and choices.

REFERENCES

Beck, A.T. (1976). *Cognitive therapy and the emotional disorders*. New York: International Universities Press.

Beck, A.T., Rush, A.J., Shaw, B.F. and Emery, G. (1979). *Cognitive therapy of depression*. New York: Guilford.

Bolton, F., and Bolton, S. (1987). *Working with violent families: A guide for clinical and legal practitioners*. Newbury Park, CA: Sage.

Briere, J.N. (1992). *Child abuse trauma: Theory and treatment the lasting effects*. Newbury Park, CA: Sage.

Coley, S. M., and Beckett, J.O. (1988). Black battered women: Practice issues. *Social Casework, 69* (8), 483–490.

Constantino, C. (1981). Intervention with battered women: The lawyer-social worker team. *Social Work, 26* (6), 456–60.

Corcoran, K, and Fischer, J. (1977). *Measures for clinical practice—A source book*. New York: Free Press.

Council on Scientific Affairs, American Medical Association. (1992). *JAMA, 267* (23), 3184–3189.

Davidson, B. P., and Jenkins, P.J. (1989). Class diversity in shelter life. *Social Work, 34* (6), 491–95.

Dziegielewski, S.F., Resnick, C., and Krause, N. (In press). Shelter based crisis intervention with abused women. In A. Roberts (Ed.), *Helping battered women: New perspectives*. New York: Oxford University Press.

Edelson, J. L. (1991). Note on history: Social worker's intervention in woman abuse: 1907–1945. *Social Service Review*, June, 304–13.

Ellis, A. (1971). *Growth through reason*. Palo Alto, CA: Science and Behavior Books.

Ellis, A., and Grieger, R. (Eds.). (1977). *Handbook of rational-emotive therapy*. New York: Springer.

Finkelhore, D. (1988) *Stopping family violence*. London: Sage.

Follingstad, D., Brennan, A., Hava, E., et al. (1991). Factors moderating physical and psychological symptoms of battered women. *Journal of Family Violence, 6* (1), 81–95.

Geffner, R., and Pagelow, M. (1990). Victims of spouse abuse. In R. Ammerman and M. Hersen (Eds.), *Treatment of family violence: A source book* (pp. 113–135). New York: Wiley.

Getz, W., Wiesen, A., Sue, S., and Ayers, A. (1974). *Fundamentals of crisis counseling*. Lexington, MA: D.C. Health.

Graham, D., Rawlings, E., and Rimini, N. (1988). Survivors of terror—battered women, hostages, and the Stockholm syndrome. In K. Yllo and M. Bograd (Eds.), *Feminist perspectives on wife abuse*, (pp. 217–233). Newbury Park, CA: Sage.

Hart, B. (1988). Beyond the duty to warn. In K. Yllo and M. Bograd (Eds.), *Feminist perspectives on wife abuse*, (pp. 234–248). Newbury Park: Sage.

Mancoske, R.J., Standifer, D., and Cauley, C. (1994). The effectiveness of brief counseling services for battered women. *Research on Social Work Practice, 4* (1), 53–63.

McDonald, P. (1989). Transition houses and the problem of family violence. In B. Pressman, G. Cameron, and M. Rothery (Eds.), *Interviewing with assaulted women: Current theory research and practice* (pp. 111–123). NJ: Lawrence Erlbaum.

Novella, A. C. (1992). From the surgeon general: U.S. Public Health Service. *JAMA, 267* (23), 3132.

Puryear, D. (1979). *Helping people in crisis*. San Francisco, CA: Jossey-Bass.

Roberts, A. R. (1991). *Contemporary perspectives on crisis intervention and prevention*. Englewood Cliffs, NJ: Prentice-Hall.

Roberts, A., and Roberts, B. (1990). A comprehensive model for crisis intervention with battered women and their children. A. Roberts (Ed.), *Crisis intervention handbook: Assessment, treatment and research (p. 106–123).* Belmont, CA: Wadsworth.

Roberts, A. (1990). *Crisis intervention handbook: Assessment, treatment and research.* Belmont, CA: Wadsworth.

Rodenburg, F., and Fantuzzo, J. (1993). The measure of wife abuse: Steps toward the development of a comprehensive assessment technique. *Journal of Family Violence, 8* (3), 203–227.

Schecter, S. (1988). A framework for understanding and empowering battered women. In M. Strauss (Ed.), *Abuse and victimization across the life span* (pp. 240–253). Baltimore, MD: John Hopkins University Press.

————— (1987). Guidelines for mental health practitioners in domestic violence cases. Washington, DC: National Coalition Against Domestic Violence.

————— (1982). *Women and male violence.* MA: South End Press.

Sigler, R.T. (1989). *Domestic violence in context.* Lexington, MA: Lexington Books.

Srinivasan, M., and Davis L.V. (1991). A shelter: An organization like any other? *Affilia, 6* (1), 38–57.

Stith, S.M., Williams, M., and Rosen, K. (1990). *Violence hits home: Comprehensive treatment approaches to domestic violence.* New York: Springer.

Tolman, R.M., and Bennett, L.W. (1991). A review of quantitative research on men who batter. *Journal of Interpersonal Violence, 5* (1), 87–118.

Walker, L. (1984). *The battered woman syndrome.* New York: Springer.

Webb, W. (1992). Treatment issues and cognitive behavior techniques with battered women. *Journal of Family Violence, 7* (3), 205–217.

Wessler, R., and Wessler, R. (1980). *The principles of practice of rational-emotive therapy.* San Francisco, CA: Jossey-Bass.

Wodarski, J. (1987). An examination of spouse abuse: Practice issues for the profession. *Clinical Social Work Journal, 5* (2), 172–179.

CHAPTER 8

Family Crisis—Life Cycle and Bolts from the Blue: Assessment and Treatment

ELAINE P. CONGRESS

The Marshall family—forty-two-year-old Tom, thirty-eight-year-old Delores, and their two children, sixteen-year-old Greg and fourteen-year-old Sandy—had been experiencing conflict for the last several years. When Greg turned fourteen he began to stay out late with his friends, while Sandy was always out with her boyfriend. Often they were too tired to go to school in the morning. In response to the children's behavior Tom and Delores had become more restrictive and tried to impose an early curfew. Four months ago Tom was killed in an automobile accident. Since that time Delores had become more depressed, often unable to leave the house for days at a time. Her children's distancing behavior became even more pronounced. Greg and Sandy were home very erratically; as Delores described it, "only to change their clothes and grab something to eat."

The Marshalls were experiencing a family crisis. The first stressor had involved their difficulty in adapting to the family life cycle stage with adolescents. An additional stressor involved the sudden death of Mr. Marshall. The Marshall family was faced with coping with two stressors within a short period of time. The usual roles and rules within the family had been challenged, and the family was at risk of dissolving.

This chapter will explore the types of family crises produced by life cycle transitions, as well as "bolts from the blue" stressors (Pittman, 1987). A model of family crisis treatment will be developed for work with families experiencing life cycle transition crises, "bolts from the blue" crises, or both types of crises as in the Marshall family. In order to help families cope with crisis, it is necessary first to assess the nature of the crisis the family is experiencing.

LIFE CYCLE CRISES

The modern family faces crisis points at each stage of its life cycle. Just as there are different stages for individual psychosocial development (Erikson, 1963; Levinson, Darrow, and Klein, 1978; and Sheehy, 1976), life cycle events for families have been identified (Solomon, 1973; Duvall, 1977; Carter and McGoldrick, 1980, 1989). The transitions between these stages have been seen to be particularly stressful and often precipitate family crisis. Similar to the disequilibrium that occurs when the individual attempts to cope with a crisis event (Caplan, 1964), family crisis usually involves a time in which the usual family equilibrium of homeostatic balance is upset, and the family individually and as a group cannot use their usual coping mechanisms. There is often increased conflict between individuals, which may even threaten the continuation of the family system.

A crisis most frequently occurs at times when families transit from one life cycle stage to another. The family life cycle has been divided into six stages (Carter and McGoldrick, 1980, 1989):

Stage 1: Between Families—The Unattached Young Adult
Stage 2: The Joining of Families Through Marriage: The Newly Married Couple
Stage 3: The Family with Young Children
Stage 4: The Family with Adolescents
Stage 5: Launching Children and Moving On
Stage 6: The Family in Later Life

There may be some differences in these stages for poorer families, as well as changes in these life cycle stages for the growing number of divorced and remarried families (Carter and McGoldrick, 1989). Also, changing roles of women within the family and the current economic recession have brought changes in what has been seen as the typical family life cycle. The following section will consider each stage in

143

greater detail, how each stage has been affected during recent years, and the type of family crisis that may arise during transition to this family life cycle stage.

BETWEEN FAMILIES:
THE UNATTACHED YOUNG ADULT

The developmental tasks for this stage include the young adult separating from family of origin, developing intimate peer relationships, and establishing self in work (Carter and McGoldrick, 1980). It should be noted that the importance of the emotional and physical separation of women from their families was not acknowledged until the latter part of the twentieth century. A traditional expectation that may still be true for some cultural groups was that women should remain at home, emotionally and financially dependent upon their parents until marriage.

Not only the young adult but also the parents and siblings must participate in the separation process of the young adult. A family crisis may arise during this time. Both parents and children may have difficulty in separating, as the following example illustrates.

Mary, a twenty-three-year-old college graduate, had just been offered a job in a distant city. She developed severe headaches that only occurred when she was traveling to this new city. Her mother worried about who would care for her if she became sick far away from home. Her father expressed concern about her safety.

The current economic recession has made this life stage particularly traumatic for many young people and their families. Many young adults have difficulties finding employment or adequate housing, which results in their living at home with parents for a much longer period. This forced physical proximity may make it more difficult for young people and their families to develop separate lives. Some parents may try to apply adolescent rules to their adult children. This "as long as you are living under my roof" attitude often produces family conflicts and creates a family crisis.

During this stage young adult children often develop serious romantic relationships. Parents' concerns about their children's love choices as well as a possible decision to live together before marriage may lead to a family crisis. Also continually changing sexual mores as well as the fear of AIDS may create stress for young adults and their families.

Physical separation from the family does not necessarily mean that young people and their families have successfully mastered this stage. Bowen (1978) described emotional cutoff, in which young people may leave home reactively and never work through this family life cycle of emotional separation, as this case example indicates.

A thirty-year-old man walked into a community clinic in Berkeley. He had never worked regularly and usually supported himself through odd jobs and checks from his family. He had had a series of girl friends, but told the social worker that they all turned out to be just like his parents. The worker learned that at the age of eighteen he had left a small New England town to come west because his family was too strict and rigid. Although he had been physically separated from his family for twelve years, his as well as his family's difficulty in coping with financial and emotional separation that occurs during this life cycle stage is quite evident.

Since in recent years young adults are often older when they marry for the first time, this first stage of separating from the family of origin may be longer for many families. It should be noted that for some families, especially poorer ones, this stage does not occur. Many adolescent girls become mothers without passing through the first two stages of the family life cycle. Separation from parents may never occur, as multiple generations continue to live together under the same roof. This may lead to family crisis in terms of parenting roles.

THE NEWLY MARRIED COUPLE

The transition from a previously unmarried stage to marriage may produce crisis for the family. Each partner must learn how to compromise, to accept that the spouse may have differing expectations and life-style choices.

Christine and Don experienced a family crisis during this stage. Very tearfully, Christine called a family counseling agency to ask for help, as after a two-month marriage their relationship was "on the rocks." Now they disagreed on everything, while during a two-year courtship, they had seemed so compatible. She discussed some of their differences—she was very neat, he was disorganized and saved everything. She wanted to go out on Saturday night; he preferred to watch VCR movies at home.

Often couples have difficulty transiting from the idealized romantic relationship of the courtship stage to a mature love relationship in which compromise and mutual respect are so important. An increasing number of couples are choosing to live together before marriage. As a consequence, the transition to marriage may seem less of a traumatic life cycle event. Yet many couples, even those who have lived together happily for several years prior to marriage, may experience conflict after marriage in coping with extended family as a couple for the first time (Carter and McGoldrick, 1989).

If families cannot successfully negotiate this life cycle crisis, divorce may be the result. The increasing divorce rate for couples during the first few years of marriage attests to family conflict and crisis during this stage of the family life cycle.

It is well known that divorce is on the increase and that one out of two marriages ends in divorce (U.S. Bureau of Census, 1990). Divorce can occur at any stage of the family life cycle and can precipitate a crisis for both the family and the individuals involved. Most of those who divorce will remarry within a short period of time. Life cycle stages for those divorcing and remarrying have been identified (Carter and McGoldrick, 1989). Often the crisis of divorce, remarriage, and blended families requires families to learn new ways of relating which may precipitate conflict.

THE FAMILY WITH YOUNG CHILDREN

A particularly difficult crisis period for many families occurs with the birth of children. The family must cope with the physical and psychosocial changes of pregnancy and childbirth. They must regroup as a triad instead of a dyad and assume new parenting roles. Often the therapist hears ''we were so happy together before the baby arrived,'' as the next case example illustrates.

Mr. and Mrs. Daniels were referred for family counseling six months after the birth of their son, Brian. Mr. Daniels complained that his wife was not ''there'' for him anymore. According to him, she spent

146

all of her time caring for Brian. While before she had prepared gourmet meals, now he was lucky if he found a TV dinner in the refrigerator. Mrs. Daniels retorted that her husband did not seem to care about her and the baby. He never offered to change a diaper or feed the baby. The last time they had gone out together was a month before the baby was born.

This period has been described as the ''pressure cooker'' phase of the life cycle, and the majority of divorces occur within this life cycle phase (Carter and McGoldrick, 1989). Current changes within American families may make this period even more stressful. Women are usually older and working when they have their first children, which may produce additional physical and psychosocial stress on families at this time. With increased numbers of divorced single parents, remarriages, and blended families, complex issues of step-siblings and stepparents may have to be negotiated at this stage.

During the early stages of marriage couples often have conflicts because of varied family of origin experiences. Having children often renews these conflicts, as the following example indicates.

Four-year-old Susan and her family were referred to a family counselor by a preschool teacher because of Susan's hostility toward other children. In talking with the parents it became apparent that Bob and Donna Evans had very different views on raising children. Bob, who came from a family of eight with an alcoholic mother, believed that it was necessary to be very strict with a child if one wanted to prevent delinquent behavior. Donna, who had been raised as an only child with very permissive parents, had an M.A. in psychology and believed it was always important to talk and reason with children about their behavior.

THE FAMILY WITH ADOLESCENTS

It is well known that adolescence is a crisis point for many families. Just as adolescents face tremendous physical and psychosocial changes when they reach this stage of development, often parents are at the same time experiencing a midlife crisis related to physical and vocational changes. Sometimes a midlife crisis leads to an extramarital affair that may threaten the very existence of the marriage. The fact that this life cycle phase has the fastest growing divorce rate attests to families' crisis experience during this stage.

Parents may be threatened by the adolescent's desire for greater autonomy and independence. The togetherness of the family with latency age children is now changed as adolescents seek out peer relationships independent of their family. While some parents have difficulty letting go and relaxing rules, others have problems imposing any restrictions or being consistent in their enforcement, as the example of the Adams family illustrates.

The Adams family seemed like a model family when their two sons were latency age. Neighbors marveled about how close they were and how happy they seemed together. Every weekend and vacation they spent together. When Tom, Jr. and Richard became adolescents, they were absent more and more from the house. In response Mrs. Adams became very depressed and did not even attempt to give her sons any restrictions. Mr. Adams, who often traveled because of increased work responsibilities, indicated that he did not think it was appropriate to impose any curfew on his sons as ''all young men have to sow their wild oats'' as part of the growing up experiences. The family was referred for family counselling after the two boys were picked up in a stolen car at 3:00 in the morning.

Cultural differences often affect family crises with adolescents and their families. Parents may have been raised in countries other than the United States where there was not an extended adolescent period. Teenagers were expected to take on adult responsibilities of work and marriage. On the other hand, American adolescence is viewed as a time for pursuing education, as well as dating a number of partners. This cultural conflict between generations often produces family crisis (Congress, 1990).

Family crisis may be aggravated during this period if adolescents become parents. Often teenage girls do not move out but raise their children within their family of origin's household. This may precipitate additional conflict between parent and adolescent about who should assume the parenting role with the adolescent's offspring.

LAUNCHING PHASE

The fifth stage has been identified as launching the children and moving on. Also described as the empty nest phase, this stage has changed dramatically over the last few decades. Increasing numbers of women now work outside the home; only part of their time and energy is devoted to raising children. Thus, when children leave home, these mothers often experience less change than their mothers did. Also this stage is not as clearly demarcated as previously, as many adult children, especially during the current recession, tend to either return to live with parents after college or drift back at times of economic hardship.

One major task for this developmental stage involves the family learning to reconstitute as a dyad. Often family crisis during this stage leads to separation and divorce, as the growing number of divorces after many years of marriage suggests.

Ted and Ann Winters' story offers evidence of a family crisis during this stage. Forty-four-year-old Ann was first seen in a mental health clinic with multiple depressive symptoms, crying spells, insomnia, and anorexia. Married when she was eighteen she had four children; the youngest, age eighteen, had just enrolled in a distant college. Ann reported that she and her husband had spent the last twenty-six years raising their four children. Now that their youngest had left they found they had nothing in common. Days went by, and they barely communicated. Ann thought they would continue like this forever. This family crisis was not acknowledged, however, until Ted asked her for a divorce.

FAMILY IN LATER LIFE

The final stage of the family life cycle, the family in later life, is the time the couple spends together after children have left the home. Sometimes this period is quite extensive, especially with increased life expectancy. A husband and wife who have launched their youngest child by the age of fifty can expect twenty-five more years together. Yet many families are deciding to postpone having children until middle age. This will greatly reduce the length of this final stage of the family life cycle. Family crisis is often precipitated during this stage as families must come to terms with intergenerational role shifts, as the Johnson family indicates.

Paul and Mary Johnson were a healthy couple in their late fifties. They had raised three children; the youngest had just bought a large home in California. Paul decided to take early retirement and, at the request of their youngest daughter, Irene, they moved into a separate apartment in her new home. A family crisis soon ensued as both Paul and Mary found themselves treated like children. Irene and her husband objected to Paul's early rising at 6:00 A.M. ("I've got up at 6:00 for fifty-seven years," he retorted). Also, when Mary babysat, Irene had nothing but criticism ("They should not have been given ice cream before dinner. They should have gone to bed by 9:00.").

Serious illness and death can also precipitate a family crisis during this final stage of the family life cycle, as this case example illustrates.

The Petersons had been married thirty-five years, and after John retired at sixty they looked forward to many happy years together. John, however, became increasingly forgetful, and their worst fears were confirmed when they learned that John had developed Alzheimer's disease. Two years later Mary seemed depressed and exhausted after attempting to provide round-the-clock care for her seriously ill husband. Yet she felt she did not want to send him to a nursing home, as caring for him was her responsibility.

BOLTS FROM THE BLUE

Family crisis is not limited to developmental stressors as the family moves through the family life cycle. In addition to developmental crises, Pittman lists "bolts from the blue" as a particularly significant precipitant of family crisis (Pittman, 1987). Any unexpected change can create stress for the family and precipitate a family crisis. Usually stressors are thought to be negative (death of spouses, serious illness, being fired at work), but even positive sudden changes can precipitate a family crisis, as the Jones family learned.

Tom and Susan Jones both worked hard to support themselves and their two children in a working-class neighborhood. All that changed when one day Tom won a $10 million lottery. Tom immediately quit a very taxing factory job, and Susan decided to work no longer as a clerk in a small real estate office. After a few weeks of leisure, though, Tom and Susan, not accustomed to spending so much time together, were continuously in conflict. To add to the family crisis, their son Bill, who was attending college, dropped out to come home, saying he did not have to study now, and that instead he would help his father invest his money. Their high school age daughter Amy became very moody and irritable. She complained that she had no friends except those who wanted to "borrow" money from her.

It is evident that each family member was affected by the family windfall in different ways. Although a "bolt from the blue" may seem to affect one member more, as for example, serious illness or being fired at work, personal stressors affect the whole family. Even though Tom won the lottery, all family members were affected by this change.

An increase of "bolts from the blue" in recent years has produced more family crisis than ever before. The current recession has led to sudden plant and office closings. Natural disasters such as the San Francisco earthquake of 1989, Hurricane Andrew in 1992, and the midwest floods of 1993 that led to extensive property loss precipitated crisis for many families. Also more individual and group incidence of violence have contributed to family crisis. Often it is not the single event but rather the cumulative effect of stressors that makes the family unable to cope, as in the following case example.

The Williamses live in a community where crime has been steadily on the increase. Last December, their nine-year-old son, Dennis, had been walking home from school with two other neighborhood children when they were caught in the crossfire of two warring drug gangs. One of the other children had been grazed by a bullet but suffered no permanent injury. The Williamses admitted that they were very concerned about the safety of the neighborhood, but all in all seemed to cope well with this stressful, unexpected life event. Then two months later, when Tom Williams was making a delivery to the sixth floor of the World Trade Center, a bombing occurred. Tom did not incur any injury and was quickly able to exit the building. This "bolt from the blue" seemed to precipitate a family crisis. Mr. Williams became phobic about making visits to highrise office buildings. Fearful that he would lose his job, Mrs. Williams was very critical of his fear, which produced much family conflict. Dennis began to have nightmares, while fourteen-year-old Denise as well as Mrs. Williams blamed Mr. Williams for going to work that day when he had a bad cold.

It is interesting to note that the family seemed to cope with the first stress with minimal difficulty, while the second stressful event precipitated a full-blown crisis for this family. Also a common response to "bolts from the blue" includes a search for blame (Pittman, 1987), and Mr. Williams was clearly blamed for bringing this problem on himself.

CRISIS INTERVENTION WORK WITH FAMILIES

Developmental crises and "bolts from the blue" affect each family member differently, as well as the family as a whole. It is "normal" for the family to experience a crisis at a life transition point or with a "bolt from the blue." Many families may resolve their family crisis without any treatment. Families often do not seek help on their own, and the majority of families seen for crisis intervention are referred by an outside source such as the school or an employer.

It is known that there are three possible outcomes for crisis resolution: (1) better functioning than previously, (2) functioning at the same level as prior to the crisis, and (3) continued impaired functioning as a result of the crisis (Golan, 1978). Applying this conceptualization to family crisis, it becomes apparent that some families may never recover from a crisis. Sometimes the crisis is so overwhelming, the conflict it produces so intense, that family dissolution is the result. In a few instances the crisis may be so traumatic for one member that psychiatric hospitalization and/or psychotropic medication may be needed. In most cases, though, short-term outpatient family crisis treatment can be used to help the family cope with the crisis. The goal of this work is to restore the family to the same or better level of functioning as compared to before the crisis.

Three models of crisis intervention work—the equilibrium model, the cognitive model, and the psychosocial transition model—can all be applied to the crisis work with families (Gilliland and James, 1993). The equilibrium model presupposes that the individuals experiencing a crisis are in a state of psychological disequilibrium in which their usual coping mechanisms and problem-solving methods are not effective. While the goal of crisis work with individuals would be to restore them to their precrisis state of equilibrium (Caplan, 1961), the goal of family crisis work would be to restore the family to their precrisis level of functioning. Either external "bolts out of the blue" or psychosocial developmental life cycle stressors can detrimentally affect the family's equilibrium. This can lead to symptom development among different members, as well as increased conflict about rules and boundaries. The use of this model is seen to be more effective at the onset of crisis work with families when they are completely overwhelmed by the crisis. Some examples of the use of this model might include work with families who lost their homes in recent floods or with families who have experienced the sudden violent death of a member.

The cognitive approach, which has been used widely with individuals in crisis (Beck, 1976; Ellis, 1962), can be applied to crisis work with families. After each crisis, individual members as well as whole families often have irrational ideas about the crisis event or their ability to cope with the stress that detrimentally affect their resolution of the crisis. Two examples of this in crisis work with families include the parent who feels that her adolescent does not love her anymore if he is not home every night, and the recent widow who states she cannot live without her husband. Cognitive techniques can best be applied to work with families after the family has been somewhat stabilized and restored to at least partial equilibrium.

The use of the psychosocial transition model has been most effective in work with families in crisis. This model focuses not only on the individual family members involved, but also on the use of social supports and environmental resources to help the family in a state of crisis (Minuchin, 1974). In family work this would involve using a family member to support another family member who has particular difficulty in coping with a crisis event. Also extended family and community resources such as the Red Cross and the welfare system can be used to provide support.

STEPS IN CRISIS INTERVENTION WORK

Crisis intervention work with families is usually short-term and time-limited, lasting from ten to twelve weeks. The following crisis intervention model (Roberts, 1990) can be applied to work with families in crisis. The seven stages of treatment include:

1. *Make psychological contact and rapidly establish the relationship.* An important beginning intervention in all treatment involves establishing rapport and building trust (Biestek, 1957). The need for the rapid establishment of trust is most essential in crisis work, because of the short-term nature of the work. The helping professional cannot afford to wait to establish a relationship, as therapeutic work with the client must begin immediately during the first session. Yet establishing a relationship is always challenging in crisis work with individuals and even more difficult with families. By definition people in crisis are overwhelmed by the event, and their usual coping mechanisms are not effective. Those in crisis may be nonverbal, very depressed, and continually crying. Others may be very angry, paranoid, and unwilling to talk with anyone. Still others may be so fearful they are mute. Even though it has been noted that people in crisis are less defensive and

thus more receptive to crisis work (Parad, 1965), the extreme emotional expressions related to crisis may make the person in crisis difficult to engage. This is compounded in work with a family in crisis, in which different family members may have varied reactions. A dilemma arises for the family crisis worker about how to establish rapport with each member but still relate to the whole family.

A challenge of family work in general and crisis family work in particular is that often one member is stigmatized and scapegoated as causing family problems, as the following example illustrates.

Fourteen-year-old Barry was the only son of Jim and Teri Aldrich. Jim and Teri had tried to have children for many years, and Barry was their only child, born after fourteen years of marriage. A good student, an all-round athlete, and popular with other children, Barry had been an ideal child during his latency years. His parents had very high expectations for him. When Barry turned thirteen, he began to be truant from school and hang out with kids whom the parents felt were bad influences. An astute school social worker realized that the family was experiencing a developmental crisis around adolescence and referred the family to a family counseling agency. For the first scheduled interview only Barry showed up, and he was an hour late for the family appointment. When the worker called later to try and engage the family, she was told that only Barry had a problem, and that Jim and Teri expected the family agency to change Barry's behavior.

The preceding example illustrates how difficult it is to engage families, especially if they view the crisis as a problem belonging to only one member. The family crisis worker must reach out to each member individually. With the Aldrich family, the family crisis worker called both parents individually and once spoke to them on a conference call. The worker was able to engage the family by stressing their concern for Barry and that the parents could provide important information about his "problem." Only after several phone contacts was a family session arranged. When this family session actually occurred, the worker did not focus on Barry's problem, but rather encouraged each parent to talk about themselves and their work (Jim was an insurance agent, Teri a realtor). The worker established a relationship with each parent before any discussion of Barry's behavior began, as this would be essential in engaging them in family crisis treatment.

2. *Establish the dimensions of the problem in order to define it.* Clarifying the problem is essential in family work with those in a developmental crisis. Often different family members have very different

views of what the problem is. This was evident with the Aldrich family. After the worker established a relationship with the family, each family member was encouraged to describe what the problem was. There were three different versions. Jim thought the major problem was that Barry had not been going to school. He had hopes that Barry would become a doctor, which is something he had always wanted for himself, as he had been forced to drop out of college to support an invalid mother. On the other hand, Teri was more concerned with Barry's friends. She pointed out that she had learned from a coworker that one of these friends had been involved in a robbery. Barry thought the problem was that both his parents, especially his mother, were too overprotective. As he stated, "They treat me like I was still nine years old." Both parents were surprised to learn that each had a different definition of the problems. Teri was surprised by Barry's statement and said, "I never knew he felt that way," as usually Barry had been very uncommunicative within the family.

3. *Encourage the exploration of feelings and emotions.* Despite the fact that families have a long history of shared experiences, nevertheless many have not had the opportunity to share feelings and emotions, especially those related to the family crisis. If feelings have been shared, they are usually only angry ones that often lead to greater distance and prevent further discussion. This was evident in the Aldrich family, who had shared only angry feelings in the previous six months. The family crisis worker was able to reach for underlying feelings. Jim shared that he felt disappointed that his only son might not achieve much in life. Barry heard for the first time how his father had always felt denied the opportunity to pursue education and the hopes he now had for his son to succeed. After a period of anger and blaming Barry for causing family trouble, Teri was able to verbalize her fears that "something bad would happen to Barry." She recalled that her cousin had been killed in an adolescent gang fight and that this might be why she was so concerned about Barry's behavior. At first Barry appeared sullen and uncooperative. During the second interview he was able to express fears about growing up, that "school was much harder now" and he would not be able to do the work required of him.

4. *Explore and assess past coping attempts.* Families have usually had a long history of handling and resolving conflict, and it is essential that the family crisis worker assess family strengths in this area. The Aldrich family had had many positive experiences in the past. Jim and Teri had coped with many years of infertility before Barry was conceived. Also the family had a solid track record of handling prob-

lems and crises that had previously occurred. Five years ago Teri's mother had become terminally ill and moved in with them. The whole family had been able to help with her physical care and also provide emotional support to each other during this crisis.

In terms of the immediate adolescent crisis the family was able to seek out family crisis treatment, and they were praised for this. It is essential in family crisis work to acknowledge how difficult it might have been for the family to pursue help. This may be particularly true of certain ethnic groups who often rely on extended family and informal support systems to provide help in time of crisis (Gilliland and James, 1993). Often the family crisis worker may be the last choice after the family has exhausted other family, school, and community resources.

5. *Generate and explore alternatives and specific solutions.* Essential in crisis work is the consideration of multiple alternatives that the family may use in handling the crisis. With the Aldrich family alternatives discussed ranged from taking out a PINS petition and having Barry placed in a residential treatment facility to doing nothing until the problem had become more acute. Finally the plan of developing a contract in which all members would have input and responsibilities was formulated, and each member participated in this formulation.

6. *Restore cognitive functioning through implementation of action plan.* This involves three steps. First, each family member must have a realistic understanding of what happened and what led to the crisis; second, each family member must understand the specific meaning of this life crisis and how it conflicts with his or her expectations; and finally, irrational beliefs must be clarified and homework assignments used to facilitate new experiences (Roberts, 1990).

Each member of the Aldrich family gained an understanding of the developmental crisis of adolescence and how this crisis had been generated. The need for more flexible family boundaries that permit adolescents to move more freely in and out of the family system (Carter and McGoldrick, 1980) became clearer to the parents. Jim and Teri Aldrich learned that it was normal for adolescents to want more independence and prefer peer relationships during this period. They realized that Barry was no longer a latency age child and the family togetherness of this period had changed. Barry was able to understand that he could move in and out of the family more freely, but he still was part of the family, and the need for some rules and regulations still existed.

The unrealistic expectations of Jim for his son became evident. Barry needed to formulate his own plans for his future. He might never become the doctor that Jim had wanted to be. Jim and Teri began to understand how much pressure they put on Barry because he was their long awaited only child. Barry gained new understanding that his parents really cared for him, and that they did not put restrictions on him because they wanted to keep him a baby or wanted to be mean to him.

The final step involves restructuring, and the worker was able to develop a contract with homework assignments. Clear rules were set, with all family members participating. For example, Barry would be permitted to stay out until midnight on weekends if he had gone to school each day the preceding week. One homework assignment involved Jim (who was often too busy with his work) taking Barry and his friends to baseball games.

7. *Follow up.* Crisis intervention work with families usually lasts only ten to twelve weeks, but the family should be made aware that they can return if there is any further crisis. The Aldrich family was seen for ten sessions, after which they reported that Barry's ''problems'' were diminished and that they felt they were handling family conflicts better than previously. They were informed that they could return if any new crisis developed. Four years later they had not returned for treatment. The family crisis worker read in a local paper that Barry had just enrolled in a premed program in college.

SUMMARY AND IMPLICATIONS FOR PRACTICE

This chapter traces the family crisis points that may occur during the family life cycle. Family crisis and conflict are most likely to occur when a family transits from one stage to the next. At that time the family system's equilibrium is disrupted, individual and family coping methods may not be effective, and intense conflict may develop. Sometimes divorce is the result of the family's difficulty in resolving the transition between stages of the family life cycle. In addition to developmental stressors, ''bolts from the blue'' may precipitate a family crisis. ''Bolts from the blue'' may include sudden death, injury, violence, and natural disasters. Although bolts from the blue may seem to strike family members differently, with one member seemingly affected the most, in reality the family system as a whole experiences a crisis.

Three models of crisis intervention treatment—the equilibrium, the cognitive, and the psychosocial transition models—are all useful in working with families in crisis. Roberts' (1990) model of crisis intervention can be applied to crisis work with families. Engaging individual family members may be challenging, especially if one member is identified as the family problem. Each family member must be encouraged to discuss feelings and emotions openly with others. The family's strengths, past and present, should be explored, as well as previous attempts to cope with the problem. The range of alternatives needs to be explored with all family members and a definite plan of action determined. Although crisis intervention work with families only extends from ten to twelve weeks, the family must understand that they are welcome to return for future help if they wish.

Although family crisis intervention treatment may not work with all families, it appears useful for the majority of families experiencing life cycle and bolts-from-the-blue crisis events. Even though individual family members may have had very traumatic life events as children that have contributed to their difficulty in coping with certain life cycle stages within their current families, family crisis treatment can still be effective with these families. Families who may not be able to benefit from this treatment model are those who were very dysfunctional prior to the crisis event. Also, if one member is so severely affected by the crisis that a suicide attempt or other psychotic behavior occurs, psychiatric hospitalization may be the preferable treatment modality. For most families experiencing a crisis, however, family crisis treatment provides the opportunity for families in a short period of time to reestablish their equilibrium and sometimes even function more effectively than prior to the crisis event.

REFERENCES

Beck, A.T. (1976). *Cognitive therapy and the emotional disorders*. New York: International Universities Press.

Biestek, F. (1957). *The casework relationship*. Chicago, IL: Loyola University Press.

Bowen, M. (1978). *Family therapy in clinical practice*. New York: Aronson.

Caplan, G. (1961). *An approach to community mental health*. New York: Grune and Stratton.

———— (1964). *Principles of preventive psychiatry*. New York: Basic Books.

Carter, E. and McGoldrick, M. (Eds.). (1980). *The family life cycle: A framework for family therapy*. New York: Gardner Press.

————, and McGoldrick, M. (1989). Overview: The changing family life cycle—A framework for family therapy. In E. Carter and M. McGoldrick, *The changing family life cycle: A framework for family therapy* (2d ed.). Boston, MA: Allyn and Bacon.

Congress, E. (1990). Crisis intervention with Hispanic clients in an urban mental health clinic. In A.R. Roberts (Ed.), *Crisis intervention handbook: Assessment, treatment, and research*. Belmont, CA: Wadsworth.

Duvall, E. (1977). *Marriage and family development* (5th ed.). Philadelphia, PA: Lippincott.

Ellis, A.E. (1962). *Reason and emotion in psychotherapy*. New York: Lyle Stuart.

Erikson, E. (1963). *Childhood and society* (2d ed.). New York: Norton.

Gilliland, B. and James, R. (1993). *Crisis intervention strategies* (2d ed.). Pacific Grove, CA: Brooks Cole.

Golan, N. (1978). *Treatment in crisis situations*. New York: Free Press.

Levinson, D.J., Darrow, C. N., and Klein, E. B. (1978). *The seasons of a man's life*. New York: Knopf.

Minuchin, S. (1974). *Families and family therapy*. Cambridge, MA: Harvard University Press.

Parad, H. J. (1965). *Crisis intervention: Selected readings*. New York: Family Services Association of America.

Pittman, F. (1987). *Turning points: Treating families in transition and crisis*. New York: Norton.

Roberts, A. (1990). An overview of crisis theory and crisis intervention. In A. Roberts (Ed.), *Crisis intervention handbook: Assessment, treatment, and research*. Belmont, CA: Wadsworth.

Sheehy, G. (1976). *Passages: Predictable crises of adult life*. New York: Dutton.

Solomon, M. (1973). A developmental conceptual premise for family therapy. *Family Process, 12*, 179–188.

U.S. Bureau of Census. (1990). *Statistical Abstract of the United States, 1990*. Washington, DC: U.S. Government Printing Office.

CHAPTER 9

An Integrative Dialectical-Pragmatic Approach to Time-Limited Treatment: Working with Unemployed Clients as a Case in Point

GILBERT J. GREENE

Joe Smith is thirty-six years old and married to Sue, also thirty-six years old. Joe and Sue have been married for fourteen years and have two children: Jim, age twelve, and Jane, age eight. Five months ago Joe was permanently laid off from his job as an appliance salesperson in a local store that went out of business. Sue works as a licensed practical nurse (LPN) at a nursing home. Sue took classes at the local community college to become an LPN and went to work two years ago when Jane started school. Money is very tight for the Smiths. Joe and Sue have had to use their savings to supplement Sue's salary and Joe's unemployment compensation. Joe's unemployment compensation is going to run out soon, as will their savings.

Joe worked for ABC appliance store for three years. Prior to working for ABC, Joe worked at XYZ appliance store for five years before the store began having serious financial problems and laying people off. When Jim was laid off by XYZ store he was able to get a job at ABC store within two weeks. The current period of unemployment is the longest Joe has ever experienced. For the first two months after leaving ABC, Joe worked very hard in his search for a new job selling appliances. No appliance stores in the city, however, are hiring due

160

to the economic recession. For the past three months Joe has been very discouraged in his job search. He has restricted his search to only appliance sales jobs since that is what he knows best and feels most competent doing. He surveys the want ads almost daily and makes approximately one telephone call per week regarding jobs. Joe has two years of college but dropped out due to the cost and lack of any specific career and educational goals. Five years ago Joe took a couple of courses in computers but made marginal grades and lost interest.

Joe was referred by his family physician for therapy for insomnia, which has been a problem for him for approximately one month.

Unemployment has increasingly become a problem in the United States in the past ten years as various types of employers downsize and reorganize to become more competitive (Jones, 1991–92; Leana and Feldman, 1992). Becoming unemployed is often experienced as a crisis by the individual and family (Jones, 1991–92). Unemployment fits Roberts' (1991) definition of a crisis in that it, like any crisis, is a problemic situation that disturbs the individual's equilibrium and often cannot be resolved by the use of his or her usual coping strategies.

According to crisis intervention theory, a person who is in a state of disequilibrium will be open to directed interventions for developing new adaptive coping methods (Roberts, 1991). Therefore, a person in crisis is willing to try new ways of thinking and behaving, which he or she would not otherwise try, in order to reduce his or her distressing feelings. The period of disequilibrium resulting from a crisis usually runs its course in four to six weeks (Parad and Parad, 1990). Four to six weeks after a crisis, individuals, with or without treatment, tend to experience either a return to their previous level of equilibrium or a new level of equilibrium that may leave them stronger or weaker than prior to the crisis. Crisis intervention as a treatment modality, therefore, is designed to last for this length of time. In a review of the literature, Ewing (1990) points out that the provisions of crisis intervention within twenty-four hours of the crisis is optimal and that clients tend not to be receptive to its more directive methodology if there is a delay of two or more weeks.

A recently unemployed person may or may not experience unemployment as a crisis. A person who would be inclined to initially experience unemployment as a crisis most likely will not have a sufficient support system and sources of self-esteem other than his or her place of employment. In other words, the place of employment is this person's primary, if not only, source of social support and self-esteem. With the loss of a job, a person such as this is likely to quickly experience a sense of disequilibrium, stress, and anxiety. Inadequate financial stability is an additional factor contributing to a person quickly experiencing unemployment as a crisis; she or he may not be able to live from week to week on the reduced income provided by unemployment compensation. A clinician working with a person in crisis due to unemployment would do well to use Roberts' (1991) seven-stage model of crisis intervention:

1. Assess lethality and safety needs.
2. Establish rapport and communication.
3. Identify the major problem.
4. Deal with feelings and provide support.
5. Explore possible alternatives.
6. Assist in formulating an action plan.
7. Follow up.

At times, losing a job will not be experienced as enough of a crisis for some people to seek professional services. Many people have a lot of hope and energy accompanied by unrealistic expectations and denial in the early stages of a job search (Jones, 1991–92). After a period of being unsuccessful in the job search, people experience a weakening in both their optimism and denial, which are replaced by feelings of depression (Jones, 1991–92). Such unemployed people may not be experiencing a crisis but rather a new equilibrium in which they are "weaker" than before. Though feeling depressed, they may not be in enough distress to seek professional services.

Frequently, when unemployed people do seek the services of a clinician, it is for a problem other than unemployment, and often they do not see a relationship between the presenting problem and their unemployment (Briar, 1988). Such clients may be experiencing psychological and/or physical discomfort, but they are not in a state of crisis. When this is the case, a somewhat longer period of treatment may be indicated. The length of this period would be longer than the four to six weeks of crisis intervention but still within the parameters of time-limited treatment, which could be anywhere from six to fifteen sessions (Parad and Parad, 1990).

Psychotherapy that is planned to be time-limited (brief) has been practiced for many years. Various approaches to time-limited treatment have been developed based on the major theories of counseling and psychotherapy: psychodynamic (Malan, 1976; Mann, 1973; Marmor, 1979; Sifneos, 1978; Strupp and Binder, 1984), cognitive (Moretti, Feldman, and Shaw, 1990), cognitive–behavioral (Lehman and Salovey, 1990), behavioral (Wilson, 1981), interpersonal (Klerman et al., 1984), solution-focused (Walter and Peller, 1992), strategic (Fisch, Weakland, and Segal, 1982), systemic (Bergman, 1985), and eclectic (Garfield, 1989; Gurman, 1981). These various approaches advocate that the clinician use active and direct methods with clients in order to get them to make changes as quickly as possible both in and outside the sessions.

All the various approaches to time-limited treatment have several common dimensions:

1. Time limits are determined in the beginning.
2. The treatment is organized around a particular problem or focus.
3. The clinician is active in the sessions as compared to a more traditional, long-term dynamic approach.
4. The client's life outside the therapeutic setting receives considerable attention.
5. A high quality collaborative, working relationship between the client and clinician is desired.

Also emphasized by most of these time-limited treatment approaches is the selection of clients who are psychologically aware and motivated enough to have a good prognosis. However, given the realities of everyday practice, clinicians cannot always carefully select clients who are appropriate for time-limited treatment. In addition, many clients, including some of those who are "good candidates" for time-limited treatment, do not respond positively to (resist) the clinician's active and direct methods. Time-limited treatment often becomes stuck in a therapeutic impasse when clients do not respond to and/or comply with the clinician's usual active and direct interventions. This paper will discuss an integrative dialectical-pragmatic approach to time-limited treatment the author has found effective with many types of clients, especially difficult and resistant ones, and client configurations (individuals, couples, and families). To illustrate the use of this model, it will be applied to clinical work with two cases of unemployed persons who initially presented with problems other than unemployment.

TIME-LIMITED TREATMENT AND DIFFICULT CLIENTS

Though long-term psychotherapy of several years length has been considered the ideal, time- limited treatment is the reality of everyday clinical practice. Regardless of treatment modality, most clients terminate after ten sessions (Koss, 1979; Taube, Burns, and Kessler, 1984) with the median number ranging between six and eight (Garfield, 1986). Consequently, most psychotherapy is time-limited by default because clients usually do not desire long-term treatment. In an extensive review of the research literature, Koss and Butcher (1986) found time-limited treatment to be just as effective as long-term, open-ended treatment. Given the effectiveness of time-limited treatment and the realities of everyday practice, it makes sense for clinicians to be adept at providing psychotherapy by design.

All but the strategic, systemic, and solution-focused approaches give some importance to selecting clients for time-limited treatment. Developers of brief dynamic therapy have especially emphasized the importance of carefully selecting clients who are most suitable for this type of treatment (Malan, 1976; Mann, 1973; Marmor, 1979; Sifneos, 1992; Strupp and Binder, 1984). The criteria for inclusion and exclusion for brief therapy eliminate up to 80 percent of all clients (Silver, 1982). Such clients are resistant to entering psychotherapy in the first place, and when they do, they are resistant to change. These criteria would eliminate all difficult clients who are not seeking long-term psychotherapeutic treatment, which includes most difficult clients. Difficult clients are generally viewed, then, as needing long-term treatment. However, to commit to open-ended, long-term treatment takes a considerable amount of motivation. Lacking enough motivation, difficult clients drop out of treatment prematurely and receive short-term treatment by default (Budman and Gurman, 1988). Thus, there is a paradox regarding length of treatment and selection of criteria: those who are most in need of long-term treatment are the least likely to "buy into it" and those most motivated for long-term treatment are also the best candidates for dynamic brief treatment.

Given that time-limited treatment is action oriented, all approaches to this method make direct requests of clients: keep appointments, come to appointments on time, report thoughts and feelings in sessions, assume responsibility for change, complete homework assignments, and experiment with different behaviors between sessions. A client who does not do any or all the above is said to be resistant or noncompliant. To deal with resistance, most approaches address the behavior directly with even more of the interventions that have not been successful, that is, increased interpreting, explaining, educating, challenging, and requesting.

The literature on dynamic brief treatment contains very little discussion on how to deal with resistant clients. Most likely, this is due to the careful selection of clients for brief therapy—they tend not to be very resistant in the first place. The primary means for dealing with resistance in the dynamic literature is for the clinician to encourage the client to examine how and why she or he keeps himself or herself locked into self-defeating patterns of feeling, thinking, and/or behavior (Strupp and Binder, 1984). Such a direct intervention of interpreting the resistance may be effective for prime candidates for brief treatment, but not for the difficult client, whether in brief or long-term treatment.

Cognitive-behavioral therapy views noncompliant clients as sabotaging their treatment (Mullin, 1986). One of the major ways clients sabotage their treatment is by failing to carry out homework assignments (Lazarus and Fay, 1982). Mullin (1986) states that such client behaviors are a result of incorrect beliefs and, therefore, should be dealt with like any other faulty belief: more explaining, questioning, and challenging. However, many clients do not respond to more of the same types of therapeutic interventions.

THE BRIEF THERAPY OF THE
MENTAL RESEARCH INSTITUTE

One major approach to brief treatment, which is applicable to a wide range of clients and has addressed working with those that are difficult and resistant, is the model developed at the Mental Research Institute of Palo Alto, California. The strategic/systemic theorists and therapists at the Mental Research Institute (MRI) (Fisch, Weakland, and Segal, 1982; Watzlawick, Weakland, and Fisch, 1974) have provided an excellent framework for understanding psychosocial problem formation and problem resolution. The MRI approach is considered *pragmatic* because it is problem-focused and emphasizes giving up interventions found to be ineffective, while identifying and using as quickly as possible only those interventions that will work.

The MRI model views problems as everyday difficulties that have been mishandled. This mishandling includes denying that a problem exists or applying the same ineffective solutions to the difficulty over and over again. The logic of the members of the social system in which the difficulty is occurring assumes that if a little of the attempted solution does not get results then "more of the same" needs to be applied, resulting in a vicious cycle. The resultant vicious cycle becomes a rigid (fixed) pattern of behavior organized around the problem; consequently, "things change but everything remains the same." Applying "more of the same'' ineffective attempted solutions to the problem is referred to as *first-order change* (Watzlawick, Weakland, and Fisch, 1974).

First-order change is logical and commonsensical according to the view of reality (the assumptive world) of members of a particular social system; that is, a family. Client systems get stuck in first-order changes when they do not have a rule (cognitive schema) for changing the rules for solving difficulties. Without such a "metarule," change cannot be made by those operating within the rules—the assumptive world—of that system.

Applying "more of the same" usually involves applying the opposite of the problem; Dowd and Pace (1989) point out that many schools of psychotherapy use techniques that are based on this principle. For example, a dynamic involved with people who have symptoms of depression is their negative self-talk and irrational beliefs about themselves. Cognitive therapy advocates the clinician challenging the irrational, negative self-talk in order for the client to develop positive self-talk and rational beliefs that will result in eliminating the depression. If the client does not respond to the initial challenging of irrational beliefs, the therapist is to do more challenging or challenge different beliefs; the answer still is in replacing irrational beliefs with rational ones. Other examples of typical first-order interventions include assertiveness training and training in parenting skills.

Clients who do not respond to first-order interventions may have rules (cognitive schemas) within their assumptive worlds stipulating that (1) guidance and advice should be given to someone who has a problem, and (2) the person with the problem is somehow deficient for having a problem. Regardless of how reassuring the clinician may be, clients may interpret such interventions as further judgment and these clients may resist first-order change as a way of maintaining some control over their lives and a sense of dignity and self-esteem. Despite the turmoil a client might experience regarding a problem, the repetitive patterns of the vicious cycle of their impasse might provide a certain amount of stability and predictability in their lives. When this is the case, first-order interventions are usually not very effective because such clients are not in a true crisis.

First-order change attempts are often assimilated according to the rules of the assumptive world of clients which usually results in no change occurring (Dowd and Pace, 1989). When clients do not respond positively to first-order interventions a therapeutic impasse exists. When this situation occurs most theoretical approaches say that the client is resistant and unmotivated. This view of the client puts the focus for responsibility of the impasse within the client. An alternative view is for the therapist to examine the assumptions about change contained in the type of therapy she or he is using (Fisch, Weakland, and Segal, 1982). The problem, then, may not be with the client but with the therapist's unwillingness to question the efficacy of his or her theory. The impasse, therefore, may be due more to the therapist's resistance than the client's. To counter such a therapeutic impasse, the MRI model advocates the use of *second-order change*.

Second-order change is illogical and "uncommonsensical" according to the rules of one's assumptive world. Change can be made by members of a particular system when there is a rule for changing the rules (a metarule). A system without such a metarule can experience second-order change when its members encounter novel experiences/ people in their environment (Dowd and Pace, 1989; Levine and Lightburn, 1989); therapy should be such an experience. In order to maintain the therapeutic relationship, clients must accommodate to the clinician, who is the source of the novelty. Accommodating means that the client must broaden and/or add rules to his or her assumptive world (Dowd and Pace, 1989). The changes in these rules allow the client system to be more flexible in responding to the world and thus break out of current vicious cycles.

One commonly used second-order change intervention is *reframing*. Reframing involves redefining or relabeling the facts of a situation so that the client might view them in a different and more workable manner. In other words, the facts do not change but their meaning does (Watzlawick, Weakland, and Fisch, 1974). Usually reframing takes the facts of a situation that have been defined negatively by the client and his/her significant others and gives them a positive meaning (connotation). An example would be suggesting to a client that depression could be a necessary prelude to a major psychological breakthrough (Weeks, 1977). An alternative, plausible redefinition such as this can interject some novelty into the client's assumptive world. The introduction of novelty into the client system should result in a small amount of disequilibrium and crisis. To reduce this disequilibrium, the client must update (accommodate) his/her rules (cognitive schemas), which in turn leads to enough second-order change to begin problem resolutions.

Some second-order interventions involve the clinician giving directives, which may seem illogical and uncommonsensical to the client system, to do something different to deal with the problematic situation. For example, parents may be instructed to just ignore their child's tantrums (Watzlawick, Weakland, and Fisch, 1974). Another example involves instructing a perfectionistic client to deliberately make one small mistake that was known only to the client (Fisch, Weakland, and Segal, 1982). For most clients, if they follow such directives, the problem may improve because they are doing something different, which forces them to go beyond their usual rules for dealing with such situations. Therefore, novelty around the problem is experienced by the client, and second-order change occurs. Other clients, however, do not comply with such directives. Such clients may react to such "second-order" prescriptions as they do to first-order interventions in that they experience such requests as implicit judgments and criticism.

When clients are noncompliant with therapeutic directives, then the clinician may want to use another second-order intervention that "restrains" the client from changing. *Restraint from change* interventions have been found to be very useful with noncompliant (oppositional) clients (Westerman et al., 1987). The idea behind such intervention is that if a client has a generalized position of opposing any advice and/or directives, then a way to get him/her to change is to request that s/he not change. Such an oppositional person may change by rebelling against the request that s/he not change.

Restraint from change interventions have been placed into categories of either "soft" or "hard" (Rohrbaugh et al., 1981). Soft restraint from change involves suggesting to clients early in treatment that they should "go slow" in attempting change, or discussing with clients the possible "dangers of improvement." A hard restraint would involve "prescribing the symptom/problem" by suggesting to clients that they try to increase the frequency, intensity, and/or location of the symptomatic thoughts/feelings/behaviors for now. Such prescriptions are preceded by a rationale that usually includes positively reframing the presenting problem.

Both soft and hard restraint from change interventions are *paradoxical*. In commenting on paradox, Dell (1981) states: "That which successfully flies in the face of 'common sense' can only be considered 'paradoxical' " (p. 38). Soft and hard restraint from change prescriptions are paradoxical because the client is given a message of not changing within a context (therapy) in which she or he is expecting help to change (Greene and Sattin, 1985). Novelty is introduced into the client system by paradoxical interventions since they are considerably different from the methods the client and/or his or her significant others have been using in attempting to bring about change in the problem. Consequently, a different solution has been applied to the problem (Watzlawick, Weakland, and Fisch, 1974). This new solution violates the old rules that have helped to perpetuate the problematic pattern of behavior. Therefore, for example, after depression has been positively reframed as perhaps being a necessary prelude to major psychological and emotional growth, the clinician can then suggest to the clients that they might want to experience the depression in a room in the house different from where they usually spend their time when depressed in order to learn more about what they need to know to enhance their emotional and psychological growth.

Despite the creativity of reframing and restraint from change (paradox), some clients still do not respond to treatment—they continue to be noncompliant. A clinician may try different forms of reframing and paradox in an attempt to find the "right combination," but this may end up in nothing more than applying "more of the same," which will continue the therapeutic stalemate. When this is the case, the clinician, in the spirit of the MRI model, should try something different.

DIALECTICS OF CHANGE

To continue existing, systems need to be able to maintain a considerable amount of stability. At the same time, however, systems need to be able to develop (grow) and make changes when there are fluctuations in the environment. Consequently, systems oscillate between stability and change within set rules and limits (boundaries) (Keeney, 1987; Keeney and Ross, 1985). In designing interventions, Keeney (1987) emphasizes that both stability and change need to be addressed. First-order interventions put major emphasis on change. The second-order interventions of restraint from change, especially prescribing the symptoms, place major emphasis on stability. Keeney (1987), however, believes that the most effective interventions are those that request change and stability at the same time.

An intervention that asks for both stability and change from the client is *dialectical*. Dialectics deals with the resolution of contradictions and opposites, which produces change (Liddle, 1984). The basis of dialectics is that *thesis* meets *antithesis* resulting in *synthesis* (change). It is through the resolution of contradictions (a dialectical process) that *development* (growth) occurs (Reigel, 1976). Such development results in a system with increased complexity in terms of its rules, beliefs, and constructs (schemata). For therapy to be effective, therefore, it should be dialectical and result in enhanced development and evolution of the client system (individual, couple, family).

169

According to Omer (1991), *"Dialectical interventions are treatment strategies that embody two antithetical moves* in such a way that as the pendulum swings from one to the other, change forces are mobilized and resistances neutralized" (p. 565). A commonsense view of dialectics might consider the thesis in the clinical situation as the client's presenting problem, that is, anxiety, and the antithesis as the opposite of the problem, which is offered by the clinician's interventions, that is, relaxation training. A more in-depth analysis of the clinical situation, however, views the thesis as the client's assumptions about the problem and change ("I need to change; I need to get rid of my anxiety; I need to learn to calm down and relax") and the antithesis as an opposite view ("Perhaps you should not change for now because of what the anxiety might be doing for you and/or others").

A dialectical intervention, therefore, offers clients both messages simultaneously, that is, "Change, and here's how" vs. "Don't change, and here's why." The restraint from change intervention of asking the client to have the symptom (stability) in a different room or at a different time of the day (change) qualifies as being dialectical. However, the simultaneous request for stability and change in such an intervention is somewhat implicit. Consequently, the client might only hear it as either a request for stability or a request for change and thus no change takes place.

In order to have a therapeutic impact on the client system, the simultaneous request of stability and change sometimes needs to be made explicit. To accomplish this, the clinician tells the client in a direct, first-order manner what he or she could do to change the presenting problem—that is, how to go about being more assertive, or to relax, or think more rationally, or manage their child's behavior—but then tells the client that she or he might not want to change just yet since they and/or significant others, especially a spouse or parent, might be deriving some benefit (the therapist does hypothesize with the client what this might be given the dynamics of the client situation and/or the family of origin) from the presenting problem (this requires positively reframing the problem and prescribing the status quo temporarily). The client is told that this is just "food for thought" and to just think it over between sessions. With such an intervention, the clinician is simultaneously and explicitly suggesting first-order change and second-order change but requiring neither. The restraint from change message introduces enough novelty and disequilibrium (crisis) into the client system so that the client will be more open to responding to the suggestions for first-order change. An intervention designed and delivered like this fosters client empowerment in that s/he decides what the change will be. It has been the experience of the author that the client usually chooses to make changes somewhere in between the clinician's requests for stability and change. Often the initial changes are not attributed by the client to the intervention itself but "just seem to have happened out of nowhere."

The disequilibrium brought about by interventions can be thought of as "loosening up" the client system; loosening up its rules, schemas, constructs (Epting, 1984). Once clients start to make some changes, regardless of how small, they are frequently more open to first-order interventions, and the pace of treatment can then be accelerated. However, some clients do not respond to this more explicit dialectical intervention or the first-order interventions that follow. When an impasse occurs at this point, it is helpful to broaden the context of the presenting problem so as to consider other factors that might be impinging on the client. The other factors in which the client's problem might be imbedded make up what Keeney (1987) has referred to as *third-order reality*.

Third-Order Reality

Extending the work of the MRI model, Keeney (see Keeney, 1987; Keeney and Silverstein, 1986) has provided an excellent therapeutic map for thinking about client resistance and problematic vicious cycles. Keeney looks at first-, second-, and third-order realities. First-order reality focuses on discrete behaviors/problems of individuals. Clients attempt to make change according to the first-order rules of the client system, which stipulate that problematic/symptomatic behaviors of individuals occur outside the interpersonal context of his or her relationships with significant others. Change within first-order reality can occur when clients are responding to only minor fluctuations in their psychosocial worlds. When demands on the client from the environment exceed her/his rules (cognitive schemas) the client and/or significant others will have to change the way they usually respond in order to experience problem resolution. To produce such a response will require going beyond first-order reality, thus allowing the problematic behavior to be considered within an interpersonal context (second-order reality).

Operating at the second-order level involves the clinician's realization that the client and his/her significant others are mutually affecting each other so that the problem is maintained. The clinician reframes the client's problem as possibly providing some "benefits" for both the client and the significant others. Sometimes, however, moving one's attention to the pattern, of behavior of the interpersonal context is not enough to effect change. When a stalemate occurs, it is necessary to situate the problematic patterns of behavior within the context of the patterns of the family of origin (*third-order reality*). The interactional patterns of the presenting problem are often parallel to interactional patterns and unresolved issues of the previous generations in the client's family of origin. Thus, there is a need to address change in the patterns by linking the client's presenting problem to his/her history within the family of origin as well as the history of those of the previous generations of the family of origin.

AN INTEGRATIVE MODEL FOR
TIME-LIMITED TREATMENT

The model of time-limited treatment discussed here is an integration of the pragmatics of the MRI approach, Keeney's extension of the MRI model, and dialectics. This model provides for both client problem solving and development (growth). This integrative approach employs an adaptation of the six steps of the MRI model (Nardone and Watzlawick, 1993):

1. Join the client system (establish a relationship).
2. Define the problem.
3. Identify the attempted solutions.
4. Define the goal.
5. Develop and implement a plan of intervention.
6. Termination.

Join the client system (Minuchin and Fishman, 1981). This is analogous to developing a therapeutic alliance (Hartley and Strupp, 1983) or a collaborative relationship (Beck et al., 1979). To join the system the therapist must demonstrate empathy, acceptance, support, genuineness, and leadership. Joining is enhanced when the therapist maintains a focus on the presenting problem and, at times, uses the client's language, metaphors, and figures of speech. Joining must continue throughout the course of treatment but is essential in the initial stages. This step is consistent with stage two of Roberts' model of crisis intervention, which involves establishing rapport and communication.

Stage four of Roberts' model is also an aspect of joining in that the clinician must deal with feelings and provide support in order to join and stay joined with the client system.

Define the problem. This gives the focus of time-limited treatment. The problem is defined by the client as concretely and specifically as possible in terms of who, what, where, when, and how. As can be seen, this step is consistent with stage three of Roberts' model of crisis intervention.

Identify the attempted solutions. Once the problem has been defined as concretely and specifically as possible, the therapist should elicit from the client what s/he and/or others tried in attempting to eliminate the problem. According to the MRI model, "the solution is the problem"; the attempted solutions are maintaining the problem. An emphasis in treatment then is to get clients and/or significant others to use different solutions in attempting to deal with the problem.

Define the goal. The goal follows from the problem and also comes from the client. Like the problem, it is important to define the goal as concretely and specifically as possible. The more concrete and specific the definition of the problem, the better one is able to define the goal concretely and specifically. Problem and goal definition are essential ingredients in the therapeutic contract (Greene, 1989) and provide the focus throughout the course of treatment.

Develop and implement a plan of intervention. The plan of intervention should follow from one's hypotheses about the dynamics of how the problem developed and is being maintained by the attempted solutions. Identifying the attempted solutions indicates what first-order interventions will not work and what second-order changes one might use or try to get the client to use. This step is somewhat different from stage six of Roberts' crisis intervention model. In crisis intervention the action plan usually consists of the clinician directing clients to carry out tasks. These tasks are of a first-order change nature. In this step of "developing and implementing a plan of intervention," the interventions would include requests for both first- and second-order change (a dialectical intervention).

Terminate. Many, if not most, clients have issues involving unresolved grief and incomplete mourning from previous loss. Termination of psychotherapy usually involves ending a relationship that has been important to the client. How the clinician handles termination impacts on the client's resolution of loss issues.

As much as possible, the problem, attempted solutions, and the goal should be identified by the end of the first or second session. Also during the first two or three sessions, it is very helpful to develop a multigenerational family *genogram* (McGoldrick and Gerson, 1985). The genogram provides the information about relevant *third-order reality* factors. In doing the genogram the following information is sought: Has anyone else in the extended family ever had at any time a similar problem? How did they get over the problem if they did? Who in the extended family has tried to help the client(s) with their problem? What advice has the client(s) received from others in the extended family? What help and/or advice has the client(s) found most useful? What losses and/or disruptions have the client and his/her family experienced in the recent and distant past such as death or serious illness of a family member, divorce, job loss, major relocation?

In obtaining information from clients and conducting interviews throughout the course of treatment, the clinician should use, as much as possible, open-ended questions in the Socratic fashion of "guided discovery" that is used in cognitive therapy (Freeman, et al., 1990). However, guided discovery should be expanded to include "circular" (see Fleuridas, Nelson, and Rosenthal, 1986; Penn, 1982) and "reflexive" questions (see Tomm, 1987) used in strategic and systemic therapies. Such questions have been found to be interventions themselves (Ferrier, 1986; Tomm and Lannamann, 1988).

It has been advocated that in sequencing interventions, one should initially start with a direct, first-order approach, and then, if this is not effective, switch to a more indirect, second-order one (Stanton, 1981). For example, Duncan, Rock, and Parks (1987) report that when clients do not respond positively to a cognitive-behavioral approach to stress management, they switch to a second-order approach based on the MRI model, then switch back to cognitive-behavioral interventions once some change has begun. In the spirit of dialectics, it is useful to make interventions that simultaneously address the first and second orders of reality and, when necessary, the third order, in the early and middle stages of treatment. Once the client(s) has begun to make some change, first-order interventions can be increasingly emphasized. It should be mentioned again that the focus throughout the course of treatment should be the problem and goal as defined by the client. As the clinician learns about family-of-origin/third-order reality variables, she or he may get sidetracked. However, the clinician should consistently hypothesize as to how these larger system variables impact on the presenting problem and goal.

In designing second-order interventions the MRI model states that they should be 180 degrees from the attempted solutions (Fisch,

Weakland, and Segal, 1982). There are numerous second-order interventions discussed in the literature (see Bergman, 1985; Fisch, Weakland, and Segal, 1982; Haley, 1987; Madanes, 1987; Watzlawick, Weakland, and Fisch, 1974), and, thus, they will not be presented here. In the integrative model discussed here, many of these second-order interventions are used as needed.

CLINICAL WORK WITH UNEMPLOYED CLIENTS

Employment provides several benefits to individuals: financial income, social networks, structure, and enhancement of self-esteem (Madonia, 1983). Losing one's job can be a major traumatic, stressful event in a person's life. Unemployment can have any number of consequences: depression, suicide, mental illness, poor mental health, marital discord, parent-child conflict, spouse and child abuse, physical ill health, and somatic and behavioral problems of children (Briar, 1988; Jones, 1991–92; Leana and Feldman, 1992; Pryor and Ward, 1985). Individuals who are unemployed for fifteen weeks or more or who lack financial resources to buffer the stress may have a particularly difficult time coping (Briar, 1988).

Searching for new employment usually takes considerable time, effort, and energy. Some unemployed people may seek ''unemployment counseling'' to help them find another job. Counselors may provide the following in working with the unemployed: empathic listening and acceptance; self-esteem counseling; stress management training; information on resources and programs; encouragement to do volunteer work; job-seeking and job-keeping skills training; ideas about alternative forms of employment; assertiveness skills training; modeling and role playing (Pryor and Ward, 1985); and cognitive restructuring (Briar, 1988).

The above interventions fit the category of ''first-order'' change and are beneficial to many people (Dowd and Pace, 1989). Individuals who are likely to benefit the most from these first-order interventions are those who already are the most self-sufficient (Pryor and Ward, 1985). Those individuals who are having the most difficulty coping are the least likely to seek professional help, and if they do, have a tendency to drop out prematurely (Pryor and Ward, 1985). These individuals, low in self-sufficiency, most likely are also very low in self-esteem and self-confidence and would thus tend to interpret first-order interventions as criticism and rejection (Briar, 1988).

As previously mentioned, when unemployed individuals come for professional therapeutic services their presenting problem(s) frequently is something other than unemployment, and they often do not attribute the presenting problem to their unemployment status. Presenting problems may include various somatic complaints, insomnia, marital problems, or a child's acting out (Briar, 1988). According to Briar (1988), "the abatement or stabilization of symptoms may be critical before long-term occupational needs can be addressed" (p. 81). To deal with the presenting problem and the problem of unemployment, dialectical interventions may be necessary.

The following will illustrate the use of dialectical interventions in the case of Joe Smith. As will be shown in the case of Joe Smith and in the case of Jan Jones that follows, these dialectical interventions are usually given at the end of a session in the form of a message or comment from the clinician to the client. The following information was obtained from Joe during the first interview.

Problem: Sleeping very poorly five out of seven nights a week. During those five nights he estimates he is able to sleep two to three hours each night. On the other two nights is able to sleep five to six hours. Joe states he cannot understand why he would have trouble sleeping since he has been able to sleep soundly for eight hours a night every night of his life.

Attempted Solutions: Joe reports that he has tried common remedies such as counting sheep, drinking warm milk before bedtime, and an occasional nonprescription sleeping pill. None of these seems to work. Sometimes he will stay in bed and toss and turn all night, but on most nights he will get up and watch television. Joe stays home and watches a lot of television on most days and he does drop off to sleep (takes short naps) during the day.

Goal: Joe states that he would like to sleep for at least seven hours a night for five nights of each week. He believes he could handle two sleepless nights if he were sleeping fairly well on the other five nights.

Joining was also used throughout the therapeutic work with Joe. Joining is a process and would require considerable verbatim dialogue to fully illustrate. Due to space limitations this process will not be illustrated here. For illustrative dialogue, see Minuchin and Fishman (1981) and Teyber (1992).

First-Order Reality

Joe's primary first-order reality concern was his sleep problem. There are several first-order interventions that could be used with this type of presenting problem, and some of them will be mentioned below. Second-order interventions can also be used with a first-order problem described as belonging only to the individual; this will be illustrated below.

During the first session the clinician listened to Joe's story, empathically responded to his distress regarding difficulty sleeping, and obtained Joe's definition of the problem, his attempts to solve the problem, and his goal definition. Joe reported that he does not think his insomnia is related to his unemployment; at this time he does not have any ideas as to the cause of the problem. At the end of the first session with Joe, the clinician used an intervention frequently used with many different types of clients.

> THERAPIST: Joe, our time is almost up for today. Between now and our next meeting I would suggest that it might be helpful for you to keep a written record—a journal or log of sorts—of exactly how much you sleep each night the exact times you sleep and the exact times you are awake, and what you are feeling, thinking, and doing when you are up in the middle of the night. This might provide you and me a better understanding of your sleep problem and what to do about it. Are you willing to do this?
>
> JOE: Yes, that doesn't sound too hard.
>
> THERAPIST: Also at this time, Joe, I want to suggest that you might want to "go slow" in changing. I know you are tired of the insomnia, but sometimes people, in their impatience, try to change too much too quickly. Trying to change too much too quickly can be a setup for failure and thus backfire. In fact, you might not want to try to make any changes for now. However, whether or not you do try to change is up to you. What do you think?
>
> JOE: Sounds OK. (pause). In fact, I'm kind of glad to hear you say that. I've been putting enough pressure on myself as it is.
>
> THERAPIST: OK. I'll see you next week.

This intervention at the end of the session suggests the *change* of keeping a written record, which is different from what he's been doing, as well as *stability* (restraint from change) in the form of the suggestion of "going slow" and "perhaps not trying to make any changes" at this point of the clinical process. The idea of going slow in change also reflects where many clients are at the beginning of treatment—ambivalent and anxious about change; it is "starting where the client is" (Goldstein, 1983). After being told to "go slow" in changing and/or "to not try to change anything for now," most clients verbally or nonverbally indicate relief that they are not being pressured to change immediately and possibly experience more failure and anxiety, regardless of the nature of the specific presenting problem.

Asking a client to keep a written record not only provides more data about the specific problem but also indicates how compliant or noncompliant a client might be. If a client tends to be noncompliant (oppositional) then she or he might resist by not keeping the written log and also by making some small positive changes in the presenting problem in reaction to the clinician's suggestion of "going slow" and "not making any changes for now" (Fisch, Weakland, and Segal, 1982).

At the beginning of the second session Joe indicated that he had not kept the written journal suggested in the first session. He states that sometimes he forgot to do it and when he did remember, he was just too "wound up" to sit down and write. Joe reported that he did have three nights of approximately five hours sleep but he thought this was just coincidental.

During this session Joe again indicated that he did not think his sleep difficulties had anything to do with being unemployed. He said that he did not like being unemployed, but he did not worry about getting another job. At the end of this session the clinician gave Joe the following message.

THERAPIST: Joe, our time is almost up for today. I want to take the last few minutes of the session and share with you some thoughts and reflections I have at this time about your situation. These thoughts and reflections can be considered as hypotheses or just educated guesses about your situation.

Joe, oftentimes people have problems sleeping when they are anxious and worried. It could be that your unemployment situation is bothering you more than you consciously realize. If this is the case, there are several things that could be done at this time to help you with your sleep problem such as relaxation training, meditation, yoga, regular exercise, not napping during the day, etc. It would be very tempting for me at this point to focus only on one or more of these routes. Another thought I have, and it is only food for thought, is that your insomnia symptoms might be occurring as a necessary prelude to some meaningful psychological and emotional change. Sometimes symptoms can be like symbols in dreams; that is, communication from one's unconscious mind. Many people believe that if they can interpret dream symbols they can learn a lot more about themselves and grow as a person. It could be that the insomnia is a type of symbolic communication from your unconscious. If this is the case then if you somehow got over your problem overnight then you would miss out on an opportunity to learn from your unconscious mind. I know this might sound a little weird and it may not be the case with you. What I am saying is just "food for thought" and you are the best judge of whether any of what I just said has any validity. If there is any validity to what I am saying, then you might not want to change too much too quickly for you would miss out on experiencing growth. Again, I want to emphasize that I am not saying this is true, only that it might be true; whether there is any truth to what I am saying can be determined only by you. What's your reaction to what I just said, Joe?

JOE: It is a little weird, but I think I see what you're saying. If nothing else, I will think about it.

By telling Joe about the techniques he could learn and use to help himself relax and increase the likelihood of sleeping, the clinician is suggesting to him the message of *change*. The positive reframing of his insomnia and the accompanying restraint for change messages suggest *stability*. For reframing to be successful the new definition has to be plausible. The reframe was not declarative and forced on him but just suggested as a possibility; it is up to Joe to determine the reframe's validity.

At the third session Joe reported that he was able to get five hours sleep for two nights and seven hours on a third night during the past week but he still wanted and needed more sleep than he was getting. He stated that he wasn't so sure about the insomnia as a prelude to growth and change, but he was becoming more concerned about his family's financial situation and getting another job. The clinician asked him what he was doing in regard to his job search activities and he reported that he was doing about the same as he has been doing for the past three months. Upon further questioning Joe stated that right before and after he was laid off he did have three sessions at an employee assistance program (EAP) on stress management and job searching skills. However, Joe said he just did not have the energy to do all that he learned at the EAP. During this session the following interaction occurred:

THERAPIST: Joe, how is your wife Sue handling what you're going through?

JOE: At first after I was laid off she was somewhat supportive, however, for several weeks and months she has really been on my case about my not doing enough to find a job. She has been especially hard on me since I started having problems sleeping. She thinks that I should just work harder at looking for a job or look for a job outside appliance sales and then I would start sleeping OK once I had another job. These days I just get either a lot of angry criticism from her or the slow-burn, silent treatment.

THERAPIST: How do you respond to her anger, criticism, and withdrawal?

JOE: I tell her that without enough sleep I don't have the energy I need for an all-out job search. Some days I feel that she's right and I will try harder for a day or so but then I back off again. . . . . Sue just doesn't know how hard it is and what I'm going through.

THERAPIST: How would you feel about Sue coming with you for the next session?

JOE: That would be OK with me but I don't think Sue will go for it. I will ask her though.

Sue did not come with Joe for the next session. Joe stated he did ask her to come but, according to him, she refused claiming that his sleep problem and unemployment were his problems and did not involve her. During the discussion Joe stated that Sue has been more temperamental and difficult to communicate with ever since her father died two years ago. It was at this point that the clinician decided that an intervention involving second-order reality was needed.

Second-Order Reality

Involuntary unemployment is a major loss and can precipitate feelings of grief in both the unemployed person and his/her significant other (Briar, 1988; Krystal et al., 1983; Madonia, 1983; Shelton, 1985). A person and/or the significant others can have a particularly difficult time coping with the losses, such as unemployment or divorce, if they have not completed the grief work over previous losses in their lives, especially the death of a family member (Walsh and McGoldrick, 1991; Worden, 1991).

Death in the family is a painful loss experience for the survivors. The grieving process takes time but most people are able to get through it without professional services. Some people do seek professional services after the death of a family member for the explicit purpose of completing the grief work. Others become "stuck in the grieving process" when they consciously and/or unconsciously cut off their painful feelings and thus the working through is incomplete. A reaction such as this is referred to as "masked grief" and can lead to the development of various physical, psychological and/or behavioral problems that can be used further to avoid grief (Worden, 1991).

Some brief therapy approaches acknowledge the importance of unresolved grief in problem/symptom formation and thus as focus for therapy (Budman and Gurman, 1988; Horowitz et al., 1984; Klerman et al., 1984) but most do not. The approaches of Budman and Gurman (1988), Horowitz, et al. (1984), and Klerman et al. assume that the client acknowledges the unresolved grief as a problem or is willing to if this connection is made for him/her by the therapist. There are situations, however, when the client is not ready to "unmask" the grief or the person in the family who has the masked grief is someone other than the client with the presenting problem. A spouse's grief at the loss of an important family member that is not acknowledged and dealt with may result in marital problems (Walsh and McGoldrick, 1991). For the unemployed client to get motivated again for the job search, the unresolved grief of the client's significant other must somehow enter into the therapeutic disclosure.

THERAPIST: How much have you and Sue talked together about her and your feelings over her father's death?

JOE: Really almost none at all. Neither one of us comes from families that talk about their feelings. Sue did say that she didn't think I was supportive of her and there for her during the last few months of her father's life and during the funeral, but I tried the best I could.

THERAPIST: So how do you feel about the death of Sue's father?

JOE: He and I weren't very close; we didn't have much in common. He didn't want me and Sue to get married in the first place. He and I got along OK but I don't think he ever stopped resenting me. But don't get me wrong, I'm sorry he died especially knowing how close he and Sue were.

THERAPIST: And how has Sue been handling her father's death?

JOE: She cried a little when he died, but during the funeral and since she has kept her feelings to herself. I could tell that his death really tore her up and even now she won't talk about him. The few times I or someone else has mentioned her father she gets real teary-eyed and changes the subject. She stays busier than ever. She works a lot at the nursing home and at our own home it seems like she does more housework than ever. She's also pissed at me all the time for not doing more housework myself since I'm unemployed and have time on my hands.

THERAPIST: Again, Joe, with the few minutes remaining I'd like to share with you some thoughts I have about your situation. On one hand, we could spend time together following up and working on what you

181

learned at the EAP about stress reduction and job searching skills. On the other hand I'm aware of what's been going on between you and Sue, especially in light of her father's death. What I'm getting at is that the two of you are angry at each other on a fairly continuous basis. It could be that your anger is somehow helping each other deal with sadness and depression. By having problems sleeping and not doing your job search in the way Sue thinks you should, you give her a reason to be angry rather than depressed about her father's death. I know that you haven't said anything about being depressed, but people who are unemployeed and having trouble finding a job frequently get depressed, and sleep problems can also be due to depression. Now I don't want to put any ideas in your head about getting depressed if you're not. Sue does know you a lot better than I do and she may be worried about you being or getting depressed. If that's the case, it may be that she is on you a lot about the job search and your insufficient housekeeping as a way to get you angry rather than depressed.

I have a theory about anger and depression in relationships. Sometimes I think people would rather have their loved ones angry at them than to see their loved ones depressed. People can become incapacitated by depression whereas when they are angry they are activated. When two people have been together for sometime they become very sensitive to each other's shifting moods almost instinctively. So when one spouse is worried that the other one is depressed or might be on the verge of getting depressed they sometimes might do or say something to get the other one angry at them. When this occurs the person is not consciously deciding to do this but rather is reponding to their unconscious sensitivity to their mate's changing moods. I'm not saying this is the case with you and Sue but I am just speculating. Again, this is just food for thought for you. If there is any truth to this theory of mine, then you might not want to change for now until you feel assured somehow that Sue no longer needs you to protect her from her grief and sadness. On the other hand, Sue might not want to change until she is assured that you are not going to become incapacitated by depression over being unemployed. Again, this may sound a little weird but it is just something for you to think about in deciding what we work on in our sessions together.

In dealing with couples' issues it is best to develop reframes that suggest mutual protection. The mutuality of the couple's situation equalizes the blame. If one spouse feels more blamed than the other then s/he may become noncompliant and sabotage treatment. The reframe of mutuality suggests the notion that their problematic situation is something that they created together and to resolve it they must both make some changes.

In the next session, Sue did accompany Joe. Sue reported that Joe did talk to her some about what the clinician said at the end of our last session, and she was curious to know more about what the clinician thought. The rest of the session was spent talking about their issues of loss, depression, and anger. Also during this session the clinician discussed with them some specific ways they could do grief work (Imber-Black, 1991; Lamb, 1988; Rubin; 1985; Whitaker, 1985; Worden, 1991). At the end of the session, the clinician pointed out that they could do some specific activities between sessions regarding the grief work and again cautioned them about trying to change too much too soon, but left it up to them to decide what they would do.

The next several sessions were spent on dealing with grief more actively and directly than before. The grief work focused on both Sue's and Joe's grief regarding her father's death and Joe's grief regarding the loss of his job. In addition, time was spent in the sessions on enhancing communication and problem-solving skills within the marital relationship. Within two weeks after Sue started coming to the sessions, Joe no longer considered himself as having a sleep problem. In addition, he started using the stress management and job seeking skills he had learned. He did not find a job as quickly as he wanted but he was back to very actively searching for a job.

Third-Order Reality

Another possible consequence of unemployment is the acting-out behavior problems of children and adolescents (Briar, 1988; Krystal et al., 1983; Madonia, 1983; Moran-Sackett and Thompson, 1983). These types of problems can be exacerbated by a parent's unresolved grief over the death of one of their parents, the grandparent of the problematic child or adolescent (Walsh and McGoldrick, 1991; Worden, 1991). Research has found that the death of a grandparent within two years of the birth of a child may be an important contributing factor to that child later developing emotional problems (Mueller and McGoldrick Orfandis, 1976; Walsh, 1978). Death in the family and unresolved grief have also been found in a high proportion of drug addiction cases (Coleman, 1991). In addition, some children and adolescents may begin engaging in problematic behavior at an age that is the same as or similar to the age of a parent when she or he (the parent) experienced the death of one of the parents or other significant family members (McGoldrick and Walsh, 1991).

A person can also have a delayed grief reaction years after the death of a family member. A delayed grief reaction can manifest itself through any of the various problems mentioned above and can be precipitated by some type of recent loss such as a job, and/or when the person reaches the age the family member was at the time of death (Walsh and McGoldrick, 1991; Worden, 1991).

THE CASE OF JAN JONES

Jan Jones was the thirty-seven-year-old single parent of Bob, age thirteen. Jan had been employed as a line worker in a unionized factory but was permanently laid off four months ago. Jan was seeking treatment for Bob, who was suspended from school for three days for swearing at and threatening a teacher. The following information was obtained regarding the situation with Bob.

> *Problem*: Bob's behavior is out of control. Jan states that for the past three months Bob has been failing almost all his subjects, getting an occasional "D." Though Bob had never been an outstanding student, he had always shown a special interest in school and made average grades. During the past two months Bob has been getting detentions at school at least three to four times a week. In addition, Jan states that Bob has been sneaking out of the apartment and staying out most of the night almost every weekend night and occasionally during the week for the past four weeks.

> *Attempted Solutions*: Jan stated that she has tried lecturing and yelling at Bob, grounding him, and taking away privileges, but nothing seems to work. She reported that she knows she has not been consistent with him, but with being unemployed and depressed she just hasn't had the energy to always follow through on discipline. Jan also stated that she would have much more energy for job searching if Bob would just start behaving himself.

> *Goal:* Bob is to (1) completely stop sneaking out at night; (2) get no more than one detention per week, and preferably none; (3) bring his grades up to at least a "C" average.

In the first two sessions the clinician focused on joining and contracting with Jan and Bob as well as completing a multigenerational genogram. During this time Bob was not very verbal or cooperative, and Jan was very willing to provide the relevant information. Jan thought Bob was just going through a phase that young people experience and that he would eventually get over it; however, the school suspension helped her realize that it was more than this. The clinician asked Jan if she or anyone else in the family had such school problems when they were young. Jan reported that she had some school and behavior problems when she was about Bob's age but did eventually get over them. The clinician then asked Jan if there had been any major events, changes, or losses in her family about the time that Bob had started having school problems. In a flat but halting manner Jan reported that her father had committed suicide when she was about thirteen years old; her father was about thirty-six years old at the time. Jan's father apparently shot himself in the middle of the night. Her parents had had a major argument, and her mother took her (Jan was an only child) to her grandparents' house late at night. In addition to strains in the marriage of Jan's parents, her father had been depressed over a failing business and heavy debts. As she was telling this story her eyes became slightly teary. The clinician asked her how she was feeling about her father's suicide and she replied that she did not have any problems about it. She stated further that right after her father's death she was told that ''she was too old to cry,'' no one talked about her father's death again, and rarely over the years did anyone ever mention her father. Currently, Jan only sees or talks to her mother occasionally and rarely has contact with any other family members.

Also during the first three sessions the clinician discussed with Jan what specific steps she taken has or could take to successfully deal with Bob's problematic behaviors. It turned out that she had taken a course on parenting skills at her church approximately four years ago. She said she knew what to do but usually did not have the energy to follow through the way she knew she could. She stated further that if she had a job she would have more energy, but Bob's problems drain her of the energy she needs for job hunting. The discussions around what could be done to deal with Bob's behavior were done in a Socratic/reflexive fashion advocated by Goolishian and Anderson (1987) and Goolishian and Winderman (1988), whereby solutions to problems are ''discovered'' by the client rather than provided by the therapist. At the end of the third session, the clinician gave Jan and Bob the following message:

THERAPIST: We've had three meetings together now, and so I'd like to share with you some thoughts I have about your situation.

On one hand, Jan, we could spend our time focusing on improving your job seeking skills and/or your consistent use of all that is involved with parenting skills such as limit setting, use of consequences and discipline, problem solving, and communication between the two of you. You already know a lot about these skills so it may be just a matter of practice on your part and support from me.

On the other hand, it may not be that simple. Something that sometimes happens in families is that a child develops a problem about the same age that a parent was when the parent experienced a major loss. From what you said, Jan, you were thirteen years old when your father died; this is the same age as Bob. Another possible factor is that you are close to the same age as your father when he died. Sometimes people have delayed grief reactions that are stirred up, frequently outside conscious awareness, when they reach an age close to that of their family member when he or she died. Also these delayed grief reactions can be stirred up by a recent loss such as a job. It is natural to experience some depression when laid off from a job; however, the depression can be magnified by delayed grief reactions. It could be that at least part of what is going on with Bob is related to these issues of loss. Sometimes the problematic behavior of children and teenagers can develop as a way to help a parent deal with depression. That is, children and adolescents would rather have their parents angry at them instead of depressed about something else. When this happens, I don't think the adolescent consciously decides to do so but rather is just very sensitive to the parent's moods. I am not saying this is the case with the two of you but it is a possibility to consider.

Another possible factor here is Bob is the same age you were, Jan, when your father died. You mentioned how no one would talk about your father much after he died. Consequently, it would be very difficult for you to deal with your grief. It could be that by exhibiting problems similar to what you had when you were his age, Bob is trying to keep this issue of your father's death and your grief alive, so to speak, as a way to help you deal with it once and for all. Again, if there is any validity to what I am saying, Bob most likely would not be doing this consciously but out of unconscious awareness of unresolved family losses and issues.

Again I am not saying that is true in your case but it is just a possibility; this is just food for thought. Of these possibilities, all could be true, one could be true, or none could be true. It is up to you to determine this. If there is any truth to any of this, then both of you may want to go slow about making changes. If there is any truth to this, then, Bob, you may not want to make any radical changes until you are sure that your mother no longer needs your help in dealing with her depression and grief. I know this all may sound a little weird but it is just food for thought.

Jan and Bob listened intently to this message. They said the message was interesting and they would think it over. This message dealt with first-, second-, and third-order realities. The discussion about the specifics of parenting operated at the first-order level. The discussion about Bob helping/protecting Jan with her depression by provoking her to anger dealt with the second-order level. Third-order reality was addressed by mentioning the possibility of Bob's behavior keeping the issue of unresolved grief alive in order to help her grief work.

At the next session Jan and Bob stated that they wanted to know more about how to deal with grief. For the next three sessions the focus was on grief work, and the clients engaged in activities between sessions to facilitate this. Over these next three sessions Bob's behavior began to improve as did Jan's depression and consistency in parenting. For three sessions after that the therapy focused some more on their relationship and Jan's unemployment. Jan did not find another factory job but did begin a job training program to help her upgrade her skills.

In the cases presented here, the process of *termination* will not be discussed due to limited space. See Kramer (1990) and Kupers (1988) for in-depth discussions of this treatment issue.

DISCUSSION

This chapter has discussed a model of working with clients that combines the use of direct and indirect interventions that can be used with client problems at the individual, interpersonal, and/or family of origin levels. The direct and indirect interventions are structured so that the request by the therapist for *stability* and *change* by the client system are communicated simultaneously. Out of this *dialectic* between stability and change, novelty is introduced into the client system, which results in some disequilibrium and crisis. The client system accommodates to this novelty, resulting in growth and change (synthesis). This dialectical process is necessary for human development, and psychotherapy should enhance one's development (Ivey, 1986).

Some of the novelty introduced into the client system is provided by the positive reframing of problems and the suggestions that result in restraint from change. One key reframe is that the problem/symptom might "help" or "protect" another family member. The idea that people develop symptoms and problems to help or protect a mate or another family member has been discussed in the literature (Allen, 1988; Jackson and Haley, 1968; Keeney, Ross and Silverstein, 1983; Selvini-Palazolli et al., 1978). This reframe of "protection" and the wisdom of the restraint from change—of "not changing for now"—must be plausible for them to be effective. The clinician should genuinely believe in the plausibility of these messages; she or he should not make something up just to try to trick the client into changing. Making up messages the clinician does not believe to be plausible goes against therapeutic *genuineness*, which the client will sense.

The integrative approach here is also consistent with a *constructivist* approach to therapy. The constructivist approach stipulates that systems are self-organizing and thus cannot be made to change in a specific direction by an outside agent. Therefore, all the therapist can do in working with a client system is "give it a bump and watch it jump" (Hoffman, 1985, p. 388). The "bump" is provided by the novelty introduced into the client system. This novelty then "perturbs" the system so that its response will result in a new organization that does not contain the problem (Goolishian and Winderman, 1988; Hoffman, 1988). An intervention will provide novelty to a client system, and thus perturb it, when it causes clients to call into question their assumptions (interpretations and definitions) about the world or a certain part of the world (Goolishian and Winderman, 1988; Dowd and Pace, 1989; Ivey, 1986; Levine and Lightburn, 1989).

A constructivist approach to therapy posits that the therapist does not change the client system from the outside, but rather, she or he must join with the clients to create a new "therapeutic system." Within the therapeutic system the clinician and client work together to "co-construct" a new reality that does not contain the problem. In order for co-construction to occur, the therapeutic relationship must be as collaborative and nonhierarchical as possible between the therapist and client. The therapist's job is to introduce novelty into the system, and the client's job is to decide how to respond to it. Such a collaborative and nonhierarchical relationship fosters client self-determination and empowerment. By providing clients some suggestions and hypotheses and advocating for none, the integrative approach discussed here allows the client to make his/her own interpretations and changes. Consequently, the changes are owned by the client, resulting in the client feeling more empowered.

The approach discussed here introduces novelty into the client system fairly early in treatment and in varying degrees. This process should result in enough disequilibrium and crisis to "loosen up" the client's schemas (the rules of the system). This loosening up can be done in the first few sessions, and then the client will be more open and cooperative with direct, first-order interventions and treatment can be accelerated. Again, these direct, first-order interventions are not forced on the client but rather introduced to him or her to try on for size.

The need to loosen up the cognitive schemas/rules is especially important with noncompliant clients. A person who has experienced involuntary job loss is often unmotivated and noncompliant with treatment when he or she has masked or delayed grief. Masked or delayed grief can exacerbate the grief from and the inability to cope with unemployment.

As mentioned earlier, the resolution of the presenting problem may have to be accomplished before the issue of unemployment can be addressed (Briar, 1988). The integrative model discussed here posits that in order for problem resolution to occur, the unresolved grief must also be addressed. The integrative dialectical-pragmatic model presented in this chapter does provide for both resolution of the presenting problem as well as ''healing'' of unresolved family-of- origin issues (developmental and growth). Both resolution of the presenting problem and development (healing) often need to be addressed in order for time-limited treatment to be effective. This dual focus applies not only to problems of unemployment but to other problem areas as well.

CONCLUSION

There are a number of approaches to time-limited treatment, and many of them emphasize carefully selecting only those clients deemed appropriate. In today's climate of managed health care and mandated time-limited treatment, practitioners increasingly cannot afford the luxury of screening clients. Clinicians need to have a model for time-limited treatment that will be appropriate for difficult, unmotivated clients as well as compliant and motivated ones. Clients who are unemployed often fall in this first category. Many people who become unemployed do not initially see this as a crisis. For those who do experience unemployment as a crisis, the use of Roberts' model of crisis intervention is indicated. Many other unemployed clients do not come to the attention of a professional clinician until they begin to experience various emotional, somatic, and family problems that they do not attribute to their unemployment. When this is the case, these clients frequently do not respond to direct methods of treatment that focus only on dealing with the unemployment; this usually results in a therapeutic impasse.

This chapter presents an approach to time-limited treatment that is an integration of the pragmatics of the Mental Research Institute (MRI) Model, Keeney's extension of the MRI Model, and dialectics, which allows for considering the multitude of factors contributing to a therapeutic impasse: treatment plans and interventions need to take into consideration these multiple factors. This integrative dialectical–

pragmatic approach is not meant to be a recipe that is applied to every type of client problem but rather a way of thinking and organizing interventions, especially when clinicians experience a therapeutic impasse. To use this approach effectively requires very sound clinical skills; beyond this, clinicians are limited only by their creativity.

REFERENCES

Allen, D.M. (1988). *Unifying individual and family therapies*. San Francisco, CA: Jossey-Bass.

Beck, A.T., Rush, A.J., Shaw, B.F., and Emery, G. (1979). *Cognitive therapy of depression*. New York: Guilford.

Bergman, J.S. (1985). *Fishing for barracuda: Pragmatics of brief systemic therapy*. New York: Norton.

Briar, K.H. (1988). *Social work and the unemployed*. Silver Spring, MD: National Association of Social Workers.

Budman, S.H., and Gurman, A.S. (1988). *Theory and practice of brief therapy*. New York: Guilford.

Castelnuovo-Tedesco, P. (1966). Brief psychotherapeutic treatment of depressive reactions. In G.J. Wayne and R.R. Koegler (Eds.), *Emergency psychiatry and brief therapy*. Boston, MA: Little, Brown.

Coleman, S.B. (1991). Intergenerational patterns of traumatic loss: Death and despair in addict families. In F. Walsh and M. McGoldrick (Eds.), *Living beyond loss: Death in the family* (pp. 260–272). New York: Norton.

Dell, P. (1981). Some irreverent thoughts on paradox. *Family Process, 20,* 37–41.

Dowd, E.T., and Pace, T.M. (1989). The relativity of reality: Second-order change in psychotherapy. In A. Freeman, K.M. Simon, L.E. Beutler, and H. Arkowitz (Eds.). *Comprehensive handbook of cognitive therapy* (pp. 213–226). New York: Plenum Press.

Duncan, B.L., Rock, J.W., and Parks, M.B. (1987). Strategic-behavioral therapy: A practical alternative. *Psychotherapy, 24,* 196–201.

Epting, F. R. (1984). *Personal construct counseling and psychotherapy*. New York: Wiley.

Ewing, C.P. (1990). Crisis intervention as brief psychotherapy. In R.A. Wells and V.J. Gianetti (Eds.), *Handbook of the brief psychotherapies* (pp. 277–294). New York: Plenum Press.

Ferrier, M.J. (1986). Circular methods/indirect methods: The interview as an indirect technique. In S. deShazer and R. Kral (Eds.), *Indirect approaches in therapy*. Rockville, MD: Apen.

Fisch, R., Weakland, J.H., and Segal, L. (1982). *The tactics of change: Doing therapy briefly*. San Francisco, CA: Jossey-Bass.

Fleuridas, C., Nelson, T., and Rosenthal, D.M. (1986). The evolution of circular questions: Training family therapists. *Journal of Marital and Family Therapy, 12*, 113–128.

Freeman, A., Pretzer, J., Fleming, B., and Simon, K.M. (1990). *Clinical applications of cognitive therapy.* New York: Plenum Press.

Garfield, S.L. (1986). Research on client variables in psychotherapy. In S.L. Garfield and A.E. Bergin (Eds.), *Handbook of psychotherapy and behavior change* (3d ed., pp. 213–256). New York: Wiley.

————— (1989). *The practice of brief psychotherapy.* New York: Pergamon Press.

Goldstein, H. (1983). Starting where the client is. *Social Casework, 64*, 267–275.

Gomes-Schwartz, B. (1978). Effective ingredients in psychotherapy: Prediction of outcome from process variables. *Journal of Consulting and Clinical Psychology, 46*, 1023–1035.

Goolishian, H.A., and Anderson, H. (1987). Language systems and therapy: An evolving idea. *Psychotherapy, 24*, 529–538.

Goolishian, H.A., and Winderman, L. (1988). Constructivism, autopsies and problem determined systems. *The Irish Journal of Psychology, 9*, 130–143.

Greene, G.J. (1989). Using the written contract for evaluating and enhancing practice effectiveness. *Journal of Independent Social Work, 4*, 135–155.

Greene, G.J., and Sattin, D.B. (1985). A paradoxical treatment format for anxiety-related somatic complaints: Four case studies. *Family Systems Medicine, 3*, 197–204.

Gurman, A.S. (1981). Integrative marital therapy: Toward the development of an interpersonal approach. In S.H. Budman (Ed.), *Forms of brief therapy* (pp. 415–460). New York: Guilford.

Haley, J. (1987). *Problem-solving therapy* (2d ed.). San Francisco, CA: Jossey-Bass.

Hoffman, L. (1985). Beyond power and control: Toward a "second order" family systems therapy. *Family Systems Medicine, 4*, 381–396.

————— (1988). A constructivist position for family therapy. *The Irish Journal of Psychology, 9*, 110–129.

Horowitz, M., Marmar, C., Krupnick, J., Wilner, N., Kaltreider, N., and Wallerstein, R. (1984). *Personality styles and brief psychotherapy.* New York: Basic Books.

Imber-Black, E. (1991). Rituals and the healing process. In F. Walsh and M. McGoldrick (Eds.), *Living beyond loss: Death in the family* (pp. 207–223). New York: Norton.

Ivey, A.E. (1986). *Developmental therapy.* San Francisco, CA: Jossey-Bass.

Jackson, D.D., and Haley, J. (1968). Transference revisited. In D.D. Jackson (Ed.), *Therapy, communication, and change: Human communication, Vol. 2.* Palo Alto, CA: Science and Behavior Books.

Jones, L. (1991–92). Specifying the temporal relationship between job loss and consequences: Implications for service delivery. *Journal of Applied Social Sciences, 16*, 37–62.

Keeney, B.P. (1987). The construction of therapeutic realities. *Psychotherapy, 24*, 469–476.

Keeney, B.P., and Ross, J.M. (1985). *Mind in therapy: Constructing systemic family therapies.* New York: Basic Books.

Keeney, B.P., and Siegal, S. (1986). The use of multiple communication in systemic couples therapy. *American Journal of Family Therapy, 14,* 69–79.

Keeney, B.P., and Silverstein, O. (1986). *The therapeutic voice of Olga Silverstein.* New York: Guilford.

Keeney, B., Ross, J., and Silverstein, O. (1983). Mind in bodies: The treatment of a family presenting a migraine headache. *Family Systems Medicine, 1,* 61–77.

Klerman, G.L., Weisman, M.M., Rounsaville, B.J., and Chevron, E.S. (1984). *Interpersonal psychotherapy of depression.* New York: Basic Books.

Koss, M.P. (1979). Length of psychotherapy for clients seen in private practice. *Journal of Consulting and Clinical Psychology, 47,* 210–212.

Koss, M.P. and Butcher, J.N. (1986). Research on brief psychotherapy. In S.L. Garfield and A.E. Bergin (Eds.), *Handbook of psychotherapy and behavior change* (pp. 627–670). New York: Wiley.

Kramer, S.A. (1990). *Positive endings in psychotherapy.* San Francisco, CA: Jossey-Bass.

Krystal, E., Moran-Sackett, M., Thompson, S.V., and Cantoni, L. (1983). Serving the unemployed. *Social Casework,* Feb., 67–76.

Kupers, T.A. (1988). *Ending therapy: The meanings of termination.* New York: New York University Press.

Lamb, D.H. (1988). Loss and grief: psychotherapy strategies and interventions. *Psychotherapy, 25,* 561–569.

Lazarus, A.A. and Fay, A. (1982). Resistance or rationalization? A cognitive behavioral perspective. In P.L. Wachtel (Ed.), *Resistance: Psychodynamic and behavioral approaches* (pp. 115–32). New York: Plenum Press.

Leana, C.R. and Feldman, D.C. (1992). *Coping with job loss.* New York: Lexington Books.

Lehman, A.K. and Salovey, P. (1990). An introduction to cognitive-behavioral therapy. In R.A. Wells and V.J. Gianetti (Eds.), *Handbook of the brief psychotherapies* (pp. 239–260). New York: Plenum Press.

Levine, K.G. and Lightburn, A. (1989). Belief systems and social work practice. *Social Casework,* March, 139–145.

Liddle, H.A. (1984). Toward a dialectical-contextual-coevolutionary translation of structural- strategic family therapy. *Journal of Strategic and Systemic Therapies, 4,* 66–79.

Madanes, C. (1981). *Strategic family therapy.* San Francisco, CA: Jossey-Bass.

———— (1987). *Behind the one-way mirror: Advances in the practice of strategic therapy.* San Francisco, CA: Jossey-Bass.

Madonia, J.F. (1983). The trauma of unemployment and its consequences. *Social Casework,* Oct., 482–488.

Malan, D.H. (1976). *The frontiers of brief psychotherapy: An example of the convergence of research and clinical practice.* New York: Plenum.

Mann, J. (1973). *Time-limited psychotherapy*. Cambridge, MA: Harvard University Press.

Marmor, J. (1979). Short-term psychotherapy. *American Journal of Psychiatry, 136*, 149–155.

McGoldrick, M., and Gerson, R. (1985). *Genograms in family assessment*. New York: Norton.

McGoldrick, M., and Walsh, F. (1991). A time to mourn: Death and the family life cycle. In F. Walsh and M. McGoldrick (Eds.), *Living beyond loss: Death in the family* (pp. 30–49). New York: Norton.

Minuchin, S., and Fishman, H.C. (1981). *Family therapy techniques*. Cambridge, MA: Harvard University Press.

Moretti, M.M., Feldman, L.A., and Shaw, B.F. (1990). Cognitive therapy: Current issues in theory and practice. In R.A. Wells and V.J. Gianetti (Eds.), *Handbook of the brief psychotherapies* (pp. 217–238). New York: Plenum Press.

Mueller, P.S. and McGoldrick Orfandis (1976). A method of co-therapy for schizophrenic families. *Family Process, 15*, 179–192.

Mullin, R.E. (1986). *Handbook of cognitive therapy techniques*. New York: Norton.

Nardone, G. and Watzlawick, P. (1993). *The art of change: Strategic therapy and hypnotherapy without trance*. San Francisco, CA: Jossey-Bass.

Omer, H. (1991). Dialectical interventions and the structure of strategy. *Psychotherapy, 28*, 563–571.

Parad, H.J. and Parad, L.G. (1990). Crisis intervention: An introductory overview. In H.J. Parad and L.G. Parad (Eds.), *Crisis intervention book 2: The practitioner's sourcebook for brief therapy* (pp. 3–66). Milwaukee, WI: Family Service America.

Penn, P. (1982). Circular questioning. *Family Process, 21*, 267–280.

Pryor, R. and Ward, R. (1985). Unemployment: What counselors can do about it. *Journal of Employment Counseling*, March, 3–17.

Reigel, K. (1976). The dialectics of human development. *American Psychologist, 31*, 686–700.

Roberts, A.R. (1991). Conceptualizing crisis theory and the crisis intervention model. In A.R. Roberts (Ed.), *Contemporary perspectives on crisis intervention and prevention* (pp. 3–17). Englewood Cliffs, NJ: Prentice-Hall.

Rohrbaugh, M., Tennen, H., Press, S., and White, L. (1981). Compliance, defiance and therapeutic paradox: Guidelines for strategic use of paradoxical interventions. *American Journal of Orthopsychiatry, 51*, 454–467.

Rubin, S.S. (1985). The resolution of bereavement: A clinical focus on the relationship to the deceased. *Psychotherapy. 22*, 231–235.

Selvini-Palazolli, M., Cecchin, G., Prata, G., and Boscolo, L. (1978). *Paradox and counterparadox*. New York: Jason Aronson.

Shelton, B.K. (1985). The social and psychological impact of unemployment. *Journal of Employment Counseling*, March, 1985.

Sifneos, P.E. (1978). *Short-term anxiety-provoking psychotherapy: A treatment manual.* New York: Basic Books.

Silver, R.J. (1982). Brief dynamic psychotherapy: A critical look at the state of the art. *Psychiatric Quarterly, 53,* 275–282.

Stanton, M.D. (1981). An integrated structural/strategic approach to family therapy. *Journal of Marital and Family Therapy, 7,* 427–439.

Strupp, H.H. and Binder, J.L. (1984). *Psychotherapy in a new key: A guide to time-limited dynamic psychotherapy.* New York: Basic Books.

Strupp, H.H. and Hadley, S.W. (1979) Specific versus nonspecific factors in psychotherapy: A controlled study of outcome. *Archives of General Psychiatry, 36,* 1125–1136.

Taube, C.A., Burns, B.J., and Kessler, L. (1984). Patients of psychiatrists and psychologists in office-based practice: 1980. *American psychiatrist, 39,* 1435–1447.

Teyber, E. (1992). *Interpersonal process in psychotherapy: A guide for clinical training* (2d ed.). Monterey, CA: Brooks/Cole.

Tomm, K. (1987). Interventive interviewing: Part II. Reflexive questioning as a means to enable self healing. *Family Process, 26,* 167–183.

Tomm, K., and Lannamann, J. (1988). Questions as intervention. *Family Therapy Networker,* Sept./Oct., 38–41.

Walsh, F. (1978). Concurrent grandparent death and birth of schizophrenic offspring: An intriguing finding. *Family Process, 17,* 457–463.

Walsh, F., and McGoldrick, M. (1991). *Living beyond loss: Death in the family.* New York: Norton.

Walter, J.L., and Peller, J.E. (1992). *Becoming solution-focused in brief therapy.* New York: Brunner/Mazel.

Watzlawick, P., Weakland, J.H., and Fisch, R. (1974). *Change: Principles of problem formation and problem resolution.* New York: Norton.

Weeks, G.R. (1977). Toward a dialectical approach to intervention. *Human Development, 20,* 277–292.

Westerman, M.A., Frankel, A.S., Tanaka, J.S., and Kahn, J. (1987). Client cooperative interview behavior and outcome in paradoxical and behavioral brief treatment approaches. *Journal of Counseling Psychology, 34,* 99–102.

Whitaker, L.C. (1985). Visiting the parental grave in psychotherapy. *Psychotherapy, 22,* 241–247.

Wilson, G.T. (1981). Behavior therapy as a short-term therapeutic approach. In S.H. Budman (Ed.), *Forms of brief therapy* (pp. 131–166). New York: Guilford.

Wolberg, L.R. (Ed.). (1965b). *Short-term psychotherapy.* New York: Grune and Stratton.

Worden, J.W. (1991). *Grief counseling and grief therapy: A handbook for the mental health practitioner* (2d ed.). New York: Springer.

CHAPTER 10

Crisis Assessment and Intervention with the Alcoholic Client: The Dilemma of Involuntariness

KATHRYN G. WAMBACH

Ralph is a forty-six-year-old alcoholic and drinks an average of two six-packs of beer and a pint of whiskey daily. For the past decade, he has experienced numerous losses of employment and three divorces associated with his drinking. While he has been in treatment for drinking several times, he had not maintained more than three weeks sobriety until the past year. With the support of his new wife (also a recovering alcoholic), Ralph has been attending Alcoholics Anonymous and working regularly for nearly eleven months. During a recent medical evaluation, he was told that his liver function was minimal and that any continued drinking would put his life in jeopardy.

After this incident, Ralph experienced an intensification of his craving for alcohol and, after several weeks of struggle, began to drink again. When his new wife discovered his lapse, she left immediately, commenting that she did not wish "to watch his death." Two days later, Ralph called a crisis hotline, angrily denouncing his wife's "desertion" and asking the worker to "give me just one reason to go on living."

Frank is twenty-eight years old and married. He and his wife are expecting their first child. As a construction worker, he drinks daily "with the boys" and views this activity as necessary in handling the stress of his job. He also likes to drink at home "to wind down" and in social situations "to have fun." He has viewed his wife's expressed concern about his drinking as "paranoia" because she grew up with an alcoholic father. He cites his job stability and the fact that he "just drinks, not gets drunk" in arguments with his wife. He has recently incurred his second DWI conviction (which he refers to as "bad luck") and has been ordered to "get treatment" as part of his probation for this offense. He calls the crisis hotline asking for a referral after his probation officer threatens to inform the court that he has not entered treatment.

Marcia is thirty-three years old. She had taught fifth grade for ten years when she married. She and her husband (age thirty-six) wanted to start a family immediately and agreed that she would quit working while their children were at home. Marcia found it difficult to adjust to being a "housewife." She began drinking with friends during "getaways" they arranged by rotating child care; later, she found that "a little wine cooler" helped her get through routine household chores. When her husband commented on the frequency with which she smelled of alcohol, she was embarrassed and stopped for several months. She missed the relief she associated with alcohol and took measures to "hide the smell" when she returned to drinking during the day. When she learned of her second pregnancy, her doctor advised her about the dangers of alcohol consumption during pregnancy. Vowing to curtail her consumption again, Marcia calls the crisis hotline, because she doesn't feel comfortable discussing her decision with anyone she knows.

REVIEW OF THE LITERATURE

The criteria for a diagnosis of addiction or dependence (i.e., DSM-IV; APA, 1994) on any substance include physiological (e.g., withdrawal symptoms), psychological (e.g., craving), and psychosocial (e.g., job loss) considerations. In contrast, the criteria for a diagnosis of abuse rest almost exclusively on the presence of psychosocial disruption.

Although there has been substantial attention to the correlates and antecedents of substance (and particularly alcohol) use and abuse, little theoretical consensus has been reached. Littieri, Sayers, and Pearson (1980) identified over forty-three distinct theories; Murray and Perry (1985) isolated nine categories of theoretical approaches in this area. Part of this confusion lies in that abuse should not be regarded as unitary but as progressing through stages of involvement, including abstinence, use, abuse, dependency, recovery, and relapse (IOM, 1990).

196

Strickland and Pittman (1984) suggested a model for understanding the initiation of usage derived from social learning theory and the consumer socialization framework. Social learning theory emphasizes learning via observation of the behavior of others, thereby providing a basis for understanding both interpersonal and media influences. In terms of interpersonal influence, both direct reinforcement of drinking and the development of attitudes and norms that support drinking in interaction with significant others may be involved. Media influences not only provide more opportunities for modeling drinking behavior but actively socialize consumer-related cognition and behaviors through the marketing of alcoholic beverages.

Liese (1994) presented a cognitive model that provides a useful framework from which to conceptualize alcohol abuse and treatment. From this perspective, abuse is triggered by a set of high risk stimuli (internal and external). Such situations activate the individual's basic drug-related beliefs, which, if based on overgeneralizations, arbitrary inferences, and other cognitive distortions that support drinking behaviors, may dominate cognitive processes in the form of urges and cravings. Paired with facilitating beliefs, which lower inhibitions regarding usage, the individual focuses on acquiring and using the substance; consequently, use continues or relapse begins.

Relapse prevention (Marlatt, 1985), a treatment approach similarly based on social learning and cognitive theories, generally has combined skill training, cognitive interventions, and lifestyle change procedures. Through this treatment process, clients learn to avoid high risk stimuli, to alter their basic drug-related beliefs, and to develop specific strategies for responding to cravings and actual relapses.

Reviews of the substance abuse treatment literature (e.g., Quinnones et al., 1979; Tims, 1981), while relying primarily on one-program studies, have indicated that addicts who undergo any kind of treatment show positive behavioral change compared to those untreated. The Drug Abuse Reporting Program (DARP) study included over 44,000 clients in fifty-two sites and found positive treatment outcomes, regardless of the specific treatment modality (with the exception of detoxification only), directly related to length of time in treatment (Simpson, 1984). The Treatment Outcome Prospective Study (TOPS) also confirmed the relationship between length of time in treatment and positive outcome (Hubbard et al., 1989).

In reviewing effectiveness of treatment with adult alcoholic subjects, Blum (1987) concluded that positive outcome was associated with a number of pretreatment conditions: residential stability, higher educational attainment, fewer arrests, higher social class, more stable social relationships, fewer psychiatric symptoms, higher psychological distress, and self-referral for treatment. Much less research has been conducted with privately funded treatment centers or self-help groups. It has been concluded that alcoholic clients have been more successful than drug-related clients in these modalities (IOM, 1990).

The major challenge to the alcoholism treatment field has been helping abusers to accept and continue treatment (Frances, Miller, and Galanter, 1989). Through the defense mechanism of denial, clients tend to minimize the nature and amount of their usage as well as the effects such usage has on their health and well-being. Denial leads to resistances to acknowledging a problem exists, to entering treatment, and to maintaining recovery (Amodeo and Liftik, 1990). Consequently, few alcoholics enter treatment in the absence of a crisis, and the use of coercion in the initiation of treatment has become commonplace (Frances and Miller, 1991). Although formal confrontation with members of the client's social system have been utilized, threats to employment or relationship status more frequently provide the impetus to acknowledge an alcohol problem and enter treatment.

THE SCOPE OF THE PROBLEM

Alcohol has been the most commonly used psychoactive substance among Americans. In 1988, the National Household Survey on Drug Abuse (NIDA, 1990) found that among household members ages twelve and older, 85 percent had used alcohol in their lifetime. Further, over two-thirds (68.1 percent) had consumed alcohol in the past year and more than half (53.4 percent) had done so in the prior month. While use of alcohol only was the most common pattern in the population (49.1 percent lifetime; 54.9 percent in the past year; 47.1 percent in the past month), the simultaneous use of both alcohol and other illicit substances has been increasing (35.9 percent lifetime; 13.2 percent in the past year; 6.3 percent in the past month).

Lifetime incidence of alcohol and drug abuse approaches one-fifth of the population; this abuse has devastating consequences for families and significant others (Helzer and Pryzbeck, 1988). It has been estimated that substance abuse plays a role in half the annual car deaths; three-fourths of robberies and felony assaults; and half of homicides, accidents, and burns (Frances and Miller, 1991).

The Institute of Medicine (IOM, 1987) reported that at least one in ten Americans has a serious alcohol problem. In 1988, 13 million

Americans were diagnosed as alcoholic (Office of the President, 1987). Harwood, Napolitano, Kristiansen, and Collins (1984) reported projections that the direct and indirect costs of alcoholism would reach $89.5 billion by 1990, far more than the projected costs of drug abuse ($46.9 billion). This estimate includes expenditures for prevention and treatment programs, costs incurred by the criminal justice system in confronting substance-related crimes, welfare support paid out to abusers and their dependents, loss of human potential (i.e., lowered productivity and impaired health), and damages suffered by crime victims. Excluded from such analysis are any consideration of nonmonetary human costs, eventual social costs associated with deficits incurred by children of abusers, and increased medical expenses incurred by abusers. Holder (1987) found that untreated alcoholics had twice the general health care costs of nonalcoholics.

Whatever the population in need of treatment, only about half a million persons enter publicly funded alcohol and/or drug abuse treatment each year (Butynski and Canova, 1988), while an additional 200,000 enter privately funded programs (IOM, 1990). Further, in this two-tiered system, private tier providers received 41 percent of the reported drug treatment expenditures while treating 22 percent of the clients; public tier providers received 59 percent of the total revenues and treated 78 percent of the clients. It has been estimated that fewer than 10 percent of addicted people either are in self-help groups or receiving professional treatment (Frances, Miller, and Galanter, 1989).

CRISIS THEORY FRAMEWORK

A crisis occurs when a person who has usually functioned and coped relatively well encounters a situation in which his or her normal coping mechanisms prove inadequate or maladaptive (Johnson, 1986). While there are common situations in which a crisis may emerge (see Baldwin, 1978), a crisis is essentially self-defined, formed in the active interaction between social circumstances and individual capacities.

The crisis state is characterized by disequilibrium, disorganization, and immobility (Golan, 1987; Parad, 1977). The individual has already engaged his or her coping skills in attempting unsuccessfully to avert the crisis. With increased anxiety and tension, the crisis may be experienced as primarily a threat, a loss, or a challenge and thereby generate additional emotional responses. In this increasingly vulnera-

199

ble state, a crisis situation may become linked to existing psychological or social conflicts.

Another characteristic of a crisis state is time limitation (Golan, 1987; Parad, 1977). While authors differ somewhat, four to eight weeks are generally regarded as upper time limits on an active crisis (Johnson, 1986). Further, within that time limit, one of two resolutions will be reached. If the crisis is not resolved, the disequilibrium will have become chronic and the individual's functioning capabilities will have been impaired.

However, if the crisis is resolved successfully, a normal state of functioning will have been restored and equilibrium regained. Indeed, with successful resolution, the individual may attain a higher level of adjustment through the acquisition of new coping skills and resultant boosts in self-efficacy. The probability of enhanced functioning is determined by the extent to which the individual views the resolution as resulting from his or her own efforts.

Finally, persons in crisis states tend to be particularly amenable to change (Golan, 1987; Parad, 1977). The characteristic emotional distress serves as a strong motivator; defense mechanisms have been weakened; and usual coping patterns have proved inadequate. An individual is consequently more likely to try new behaviors or ways of thinking as well as gain perspective on pervious coping patterns. For the alcoholic, the potential benefits associated with change and/or the potential losses of continued drinking may be visible enough to challenge denial.

Crises are common occurrences in the lives of those abusing alcohol or other psychoactive substances; indeed, the crises and alcohol abuse may form an interactive, self-maintaining relationship (Liese, 1994). The psychosocial impairment associated with addiction and/or abuse usually generates a variety of interpersonal, psychiatric, legal, financial, and/or medical problems. Among those persons who abuse alcohol, drinking serves as a primary or exclusive coping mechanism. This interactive pattern, in which a crisis is triggered by substance abuse and further drinking occurs in response, nearly inevitably leads to an escalation in the intensity of the crisis state.

Crisis Reactions and Emotional Trauma

A crisis state must be understood as a time of stress during which the intensity of the emotional response reflects the degree of disruption to one's normal steady state (Johnson, 1986). At a point where prob-lem-solving and coping skills are most needed, cognitive capabilities may be effectively inaccessible due to emotional distress.

The most characteristic emotion of a crisis state is anxiety (Golan, 1987; Parad, 1977). Disequilibrium, along with feeling out of control, heightens anxiety and discourages effective problem solving. In many situations, reasonable predictions may be made regarding stages and sequencing of emotional reactions and behavioral responses; being able to anticipate stages, however, may return some sense of control in a crisis.

Crises, when perceived as loss, generally are accomplished by depression and mourning. An association between alcoholism and depression has been well documented; further, alcohol has shown detrimental effects on mood among alcoholics (Frances, Franklin, and Flavin, 1987). However, less attention has been given to mourning the loss of drinking behavior itself. Sobriety may be associated with the perceived loss of roles and/or capabilities. In recovery, most clients must form new support systems, and engage in new activities and patterns. This usually entails leaving behind prior social systems and habits.

The immobility characteristic of a crisis state (Golan, 1987; Parad, 1977) may be viewed simply as an inability to access effective problem-solving capacities. Generally, the emotional trauma associated with a crisis state is considered the primary barrier to cognitive access. How-ever, cognitive theory would suggest that mourning the perceived losses framed within the individual's basic drug-related beliefs, rather than addressing the validity of those beliefs, may be inhibiting motiva-tion and blocking cognitive access. In contrast, perceiving the crisis as a challenge would tend to direct anxiety, releasing energy for problem solving and heightened expectations.

Restabilization and Crisis Management

Successful crisis resolution involves relief from the immediate impact of the crisis situation as well as a strengthening of the individual's coping and adaptive skills (Parad, 1977). Similarly, Rapoport (1970) suggested two levels of outcome: (1) identification of internal and ex-ternal resources to remediate the particular crisis situation and return to premorbid functioning; or (2) through using new skills (perceptual, cognitive, or affective) and/or integrating new experiences with past conflicts, to enhance premorbid functioning.

To achieve successful resolution involves active problem-solving activities (Golan, 1987). Internal and external systems must be evaluated in terms of potential resources and/or barriers. Alternatives, once generated, must be evaluated and compared. Finally, a plan for moving from the crisis state to equilibrium and enhanced functioning must be made and followed, with adjustments linked to evaluation of progress.

For the alcoholic client, restabilization may need to include detoxification to manage withdrawal. Alcohol withdrawal involves a wide range of physical and psychological symptoms and can be life threatening (Gorelick and Wilkins, 1986; Naranjo and Sellers, 1986). Both withdrawal syndrome and simple intoxication serve to compromise cognitive functioning. Ideally, sobriety should serve as a restabilization step with all alcohol-involved clients, so that maximal cognitive capabilities are available for crisis management.

Value and Ethical Issues

Crises, while characterized by anxiety and disequilibrium, may also be viewed as opportunities (Parad, 1977; Golan, 1987). A crisis may provide a turning point at which the potential for growth is greatly enhanced by the willingness to change. For the crisis worker, "a minimal effort at such a time can often produce a maximal effect; a small amount of help, appropriately focused, can prove to be considerably more effective than more extensive help at periods of less emotional accessibility" (Golan, 1987, p. 365). Crisis resolution that includes increasing the client's coping and adaptive skills exemplifies the concept of empowerment.

A nonjudgmental atmosphere is critical to effective intervention (Roberts, 1991). However, an open, caring, supportive environment may be particularly hard to achieve with certain clients. Alcoholic clients have been described as "among the hardest patients to treat, the most ungrateful, the angriest, the most sociopathic, and the most dependent and in need of support" (Frances and Miller, 1991, p. 6). Such descriptions reflect social attitudes as well as alcoholic behavior. Stigmatization of alcoholic clients, labeling behaviors as entirely willful rather than part of a treatable condition, can contribute to denial, neglect, fear, and suffering (Frances and Miller, 1991).

A worker must become aware of his or her own biases and how these are communicated to others (Gambrill, 1983). Expressing disapproval is highly detrimental to the helping process, producing client defensiveness and disrupting communication (Hepworth and Larsen,

1986). At the same time, being nonjudgmental does not imply making no distinction between behaviors that help people achieve their goals (and should be supported) and those that interfere with achieving such goals (and should not be supported). The critical distinction in promoting a nonjudgmental atmosphere is between the client's behavior and the client him- or herself (Gambrill, 1983).

PRACTICE FRAMEWORK

Roberts (1991) expanded on previously developed models of crisis intervention (e.g., Baldwin, 1978; Caplan, 1964; Golan, 1978; Rapoport, 1970), deriving a seven-step model that stresses the problem-solving approach to crisis resolution: (1) assess lethality and safety needs; (2) establish rapport and communication; (3) identify the major problem; (4) deal with feelings and provide support; (5) explore possible alternatives; (6) assist in formulating an action plan; and (7) follow up. This framework has been viewed as compatible with cognitive approaches to substance abuse treatment (Liese, 1994) and was used to formulate crisis intervention strategy for use with cocaine addicts (Cocores and Gold, 1990).

Alcoholism is characterized (and maintained by) denial of the effects of drinking on the client's health and well-being (Amodeo and Liftik, 1990). Consequently, the most critical aims of intervention with this population include problem identification and motivation for treatment. Alcoholic clients seldom seek treatment in the absence of a precipitating crisis, referred to in the language of Alcoholics Anonymous as "hitting bottom" (Frances and Miller, 1991). Further, coercion by employers, family members, friends, health professionals, and/or the legal system is often involved in creating the precipitating crisis. These dynamics create a relative lack of voluntariness and, thereby, particular dilemmas in crisis intervention with alcoholic clients.

The central issue in these dilemmas involves achieving a balance between the confrontation needed to combat denial and the supportive, accepting relationship critical to accomplishing crisis resolution. Successful intervention with alcoholic clients generally requires "a caring relationship; greater activity on the part of the therapist . . .; a degree of therapeutic zeal, with guards against overidentification; and a high degree of empathy" (Frances and Miller, 1991, p. 17). Other essential qualities include flexibility, persistence, patience, the capacity to listen, honesty, integrity, and wisdom (Frances and Franklin, 1989).

Further complicating intervention with alcoholic clients is the likely presence of intoxication. Alcohol intoxication is "characterized by an alteration in behavior with various stages, depending on the amount of alcohol used and upon individual variation and tolerance" (Nace and Isbell, 1991, p.53). More specifically, the most common maladaptive behavioral effects of alcohol intoxication include impaired judgment, mood lability, and disinhibition of aggressive impulses. These situations potentially both impair the client's ability to participate in problem solving and test the intervener's patience and good will. Also, although the crisis framework will be discussed in sequential order, working with alcoholic clients frequently demands reordering and repetition of stages.

Assessing Lethality and Safety Needs

The essential thrust in this stage of Roberts' (1991) model is to determine the person's degree of risk for serious injury or death. Common potential threats include self-destructive activities as well as violent acts of other persons. Several additional considerations may be particularly important when working with alcohol-involved clients. Along with overt suicidal behavior, a person under the influence may endanger her/his well-being more indirectly. For example, driving while intoxicated clearly places people at risk of harm. Also, chronic alcoholism can result in a number of serious medical conditions (e.g., cirrhosis of the liver, pancreatic disease, etc.) that may be life-threatening, including alcohol withdrawal (Alterman, O'Brien, and McLellan, 1991). Finally, the association between alcohol and violent behavior necessitates considering the safety needs of others (i.e., assessment for homicidal risk) along with those of the client.

Suicide assessment is particularly imperative with alcoholic clients. Approximately 15 percent of alcoholics will die of suicide, and alcohol use has been found to increase the risk of suicidal behavior for both alcoholic and nonalcoholic populations (Frances, Franklin, and Flavin, 1987). Although suicidal intent frequently clears during a sobering-up process, the likelihood of a quick return to drinking should be considered in predicting ongoing risk. Determining the need for involuntary commitment should include consideration of prior suicide attempts, frequency of intoxication, degree of depression, and other comorbid psychiatric conditions, and client insight, support networks, and commitment to treatment (Frances, Franklin, and Flavin, 1987).

See chapter 3 for an in-depth discussion of working with suicidal clients.

> RALPH: I'm just not sure life is worth living anymore.
> WORKER: Does this mean you've thought about or tried to kill yourself?
> RALPH: Sure, who hasn't?
> WORKER: Do you have a specific plan for hurting yourself now?
> RALPH: No, not really. With my liver the way it is now, I don't really need to plan anything special, just keep drinking.
> WORKER: Is that why you've been drinking tonight? To kill yourself?
> RALPH: I hadn't thought about it. I'm just under a lot of stress.

Assessing homicidal potential is generally more difficult than assessing suicide risk (Lieb, Lipsitch, and Slaby, 1973). As with suicide risk, the presence of a plan to inflict harm on others, a history of prior assaultive behavior, the potential for continued intoxication, comorbid psychiatric conditions, and the availability of environmental controls should be considered. Again, involuntary commitment and/or breaking confidentiality to inform potential victims may prove necessary.

> RALPH: That bitch just walked out on me. Somebody should teach her a lesson. Who does she think she is? I'd like to hurt her as bad as she's hurt me and see how she likes it.
> WORKER: You're really angry at her. Do you really want to hurt her?
> RALPH: You bet I do.
> WORKER: How would you go about it, hurting her as badly as she's hurt you?
> RALPH: Well, she's walked out on me already, so that's out. Maybe just scare her really badly somehow so she knows what it's like to have no control.
> WORKER: How would you do that?
> RALPH: I don't know. I'm just angry. It's not like I want to plan some way to hurt her. I'm just angry.

Finally, consideration of an alcoholic client's medical status should be included in insuring basic safety. Because of the numerous serious medical complications of abusive drinking and its related dietary and nutritional neglect, emergency medical referrals may be warranted (Nace and Isbell, 1991). Severe confusion, disorientation, and depressed mental status may indicate encephalopathy. Pain and gastrointestinal disruption may be symptomatic of liver or pancreatic deterioration. Any recent, serious change in the client's physical or mental health requires medical evaluation, either immediately or as part of restabilization in the action plan, depending on the apparent severity of symptoms.

> WORKER: I'm glad you're feeling calmer now but I'm still worried about your health. You said your doctor said drinking would be really dangerous, and I know you've been drinking tonight. Do you think you need to see a doctor?
>
> RALPH: I'm not sure.
>
> WORKER: Well, how are you feeling? Since you started drinking again, have there been any changes in your health?
>
> RALPH: No, but I haven't stopped, so I probably wouldn't notice if there have been changes.
>
> WORKER: Did you have a bad time with withdrawal when you've stopped drinking before?
>
> RALPH: You mean like DTs? No, nothing that bad; just seeing bugs and feeling lousy.

Establishing Rapport and Communication

For most people, seeking help is accompanied by an array of adjunctive concerns, including ambivalence about investing time, effort, and resources to accomplish desired changes; worries about submitting to the influence of a helper; doubts if he or she can trust a stranger; feelings of being overwhelmed by problems; questions about whether they will be judged by the helper, about the competencies of the helper, and about the degree of self-revelation that will be demanded (Gambrill, 1983). To quickly establish initial rapport, skills in attentive listening, observation, and empathic responding will serve to help people feel more comfortable.

Attentive listening involves an active process of responding and is grounded in an assumption of ignorance and a commitment to perception checking (Brammer, 1979; Kadushin, 1972). Certain verbal responses communicate the intervener's interest and concern to the client. Reflection of feelings helps to establish rapport through encouraging affective release and conveying understanding and respect. Paraphrasing and/or asking for clarification serve to acknowledge the intervener's interest and concern as well as to check out (and correct) his or her perceptions. Summarization conveys attentiveness and may help to organize information to identify central themes or problems. Likewise, empathic responding lets clients know you are listening and that you understand what is being said. Primary-level empathy, letting the client know you have heard and understand explicit expressions of emotion, is crucial to establishing rapport (Egan, 1975).

> FRANK: I just need to go to treatment to get the court off my back.
> WORKER: Sounds like a lot of pressure. Have they told you what kind of treatment you're supposed to be getting?
> FRANK: No. They said it was routine after two DWIs.
> WORKER: So do you think they mean treatment for alcohol?
> FRANK: I guess so. Does it make any difference?
> WORKER: Well, I'm sure the court had something specific in mind. I want to make sure we figure out the right thing so you can straighten things out with the court.
> FRANK: Okay, good. I just want them off my back.
> WORKER: Since they're making you get treatment, maybe we can find something you think will be useful.

> MARCIA: I don't know what to say. I'm not sure why I called. I guess I don't have anyone else to talk to.
> WORKER: That sounds pretty lonely. I'd be happy to talk with you.
> MARCIA: Thanks. I guess it's your job.
> WORKER: Well, I want to help you if I can. Why don't you tell me what's been going on in your life?

To provide an atmosphere conducive to positive crisis intervention, warmth, respect, and genuineness must be conveyed along with understanding. Conveying respect includes being an attentive listener, suspending judgment about the person, not imposing stereotypes, and acknowledging the client's assets and abilities to change (Egan, 1975). Being nonjudgmental does not imply that one makes no distinction between functional and dysfunctional behaviors, but that the worker avoids criticism, blame, and assumptions of negative outcomes (Gambrill, 1983).

> RALPH: I don't know if I deserve any more chances. This is my fourth marriage I screwed up with alcohol.
> WORKER: It certainly seems that drinking has interfered with your relationships. But you've said you had a better relationship this time. Plus, she said she'd come back if you stopped drinking. Whether you think you deserve it or not, it sounds like you have another chance.
> RALPH: Another chance to screw up.
> WORKER: Hey, don't forget you stayed sober for almost a year. You can do it again. You can learn from this slip and stay sober even longer next time.

Identifying the Major Problem

Although alcoholic clients usually present with an array of problems and precipitating events, their alcoholism should be considered the primary focus of intervention (Budman and Gurman, 1989). However, given the dynamics of denial and the likelihood of situational crises in the lives of alcoholics, alcoholism treatment is unlikely to be the client's initial focus. Frequently, there may be no acknowledgment of drinking as a dynamic in the precipitating crisis during the initial crisis contact. Nonetheless, the dilemma for an intervener is to overcome denial while maintaining rapport and communication.

> RALPH: I don't know what you can do to help me. My wife just walked out, deserted me. Can you believe that? Just gets mad and walks away. Now what am I supposed to do?

> FRANK: I need some information. A man from the court said I should call you. They said I have to have treatment or go to jail. So where do I have to go and how much will it cost?

Several techniques may prove useful in bringing alcohol problems into focus. It is important to retain focus on the client's problems, not those of third parties (Lieb, Lipsitch, and Slaby, 1973). This situation may frequently occur when the specific crisis revolves around coercive efforts of significant others. Advanced empathy skills, acknowledging both what has been explicitly expressed and what has been implied and left unstated (Egan, 1975), may help separate emotions supporting denial (e.g., guilt, fear) from anger at a concerned third party.

> RALPH: She's been an alcoholic too. She knows she's making things worse. I don't need this stress.
> WORKER: How is her leaving causing you stress?
> RALPH: Well, I miss her. And people want to know where she is. What am I supposed to say?
> WORKER: So it's embarrassing you that she's left?
> RALPH: Sure, everybody thinks it's my fault.
> WORKER: Do you think it's your fault?
> RALPH: Not entirely, but, sure, some of it's my fault.
> WORKER: Have you been feeling guilty along with missing her?

Ewing (1984) suggested a series of questions useful in establishing the presence of a drinking problem (CAGE Questionnaire): (1) has anyone ever recommended you *cut* back or stop drinking; (2) have you

208

ever felt *annoyed* or angry if someone commented on your drinking; (3) have there been times when you've felt *guilty* about or regretted things that occurred because of drinking; (4) have you ever used alcohol to help you get started in the morning (an *eye*-opener), to steady your nerves? Answering three out of these four questions positively, strongly suggests alcoholism. Most importantly, these questions provide a framework for exploring and confronting denial through discussing the client's affirmative responses in depth.

FRANK: So, do you think I have a drinking problem?

WORKER I don't think I know enough about you to say. I know some questions that are supposed to help you figure out if drinking is a problem for you. Do you want to go through them?

FRANK: Okay. Why not?

WORKER: Has anyone ever recommended you cut back or stop drinking?

FRANK: Sure, lots of people try to tell everyone else how to live their lives.

WORKER: Is that what you think was going on with the people who told you to stop drinking?

MARCIA: I was really embarrassed when my husband would mention my drinking, but not annoyed.

WORKER: Hmmm. I usually get annoyed at people who embarrass me.

While the term confrontation implies conflict and negative impact, confrontation of alcoholism in crisis intervention may be defined as "a responsible unmasking of the discrepancies, distortion, games and smoke screen the client uses to hide both from self-understanding and from constructive behavior change" (Egan, 1975, p. 158). From a cognitive viewpoint (see Liese, 1994), confrontation involves recognizing and addressing basic drug-related beliefs (e.g., "Life is more fun when I drink"; "I cannot function without drinking"; etc.) and facilitating beliefs (e.g., "One drink won't hurt me"; "I'll quit after this time"; etc.).

FRANK: I don't want to stop drinking. I wouldn't have any friends or any fun if I did.

WORKER: Drinking's the only thing you enjoy?

FRANK: Of course, there's other things; but all my friends drink.

WORKER: Do you think they'd stop being friends with you if you quit drinking with them?

FRANK: I don't know. Maybe.

WORKER: You don't sound sure of that.

FRANK: Well, there are guys at work who don't drink when we go out. But that's just them. Nobody expects them to party.

WORKER: So, nobody minds.

FRANK: Not really.
WORKER: But you think it might be different if you changed?

Motivational interviewing (Miller, 1989a) is a confrontational process intended to bring the client to greater awareness of and personal responsibility for his or her problem with alcohol while instilling and supporting a commitment to change. Designed to minimize client resistance, the goal is to have the client verbalize his or her concern about drinking and its effects, to state that drinking is a problem, to acknowledge the need for change, and to commit to a plan for treatment. Further, in this approach, client resistance is met with reflection; labels are deemphasized; feedback is objective and low-keyed; and personal choice is emphasized in formulating treatment goals and course. From this perspective, it is not necessary that the client accept the "alcoholic" label, but rather that he or she acknowledge that a problem exists (Amodeo and Liftik, 1990).

MARCIA: You'd think I was an alcoholic the way my doctor harped about drinking while I'm pregnant.
WORKER: Did he say that?
MARCIA: No, but he really stressed the alcohol thing.
WORKER: Was that different from the first time you were pregnant?
MARCIA: Hmmm. I guess he mentioned it then, too.
WORKER: So maybe you feel differently about drinking now?
MARCIA: That's true. You know my husband thought it was a problem.
WORKER: So, what do you think about your drinking?

Dealing with Feelings and Providing Support

Roberts' model (1991) addresses the need for dealing with the affective domain to prepare for problem solving and providing support and encouragement to pursue change. Through active listening, communication, and empathic responses, the intervener encourages and gives permission for the expression of feelings. Feelings may be viewed as important clues to understanding contingencies (i.e., relationships between behaviors and environmental events; Gambrill, 1983). Helping the client to ascertain any cognitive distortions, misconceptions, and irrational beliefs is particularly useful when the client makes such discoveries independently.

MARCIA: I was really miserable when I stopped drinking before. It was hard to get through each day.

WORKER: What was it like?

MARCIA: Just miserable. I was bored and anxious all the time. I'd think about drinking and relaxing, then I'd feel guilty.

WORKER: Where did the guilt come from?

MARCIA: I don't want to let my husband down. We have all these plans about our lives and our families. I don't want to ruin everything.

WORKER: That sounds like a lot of pressure.

Shulman (1979) identified three related skills useful in dealing with feelings and providing support: (1) reaching for feelings (i.e., bringing emotions into focus); (2) displaying understanding of feelings (i.e., accurate identification, integration with behaviors, and acceptance); and (3) putting feelings into words (i.e., labeling and consequent feeling of control). Relieving emotional distress is critical in preparation for formulating an action plan. People often experience relief (and liberation of energy to pursue change) through simple ventilation of negative emotions (Hepworth and Larsen, 1986). Normalization of experiences, behaviors, and/ or feelings is a critical aspect in initial contact with clients so that resolution may be pursued without emotional blockage (Gamrbill, 1983).

"Subjectively, the alcoholic struggles with prolonged craving for the substance, fear of functioning without alcohol, and doubts about his or her ability to abstain and hence to recover. Concomitant with the ambivalent struggle to change, the alcoholic endures remorse, regret, guilt, and shame" (Nace and Isbell, 1991, p. 65). In addition, any nonvoluntary aspect of the person's contact will likely be accompanied with anger and resistance (Gambrill, 1983).

FRANK: So that's the story. I have to do what the court says.

WORKER: Okay, I know we can figure out what you need to do. Can you tell me how you're feeling about this? It seems like a lot of pressure for you.

FRANK: You bet. I know I have to do it but I don't really want to.

WORKER: So you've put it off?

FRANK: I guess so. I don't really want to deal with this.

WORKER: Frank, are you angry about all of this? I can see how being ordered to do something you don't want would make you feel that way.

FRANK: Yeah, I'm pissed off. And scared, too. They can take away my license and I'd lose my job. Hell, they could put me in jail.

Exploring Possible Alternatives

In the Roberts' model (1991), the initial step in exploring alternatives involves a review of past coping attempts. This process encourages

211

the identification of adaptive and maladaptive aspects of the client's coping skills. With a resistant client, this process may offer another opportunity to clarify and prioritize problem areas. While the focus of exploration is generally aimed at the precipitating crisis event, at least tentative consideration of addressing drinking behaviors is crucial in assisting alcoholic clients (Miller, 1989a).

> WORKER: How did you manage it when you stopped drinking before?
> MARCIA: I just did it.
> WORKER: Think that will work this time?
> MARCIA: Well, it only worked for a little while last time. I was miserable.
> WORKER: So you think you'll need to approach it differently now?

> FRANK: So, what are my options?
> WORKER: There are a lot of possibilities. We can make a list and have your probation officer look at them too.
> FRANK: Good idea. I want to make sure it's settled.
> WORKER: How about you? Can you tell me what you want to get out of this for yourself?
> FRANK: Just get everyone off my back, I guess.
> WORKER: Everybody?
> FRANK: Yeah, my wife wants me to stop drinking altogether.
> WORKER: How do you feel about that idea?

A wide variety of treatment options have been utilized successfully with alcoholic clients. In most instances, detoxification is considered a necessary pretreatment consideration (Alterman, O'Brien, and McLellan, 1991). In crisis situations, detoxification may well be necessary before cognitive activities (i.e., exploring possible alternatives) may be pursued. Inpatient (as opposed to outpatient ambulatory) detoxification is warranted when there is a history of alcohol-related seizures or a history of delirium tremens (Alterman, O'Brien, and McLellan, 1991). Further, clients without housing and/or employment are more likely to complete inpatient than outpatient detoxification programs.

> WORKER: Okay, so you want to start over again. Where do we go from here? What's the first step?
> RALPH: I'm not sure. I need to talk with my wife but not like this. I guess I need to get sober again.
> WORKER: How have you done that before?
> RALPH: Lots of ways: white-knuckle, detox, the whole bit.
> WORKER: I'm worried this time might be different. You've had hallucina-

212

tions and shakes before. Now, your doctor said your liver was shot. I'm afraid the withdrawal might be worse.

RALPH: Me too. Think I should check into detox?

WORKER: Maybe. Or at least talk with your doctor.

RALPH: I'd rather go to detox. They'll probably remember me.

WORKER: Well, I think that's a good start, but it seems like there's a lot more to figure out.

RALPH: Yeah, but I feel lousy now. I don't think I can think anymore.

WORKER: Maybe we can figure out the rest later . . . after you're sober and feeling better.

RALPH: Okay.

Outcome research has failed to endorse any particular treatment approach as superior and has supported the generalization that different individuals respond best to different approaches (Miller and Hester, 1989). Individual clients may be restrained by economics and the availability of treatment resources. In any event, alcoholism treatment approaches may be viewed on a continuum of intensity of intervention: no formal treatment; brief intervention; self-help groups; outpatient consultation; intensive nonresidential treatment; and residential care in a hospital or specialized treatment setting. Several guidelines may be useful in determining the appropriate level of care for an individual client (Miller, 1989b): (1) it is prudent to try the least intensive intervention likely to meet the client's needs; (2) more supervised care may be warranted by comorbid medical or psychological conditions; and (3) clients tend to respond differentially (i.e., more intensive approaches work better with socially unstable persons with severe problems, while less intensive approaches work better with socially intact individuals with less severe dependence).

FRANK: So if I want to try not drinking, do I have to go to one of those hospitals?

WORKER: Actually, there are a lot of options: from AA to some kind of outpatient program to things like the hospital. Have you tried any of these before?

FRANK: No.

WORKER: Well, people have gotten sober all kinds of ways. We need to think about what the court wants too. I think we can start with trying something less expensive and disruptive than the hospital, though.

FRANK: Good, I don't want to lose my job or anything.

Clients should be encouraged to generate their own alternatives to help combat feelings of helplessness and despair (Roberts, 1991). The crisis worker may suggest additional options and supply concrete informational detail about any alternatives. Once identified, each alternative should be explored thoroughly in terms of client feelings, potential outcomes (positive and negative), and potential obstacles or pitfalls (Gambrill, 1983).

MARCIA: Well, I have thought about trying an AA meeting.

WORKER: You sound hesitant. What's kept you from going to AA before?

MARCIA: I hear you have to say you're an alcoholic.

WORKER: Actually, you can go to an open meeting and see for yourself what it's like.

MARCIA: Well, what if someone sees me there and tells my husband?

WORKER: AA is supposed to be anonymous. I don't think it's likely anyone would tell your husband.

MARCIA: I don't know.

WORKER: Maybe we should talk about this more. It may be hard to get any help if you're too worried your husband will find out.

Assisting in Formulating an Action Plan

Once alternatives have been generated and explored, a plan for resolving the crisis should be formulated (Roberts, 1991). The focus of the plan may be directed toward immediate steps and short-term strategies for restabilization, but it should ultimately include consideration of improving coping and adaptive skills and of achieving cognitive mastery. Finally, encouraging and mobilizing clients are critical in insuring follow-through with the action plan.

Alcoholics typically present with complex problems, multiple precipitating factors, and impaired abilities to engage in active coping (Liese, 1994). Effective action plans for this population are inevitably multifaceted, including provisions for detoxification/restabilization, resolution of precipitating psychosocial situations, and some level of alcohol treatment. Frequently, formulating plans with alcoholics will necessarily proceed in stages both so that the client is able to actively participate in the process and that the full complexities of the plan may be developed.

Attention to resolving psychosocial disruption(s), which may have been precipitating events, may be particularly important with alcoholic clients. Socially unstable (e.g., unemployed, homeless, indigent) clients have decreased likelihood of successful treatment (Blum, 1987) and require more intensive treatment methods (Miller, 1989b). Further, continued psychosocial problems may trigger further drinking and crises (Liese, 1994). Finally, unresolved precipitating events may impose actual barriers to treatment entry (Miller, 1989a).

While the worker may offer recommendations in the process, self-matching has proven to be desirable in selecting treatment alternatives with alcoholic clients (Miller and Hester, 1989). Choosing a course of action from an array of alternatives may enhance motivation and reduce resistance, particularly with non-voluntary clients (Gambrill, 1983). Also an alcoholic client should be prepared to monitor, assess, and re-evaluate the action plan as needed through routinely scheduled follow-up or emergency sessions.

As has been indicated, alcoholic clients are frequently coerced into treatment, gaining motivation to avoid the negative consequences and risks associated with continued drinking (Miller, 1989a). Two additional strategies for motivating alcoholic clients involve increasing the attractiveness of the new behavior and lifestyle associated with drinking cessation, and helping reduce fears and concerns about change. From a cognitive perspective, combating basic drug-related and facilitating beliefs is critical to enhancing motivation (Liese, 1994).

Following Up

The final stage in Roberts' model (1991) of crisis intervention entails setting a specific, future time to assess the client's progress toward resolution and to revise the action plan, if needed. As mentioned above, crisis intervention with alcoholic clients may take place over a series of contacts; these may be viewed as a succession of follow ups (or a string of crisis interventions since most of the stages will be repeated in each contact).

With alcoholic clients, "lapses" and "relapses" are common even in the course of successful recovery (Marlatt, 1985). Follow-up sessions provide opportunities for relapse prevention, early intervention in the event of relapse, continued attention to enhancing self-efficacy through review of accomplishments and gains (Gambrill, 1983), and continued skill building (Marlatt, 1985).

SUMMARY AND CONCLUSION

Alcoholism is characterized by denial and compromised cognitive capabilities. Consequently, the most critical aspects of intervention with this population in a crisis situation include problem identification and motivation for treatment. Confrontation, coercion, and crises are frequently involved in bringing alcoholic clients to treatment.

The Roberts (1991) seven-stage crisis intervention model provides an integrated problem-solving approach. However, the relative lack of voluntariness creates particular dilemmas in crisis intervention with alcoholic clients. In assessing lethality, there are additional risk factors associated with this population. Assessment may be difficult and de-toxification may prove necessary both to insure client safety and to enable active client participation in the problem-solving process.

Establishing and maintaining rapport may prove difficult when confrontation is necessary in problem identification. Further, if sub-stantial coercion has been involved in the crisis contact, more difficulty in establishing communication will likely be encountered. Hostility may well be present and strain an intervener's ability to deal with the client's feelings. Indeed the worker's attitudes toward alcohol and alcoholism may present barriers to empathic response. Coercion may also imply limitations in available options, concomitant psychosocial disruption, and increased resistance to action planning. Finally, follow up is particularly crucial with the alcoholic client due to the ongoing dynamics of denial and the likelihood of relapse.

Although crisis intervention with alcoholic clients presents unusual challenges and dilemmas to the worker, the potential benefits associated with successful crisis resolution are also particularly important. Although conventional wisdom maintains that an alcoholic client must "hit bot-tom," persons entering treatment earlier in the personal and social deteri-oration associated with chronic abuse may well have more strengths and supports available with which to face the challenge of recovery. Further, earlier intervention minimizes the potential costs incurred by the client, his or her significant others, and society as a whole.

REFERENCES

Alterman, A. I., O'Brien, C. P., and McLellan, A. T. (1991). Differential therapeutics for substance abuse. In R. J. Frances and S. I. Miller (Eds.), *Clinical textbook of addictive disorders* (pp. 369–390). New York: Guilford.

American Psychiatric Association (APA). (1994). *Diagnostic and statistical manual of mental disorders* (4th ed; DSM-IV; *DSM-III-R*). Washington, DC: APA.

Amodeo, M., and Liftik, J. (1990). Working through denial in alcoholism. *Families in Society, 71* (3), 131–135.

Baldwin, B. A. (1978). A paradigm for the classification of emotional crises: Implications for crisis intervention. *American Journal of Orthopsychiatry, 48* (3), 538–551.

Blum, R. W. (1987). Adolescent substance abuse: Diagnostic and treatment issues. *Pediatric Clinics of America, 34* (2), 523–537.

Brammer, L. (1979). *The helping relationship: Process and skills* (2d ed.). Englewood Cliffs, NJ: Prentice-Hall.

Budman, S. H., and Gurman, A. S. (1989). *Theory and practice of brief therapy.* New York: Guilford.

Butynski, W., and Canova, D. (1988). *An analysis of state alcohol and drug abuse: Profile data.* Washington, DC: National Association of State Alcohol and Drug Abuse Directors.

Caplan, G. (1964). *Principles of preventive psychiatry.* New York: Basic Books.

Cocores, J. A., and Gold, M. S. (1990). Recognition and crisis intervention treatment with cocaine abusers: The Fair Oaks Hospital model. In A. R. Roberts (Ed.), *Crisis intervention handbook: Assessment, treatment and research* (pp. 177–195). Belmont, CA: Wadsworth.

Egan, G. (1975). *The skilled helper: A model for systematic helping and interpersonal relating.* Monterey, CA: Brooks/Cole.

Ewing, J. A. (1984). Detecting alcoholism: The CAGE questionnaire. *Journal of the American Medical Association, 252* (14), 1905–1907.

Frances, R. J., and Franklin, J. E. (1989). *A concise guide to treatment of alcoholism and addictions.* Washington, DC: American Psychiatric Press.

Frances, R. J., and Miller, S. I. (1991). Addiction treatment: The widening scope. In R. J. Frances and S.I. Miller (Eds.), *Clinical textbook of addictive disorders* (pp. 3–22). New York: Guilford.

Frances, R. J., Franklin, J. E., and Flavin, D. K. (1987). Suicide and alcoholism. *American Journal of Drug and Alcohol Abuse, 13* (3), 327–341.

Frances, R. J., Miller, S. I., and Galanter, M. (1989). Psychosocial treatment of addictions. In A. Tasman, R. J. Hales, and A. Frances (Eds.), *Review of psychiatry* (Vol. 8, pp. 341–359). Washington, DC: American Psychiatric Press.

Gambrill, E. (1983). *Casework: A competency-based approach.* Englewood Cliffs, NJ: Prentice-Hall.

Golan, N. (1978). *Treatment in crisis situations.* New York: Free Press.

——— (1987). Crisis intervention. In A. Minahan (Ed.), *Encyclopedia of social work* (18th ed.; Vol. 1; pp. 360–372). Silver Springs, MD: National Association of Social Workers.

Gorelick, D. A., and Wilkins, J. N. (1986). Special aspects of human alcohol withdrawal. In M. Galanter (Ed.), *Recent developments in alcoholism* (Vol. 4). New York: Plenum Press.

Harwood, H. J., Napolitano, D. M., Kristiansen, P. L., and Collins, J. J. (1984). *Economic costs to society of alcohol and drug abuse and mental illness: 1980*

(Pub. No. RTI/2734/00001FR). Research Triangle Park, NC: Research Triangle Institute.

Helzer, J. E., and Pryzbeck, F. R. (1988). The co-occurrence of alcoholism with other psychiatric disorders in the general population and its impact on treatment. *Journal of Studies on Alcohol, 49* (3), 219–244.

Hepworth, D. H., and Larsen, J. A. (1986). *Direct social work practice: Theory and skills* (2d ed.). Chicago, IL: Dorsey Press.

Holder, M. D. (1987). Alcoholism treatment and potential health care cost savings. *Medical Care, 25* (1), 52–71.

Hubbard, R. L., Marsden, M. E., Rachal, J. V., Harwood, H. J., Cavanaugh, E. R., and Ginzburg, H. M. (1989). *Drug abuse treatment: A national study of effectiveness.* Chapel Hill: University of North Carolina Press.

Institute of Medicine (IOM). (1987). *Causes and consequences of alcohol problems.* Washington, DC: National Academy Press.

———— (1990). *Treating drug problems* (Vol. 1). Washington, DC: National Academy Press.

Johnson, L. C. (1986). *Social work practice: A generalist approach* (2d ed.). Boston, MA: Allyn and Bacon.

Kadushin, A. (1972). *The social work interview.* New York: Columbia University Press.

Lettieri, D. J., Sayers, M., and Pearson, H. W. (Eds.). (1980). *Theories on drug abuse: Selected contemporary perspectives* (National Institute on Drug Abuse Research Monograph No. 30, DHHS Pub. No. ADM 84–967). Washington, DC: U.S. Government Printing Office.

Lieb, J., Lipsitch, I. I., and Slaby, A. E. (1973). *The crisis team: A handbook for the mental health professional.* New York: Harper and Row.

Liese, B. S. (1994). Brief therapy, crisis intervention and the cognitive therapy of substance abuse. *Crisis intervention and Time-limited Treatment Journal, 1* (1), 11–31.

Marlatt, G. A. (1985). Relapse prevention: Theoretical rationale and overview of the model. In G. A. Marlatt and J. R. Gordon (Eds.), *Relapse prevention: Maintenance strategies in the treatment of addictive behaviors* (pp. 3–70). New York: Guilford.

Miller, W. R. (1989a). Increasing motivation for change. In R. K. Hester and W. R. Miller (Eds.), *Handbook of alcoholism treatment approaches: Effective alternatives* (pp. 67–80). New York: Pergamon Press.

———— (1989b). Matching individuals with interventions. In R. K. Hester and W. R. Miller (Eds.), *Handbook of alcoholism treatment approaches: Effective alternatives* (pp. 261–271). New York: Pergamon Press.

————, and Hester, R. K. (1989). Treating alcohol problems: Toward an informed eclecticism. In R. K. Hester and W. R. Miller (Eds.), *Handbook of alcoholism treatment approaches: Effective alternatives* (pp. 3–14). New York: Pergamon Press.

Murray, D. M., and Perry, C. L. (1985). The prevention of adolescent drug abuse: Implications of etiological, developmental, behavioral, and environmental models. In C. L. Jones and R. J. Battjes (Eds.), *Etiology of drug abuse: Implications for prevention* (National Institute on Drug Abuse Research Monograph, 56, DHHS Pub. No. ADM 83–1335, pp. 236–256). Washington, DC: U.S. Government Printing Office.

Nace, E. P., and Isbell, P. G. (1991). Alcohol. In R. J. Frances and S. I. Millers (Eds.), *Clinical textbook of addictive disorders* (pp. 43–68). New York: Guilford.

Naranjo, C. A., and Sellers, E. M. (1986). Clinical assessment and pharmacotherapy of the alcohol withdrawal syndrome. In M. Galanter (Ed.), *Recent developments in alcoholism* (Vol. 4). New York: Plenum Press.

National Institute on Drug Abuse (NIDA). (1990). *National household survey on drug abuse: Main findings 1988* (DHHS Publication No. ADM 90–1682). Washington, DC: U.S. Government Printing Office.

Office of the President. (1987). *National drug control strategy*. Washington, DC: U.S. Government Printing Office.

Parad, H. J. (1977). Crisis intervention. In J. B. Turner (Ed.), *Encyclopedia of social work* (17th ed.; pp. 228–237). Washington, DC: National Association of Social Workers.

Quinnones, M. A., Doyle, K. M., Sheffet, A. M., and Louria, D. B. (1979). Evaluation of drug abuse rehabilitation efforts: A review. *American Journal of Public Health, 69* (11), 1164–1169.

Rapoport, L. (1970). Crisis intervention as a model of brief treatment. In R. Roberts and R. Nee (Eds.), *Theories of social casework*. Chicago, IL: University of Chicago Press.

Roberts, A. R. (1990). An overview of crisis theory and crisis intervention. In A. R. Roberts (Ed.), *Crisis intervention handbook: Assessment, treatment and research* (pp. 3–16). Belmont, CA: Wadsworth.

Roberts, A. R. (1991). Conceptualizing crisis theory and the crisis intervention model. In A. R. Roberts, *Contemporary perspectives on crisis intervention and prevention* (pp. 3–17). Englewood Cliffs, NJ: Prentice-Hall.

Shulman, L. (1979). *The skills of helping*. Itasca, IL: Peacock.

Simpson, D. D. (1984). National treatment system evaluation based on the Drug Abuse Reporting Program (DARP) follow-up research. In F. M. Tims and J. P. Ludford (Eds.), *Drug abuse treatment evaluation: Strategies, progress and prospects* (Research Monograph 51, DHHS Pub. No. ADM 84–1329). Rockville, MD: National Institute on Drug Abuse.

Strickland, D. E., and Pittman, D. J. (1984). Social learning and teenage alcohol use: Interpersonal and observational influences within the sociocultural environment. *Journal of Drug Issues, 14* (1), 137–150.

Tims, F. M. (1981). *Effectiveness of drug abuse treatment programs: Treatment research report* (DHHS Pub. No. ADM 81–1143). Rockville, MD: National Institute on Drug Abuse.

219

GLOSSARY

A-B-C model of crisis management: A three-stage sequential model for intervening with persons in crisis. The "A" refers to "achieving contact," the "B" to "boiling down the problem," and the "C" to "coping."

ABCD format: A part of rational emotive therapy in which thought processes are divided and identified in the following fashion: *A*, which is the activating experience; *B*, which is the belief about *A*; *C*, which is the consequence (emotional, behavioral, or both) that results, from A and B; *D*, which is the disputation of distorted beliefs; and *E*, which is the new effect of philosophy that evolves from the rational belief that replaces the original faulty belief.

Abduction: A situation in which a parent takes a child with the express purpose of concealing the child's whereabouts.

Acute stress disorder: The development of anxiety, dissociation, and other symptoms that occur within one month after exposure to a traumatic event.

Alcohol abuse: When the ongoing consumption of alcohol leads to disruptions in one's life such as the deterioration of school or job performance, neglect of child-care responsibilities, and so forth. In addition, a person may use alcohol in hazardous ways, such as driving an automobile or operating machinery while intoxicated. An individual may continue to abuse alcohol despite knowing that significant problems are very likely to occur, which may, in turn result in legal difficulties.

Alcohol dependence: The development of physiological dependence on alcohol as evidenced by tolerance or withdrawal symptoms.

Withdrawal symptoms develop approximately twelve hours after the reduction of alcohol consumption following extended, heavy, alcohol ingestion.

Ambivalence: Behavior that is inconsistent in thought and action. For example, a client may urgently request an appointment with a clinician and then fail to attend the session.

Battered spouses: Men or women who are subjected to and involved in either physical or emotional violence generated by the domestic relationship.

Battered women's hotlines and shelters: Services whose primary focus is to ensure women's safety by crisis telephone counseling or provision of short-term housing at a safe residential shelter. Many shelters not only provide safe lodging but also peer counseling, support groups, information on women's legal rights, and referral to social service agencies. In some communities, emergency services for battered women have expanded further to include parent education workshops, assistance in finding housing, employment counseling and job placement, and group counseling for batterers. These crisis intervention services for battered women and their children exist in every state and major metropolitan area in the United States.

Circular causality: The belief, to which most family therapists subscribe, that causality is nonlinear, that an individual family member's symptom or behavior may have multiple causes as well as multiple effects on family functioning.

Constructivism: The belief that one's reality (worldview), including one's self-concept, emerges from interaction with significant others and their environment. A constructivist approach to clinical work views change occuring from the interaction between the client and the clinician. Clinical constructivism asserts that clients are self-organizing and self-determining and that therapeutic effectiveness is enhanced when the clinician takes a collaborative rather than a hierarchical stance toward the client.

Contract: An understanding between the social worker and client concerning the time frame for work, the problems to address, goals to pursue, interventive approaches to use, and evaluation procedures to incorporate. The contract may be written or oral. It is usually explicit but may, in some circumstances, be implicit. The contract may be revised by mutual consent of the worker and client.

Crisis: The subjective reaction to a stressful life experience that threatens the individual's stability and ability to cope or function. The main cause of a crisis is a stressful or hazarous event, but two other conditions are also necessary: (1) the individual's perception of the stressful event as the cause of disruption; and (2) the indivdual's inability to resolve the disruption with previously used coping methods. Crisis also refers to "an upset in the steady state." It often has five components: a hazardous event, a vulnerable state, a precipitating factor, an active crisis state, and the resolution of the crisis. Crisis seems to be derived from the Greek word for "decision," or more broadly, "a turning point." In addition, a Chinese ideograph for crisis can be interpreted as a "danger," in that it threatens to overwhelm the individual and may result in serious consequences. A crisis may also be viewed as an opportunity, because during periods of crisis one tends to become open to new, outside influences.

Crisis intervention: A scenario in which a clinician enters into the life situation of an individual or a family to alleviate the impact of a crisis and to help mobilize the resources of those differentially affected. This clinical assistance may be given over the telephone or in person.

Diagnostic related groups (DRG): A system that attempts to manage the spiraling costs of hospital services for Medicare patients. Hospitals receive payment based on the disorder treated rather than on length of stay or the nature and extent of services provided. Some 467 DRGs have been identified.

Diagnostic school: A social work school of thought, popular during the first half of the twentieth century, that embraced Freudian psychoanalytic theory and practice.

Dialectic: The process of change that occurs through the resolution of opposites or contradictions. A dialectic is a developmental process that involves a person's present belief system (thesis) encountering new experiences and ideas (antithesis) that cannot be explained by that belief system. Such an encounter usually produces a "crisis," which is eventually resolved by the expansion of one's present belief system (synthesis). In dialectical approach to time-limited treatment, the clinician's job is to introduce novelty to the client's current, homeostatic belief system (worldview).

Disequilibrium: An emotional state that may be characterized by confusing emotions, somatic complaints, and erratic behavior. The severe emotional discomfort experienced by the person in crisis propels him or her toward action that will reduce the subjective discomfort. Crisis intervention usually alleviates the early symptoms of disequilibrium within the first six weeks of treatment, and hopefully soon restores equilibrium.

Epidemiology: A concept or term that refers to uncovering either a modifiable or an attributable risk factor. A risk factor is modifiable when it can be changed through individual or community response(s) with the goal of lowering the incidence of an illness, mental disorder, disease, developmental disability, or death. An attributable risk factor refers to the rate of growth of a medical disease or mental disorder in a population of exposed individuals that can be attributed to a certain factor(s). Epidemiologists generally study risk factors, causation, incidence, and prevalence rates of particular diseases, disabilities, and disorders.

Family crisis therapy: A crisis-oriented therapeutic approach that focuses on helping the family system return to its previous level of functioning.

Family life cycle: The series of life events through which a family passes. Individuals and families as a whole may experience crisis in passing through one or more stages.

Family systems theory: The basis of most family therapy models. The family is seen as an emotional unit of interlocking relationships that is affected by the external environment as well as the behavior of individual members.

First-order change: A person's attempt to change him/herself or the world around her in accordance with his/her present belief system/assumptions/rules. A first-order approach to change is, therefore, logical and commonsensical to the person. If this attempt at change does not achieve the desired result, the person is inclined to attempt even more of the same ineffective behavior because it is consonant with his assumptions about the world. When ongoing first-order change attempts continue to be ineffective, a vicious cycle usually results in which the attempted solution maintains and *becomes* the problem that needs to be changed.

First–order reality: A person's discrete problematic behaviors that do not take into consideration the larger interpersonal or social context.

Functional school: A social work school of thought, popular during the 1930s and 1940s, that moved away from psychodynamic theory to adopt some of Otto Rank's concepts. The functional approach emphasized time limits and boundaries, and used the term "client" rather than "patient."

Future linkage: A purposeful effort on the part of the crisis clinician to shift the suicidal patient's focus from past or present pain and struggle to future sessions, events, and goals. Future linkage helps create a future orientation for a depressed and cognitively constricted suicidal patient who may have difficulty being able to look ahead with any sense of hope or purpose.

Health maintenance organization (HMO): A health care group that provides medical care services to its members at a predetermined annual cost. Often, both mental and physical health treatment are available in the HMO's facilities.

Homeostasis: The balance or equilibrium that each family needs to achieve and maintain. A family's homeostasis is often upset by a crisis.

Incest: Sexual contact between two people too closely related to marry legally. One of the individuals involved is typically under the age of majority.

Incestuous desire: This is a yearning to engage in sexual activity with someone who is considered inappropriate due to family relationship ties.

Incest victims: Individuals who have been forced, either physically or emotionally, to have sexual intercourse or engage in other sexual activities with family relatives. The victim does not have to be biologically related to the perpetrator; however, this may be the case.

Incidence: The number of new cases of a physical disease or mental disorder that occur during a particuar interval.

Instrumental suicide behavior: Suicide-related behaviors that may consciously or unconsciously serve as a means to an end. Typically, such behaviors elicit the involvement of others. An example of instrumental suicidal behavior would be an adolescent who takes an overdose in front of his/her parent following an argument. In such a case, the goal is not to die, but rather to express one's dismay and/or anger to the parent.

Kidnapping: (See Abduction).

Learned helplessness: A pattern of behavior often noted in situations where an individual has been victimized, such as domestic violence or incest. Here an individual responds passively to risk of harm and generally believes that nothing can be done to better the current situation.

Lethality: In relation to the clinical evaluation of suicide risk, lethality refers to the objective medical/biological danger of a potential method of suicide. For example, using a gun to attempt suicide is considered much a more lethal method than taking an overdose of pills.

Perpetrators of child abuse: Individuals who inflict physical or emotional harm on children. Generally, they are known to the child and often are part of the child's family system.

Powerlessness: A feeling that one's situation is hopeless and unsolvable. This feeling is later translated into inactivity on the part of the abused individual, resulting in no action being taken to change the current situation.

Pragmatism: A practical approach to problem solving and functioning in the world that primarily concerns itself with actual effects of ideas and behavior, often to the exclusion of the intellectual or aesthetic aspects of life.

Premorbid psychological history: A client's history that contains references to previous psychiatric treatment, hospitalizations, medications, depressions, and suicide attempts.

Prevalence: A widely accepted view existing within a particular time period—usually one year or a lifetime. Prevalence rate includes all new cases that have developed in the time period in question, as well as those whose onset occurred at an earlier period but continue into the present.

Psychosocial crises: Crises that are characterized primarily by psychosocial problems such as homelessness, extreme social isolation, and unmet primary care needs. Such crises contribute to physical and psychological trauma and illness.

Rational emotive imaging (REI): A form of treatment based on the same principles as rational emotive therapy but adds the use of imagination to pattern nerve impulses.

Rational emotive therapy (RET): A form of treatment, espoused by Albert Ellis and his colleagues, in which irrational, unrealistic thoughts are identified, addressed, and hopefully extinguished.

Recovering parent: A searching parent reuniting with a missing child (in the context of child abduction).

Reunification: Reunification of a child and searching parent following abduction of the child.

Scapegoat: A family member, often the identified patient, who receives the bulk of the critism and blame within the family.

Secondary adolescent suicide prevention: Process involving the identification of the at-risk adolescent and his or her family. The at-risk adolescent is often difficult to approach and may have withdrawn from friends, school, and family.

Second-order change: An approach to change that goes beyond one's current beliefs/assumptions/rules about the world. Because this approach to change is different from a person's current beliefs/assumptions/rules about the world, the person usually experiences it as illogical, contrary to common sense, and strange.

Second-order reality: Involves situating problematic behaviors an interpersonal context and taking that context into consideration when developing and implementing therapeutic interventions.

Socialized obedience: A phenomenon noted with victims of abuse that results from being forced to exist in the abusive situation. Often these victims suffer from feelings of deflated self-worth and lack trust, which can affect future ability to bond in relationships.

Spouse abuse: The infliction of physical and/or emotional pain on one's domestic partner.

Suicide risk factors: The various demographic, social, and clinical variables that have been found to be correlated with suicide completions according to epidemiological and psychosocial research. For example, the data suggest that variables such as being male, white, socially isolated, and having a DSM-IV diagnosis are all risk factors for completed suicide.

Substance dependence: A configuration of cognitive, behavioral, and physiological symptoms that indicate a person persists in continuing to use a substance despite significant problems related to that substance. The substance is repeatedly self-administered, usually resulting in tolerance for and as well as continued compulsive use of the substance.

Survivors of domestic violence: Individuals who were once victims of domestic violence and are able to escape these negative influences and proceed toward a healthier personal and social equilibrium.

Survivors of incest: Individuals who were once victims of childhood incest and are able to escape these negative influences and proceed toward a healthier personal and social equilibrium.

Task-centered treatment: A short-term model of social work practice that emphasizes a clear or continuing focus on tasks needed to resolve the problems for which service was sought. Worker and client typically meet for no more than six to eight sessions.

Tertiary adolescent suicide prevention: Prevention that requires the availability of a variety of sources to proved peer group support. Self-help groups, whether directly focused on suicide or not, allow the adolescent an opportunity to express and work out troublesome feelings before they become critical. Some of these groups are Alcoholics Anonymous, Al Anon, Narcotics Anonymous, Alateen, and Mental Health Anonymous.

Third-order reality: The larger social context of a presenting problem and its interpersonal context. This context involves a client's family of orgin and any others who contribute to the problem, such as school teachers, probation officers, and child protection workers.

Time-limited treatment: Therapeutic services in which a limited number of sessions are predetermined by either a third-party payor or mutual agreement between clinician and client. Such treatment usually involves focusing on a specific problem and having the client do homework tasks between sessions.

Traumatic stress: A type of crisis that refers to the highly intense level of psychological stress experienced as a direct result of some catastrophic event such as a devastating fire, serious illness, rape, or major operation.

Victim: An innocent person, such as someone who experienced a violent crime or a disaster, who encounters physical injury, trauma, fear, acute anxiety, and/or loss of belongings.